EARLY COLLECTED POEMS

1965–1992

Gerald Stern

EARLY COLLECTED POEMS

1965–1992

W. W. NORTON & COMPANY

New York · London

For information about permission to reproduce selections from this book,
write to Permissions, W. W. Norton & Company, Inc.,
500 Fifth Avenue, New York, NY 10110

For information about special discounts for bulk purchases, please contact
W. W. Norton Special Sales at specialsales@wwnorton.com or 800-233-4830

Manufacturing by Courier Westford
Book design by Chris Welch
Production manager: Devon Zahn

Library of Congress Cataloging-in-Publication Data

Stern, Gerald, date.
[Poems. Selections]
Early collected poems, 1965–1992 / Gerald Stern.
p. cm.
Includes index.
ISBN 978-0-393-07666-0 (hardcover)
I. Title.
PS3569.T3888E37 2010
811'.54—dc22

                                2010003169

W. W. Norton & Company, Inc.
500 Fifth Avenue, New York, N.Y. 10110
www.wwnorton.com

W. W. Norton & Company Ltd.
Castle House, 75/76 Wells Street, London W1T 3QT

1 2 3 4 5 6 7 8 9 0

For the sorrowful.

Contents

Author's Note XVII

Rejoicings

Rejoicings 3
The Naming of Beasts 5
This Is Lord Herbert Moaning 6
In Kovalchick's Garden 7
The Blessed 8
The Unity 9
His Animal Is Finally a Kind of Ape 10
The Goons Are Leaving 12
Bird Cursing 13
I Will Be a Romantic 14
On the Far Edge of Kilmer 15
By Coming to New Jersey 16
Going North on 202 17
The Poem of Life 18
The Weeds 20
The Supreme Subject 22
When I Have Reached the Point of Suffocation 24
My Flow: His Stoppage 26
No Mercy, No Irony 27

Lost with Lieutenant Pike 28

Goodbye, Morbid Bear 30

Immanuel Kant and the Hopi 31

Pleistocene 33

The Anger of Age 34

I Called the Wolf Josephus 35

The Heat Rises in Gusts 36

Burst of Wind Between Broadway and the River 37

Top Rock 38

Columbia the Gem 39

Delaware West 40

Planting Strawberries 41

Look at Us Play with Our Meat 42

Two American Haikus 44

The Stick of Wrath 45

The Bite 48

Two Birds 49

It Is Not Berenson's Blood 50

Dog in the House 51

In Carpenter's Woods 53

Eroica 55

From the Pennsylvania Side 57

Turning into a Pond 60

Lucky Life

The Power of Maples 65

The Last Self-Portrait 66

At Bickford's 67

One Foot in the River 68

Straus Park 69

Let Me Please Look into My Window 71

I Need Help from the Philosophers 72

I Am So Exhausted 74

On the Island 75

County Line Road 77

Margie Moser's Garden 78

When It Gets Cold 80

The Days of Nietzsche 81

Burying an Animal on the Way to New York 82

The Sensitive Knife 83

The One Thing in Life 85

Four Sad Poems on the Delaware 86

On My Poor Road 87

Blue Skies, White Breasts, Green Trees 88

The Sounds 90

Sometimes When I Close My Eyes 91

The Blue Tie 92

Mentioning of the Souls 93

Self-Portrait 94

Lobelia 97

Three Tears 98

Climbing This Hill Again 100

Lucky Life 102

Malagueña 105

Pile of Feathers 106

Feeding Prisoners 107

Gold Flower 108

Honey Locust 109

Proverbs 110

Gert's Gifts 111

Stepping Out of Poetry 112

Behaving Like a Jew 113

Love for the Dog 114

Psalms 115

This Is It   116

The Cemetery of Orange Trees in Crete   119

96 Vandam   120

If You Forget the Germans   121

The Hungarian   123

Bob Summers: The Final Poem   124

God of Rain, God of Water   125

Home from Greece   127

Long Nose   128

If You Saw Me Walking   129

The Thaw   131

Morning Harvest   133

Peddler's Village   135

The Sweetness of Life   136

Too Much, Too Much   137

Underground Dancing   140

Something New   141

The Red Coal

The Faces I Love   145

Little White Sister   146

Swan Song   147

Immensity   148

Rotten Angel   149

Dangerous Cooks   151

Good Friday, 1977   152

Pick and Poke   153

Royal Manor Road   155

Modern Love   156

Little Did the Junco Know   158

Lord, Forgive a Spirit   159

Elaine Comparone   160

Ice, Ice   162

One More Time the Lambs   163

The Sacred Spine   164

I Remember Galileo   165

Potpourri   166

Magritte Dancing   168

The Shirt Poem   170

June First   174

Thinking About Shelley   175

Cow Worship   177

Joseph Pockets   178

Phipps Conservatory   183

Days of 1978   184

No Wind   185

June Fourth   186

The Angel Poem   187

St. Patrick's Day, 1979   193

Visiting Florida Again   195

Hanging Scroll   197

A Hundred Years from Now   199

The Poem of Liberation   200

Acacia   204

Your Animal   206

The Rose Warehouse   208

The Red Coal   210

There Is Wind, There Are Matches   213

The-Way-We-Were Lounge   215

Waving Good-by   216

In These Shadows   217

Dear Mole   218

My Hand   219

These Birds   220

Arthur's Lily   221

The Picasso Poem   222
The Roar   225
For Night to Come   226
Here I Am Walking   228

Paradise Poems

Orange Roses   233
Later Today   234
Rhododendron   235
Picking the Roses   236
Clay Dog   239
In Memory of W. H. Auden   240
Steve Dunn's Spider   242
Romania, Romania   244
It's Nice to Think of Tears   246
Souls from Emerson   248
Song   249
Weeping and Wailing   251
Hidden Justice   252
Christmas Sticks   253
The Same Moon Above Us   255
Leaving Another Kingdom   260
Near Périgord   263
For Song   266
My Swallows   267
Berkeley   269
The Dancing   270
Moscow   271
May 15   272
Bee Balm   273
Vivaldi Years   274
Saying the First Words   275

Night Again   276

Today a Leaf   277

The New Moses   278

Singing   279

The Seine at Night   280

At Jane's   281

John's Mysteries   284

Soap   288

I Pity the Wind   292

82/83   294

Romance   297

Villa-Lobos   298

The Nettle Tree   299

Sycamore   300

Baja   304

Of Blessed Name   306

Kissing Stieglitz Goodbye   308

Two Trees   311

One Bird to Love Forever   313

Fritz   317

Three Skies   319

Red Bird   323

Adler   325

The Expulsion   329

Groundhog Lock   333

July 2, 1983   335

The Dogs   336

Lovesick

Nobody Else Living   339

Lovesick   340

All I Have Are the Tracks   341

I Do a Piece from Greece 342

I Hate My Moaning 344

This Was a Wonderful Night 345

I Sometimes Think of the Lamb 347

Stopping Schubert 348

I Am in a Window 349

Béla 351

A Song for the Romeos 355

A Slow and Painful Recovery 357

My First Kinglet 360

I Slept Like That 362

Lillian Harvey 363

There I Was One Day 364

One Animal's Life 366

Silver Hand 368

Washington Square 369

Arranging a Thorn 370

The Dog 372

Shaking Myself and Sighing 374

A Pair of Hands 376

Bob Summers' Body 377

It Was in Houston 378

Neither English nor Spanish 380

I Am in Love 383

My Favorite Demon 385

Another Insane Devotion 386

The Blink of an Eye 388

Making the Light Come 390

It Was a Rising 391

Hobbes 393

Grapefruit 397

A Garden 400

No Longer Terror 402

Nobody Else Alive   406

Knowledge Forwards and Backwards   407

Two Moons   411

Lyric   414

My Favorite Farewell   415

For Once   419

Stolen Face   421

Steps   427

Bread Without Sugar

1

Sylvia   435

Three Hearts   437

The Bull-Roarer   438

My Death for Now   442

One Day an Arbor Vitae   444

Brain of My Heart   446

The Founder   448

The First Lewd Offering   450

Nice Mountain   451

Love Is the Opposite   453

The Age of Strolling   455

Sending Back the Gloom   458

One Gift   461

First Day of Spring   463

R for Rosemary   469

How Would It Be?   471

Saving My Skin from Burning   472

Shouting   473

The Eyes Are Always Brown   475

2

A Song for Kenneth Burke   479

Aspiring to Music   483

Grinnell, Iowa   488

Ukrainian   491

Coleman Valley Road   492

What It Is Like   493

Two Daws   495

3

Her Right Eye Catches the Lavender   501

Those Things   503

His Song of the Green Willow   506

If the Lark Had Thorns   508

The Smell of Death   511

Red with Pink   515

Someone Will Do It for Me   520

I Would Call It Derangement   523

The Thought of Heaven   526

4

Bread Without Sugar   533

Acknowledgments   547

Index   549

Author's Note

What I attempted to do in this *Early Collected*—the first six books of my collected poems—is to reach out simultaneously for a new language and a new subject matter. I was interested in that which was overlooked, neglected, and unseen, from a political, religious, and personal point of view and a voice that bespoke this in the simplest, most honest manner. I found myself returning to early— to fundamental—experiences, as I found myself discovering a new language. This constituted a celebration as well as a kind of mourning or elegy, and the results can be seen in such poems as "Lucky Life," "The Blue Tie," "Stepping Out of Poetry," and "Bob Summer: The Final Poem." This was a difficult road to hoe, for it expressed neither formal, academic niceness nor bohemian madness. If there are sources they are variously in the Hebrew prophets, in Blake, in Whitman, in Ovid, in Coleridge, and, as far as modern poets, in Yeats, Stevens, Pound, and Hart Crane.

I believe the search for the oppressed became identified, in my poetry, with the very particulars of my own life: including the oppression of working-class people in the city of Pittsburgh, where I came from, and the abuse of minorities, particularly Jews and blacks. This even includes the attention I gave not just to individuals but to plants—weeds, say—which are also hated and neglected. But most of all, the death of my sister, Sylvia, at an early age, who became, as it were, the muse of my poetry. I spent my earliest years reading a little but mostly wandering—endlessly— through the streets of Pittsburgh. The results of this would show twenty, thirty years later.

Rejoicings

Rejoicings

I put the sun behind the Marlborough Blenheim
so I can see the walkers settling down
to their long evening of relaxation
over the slimy piers.

I put the clouds in their place and start the ocean
on its daily journey up the sand;
I reach the beach a minute after the guards
have chased the last sleepers from their blankets.

Haley's blimp
drags its long tail across the sky
as the light from Greenland dips down
for a quick look at my broken stick.

I make a good circle before digging
so I can close the whole world in my grip
and draw my poor crumbling man
so that his tears fall within the line.

The sand, half out of focus, lightens and darkens
according to the clouds and the sun
and takes all I have of pity and fear
like a weak and devoted friend.

A few black puffs, the end of some great violence,
blow into the wind before their dispersal.
I move my lips and raise my quiet hand
in all the craziness of transferred emotion.

After twenty years of dull loyalty
I have come back one more time to the shore,
like an old prisoner—like a believer—
to squeeze the last poetry out of the rubbish.

I pour a little mud on my head
for the purification
and rub the dirty sand into my shirt
to mix everything with crystal.

I put a piece of shell for killing birds
in the open hand
and all the paraphernalia of the just,
bottle and paper and pencil,

for the work to come.
I wait one hour. That is the time it takes
to free the soul, the time it takes
for reverence.

Once or twice I have to alter the grave
so the water can come in quietly.
I am burying our Nietzsche;
I am touching his small body for the last time.

The Naming of Beasts

You were wrong about the blood.
It is the meat-eating lamb we are really terrified of,
not the meat-eating lion.
The noisy Soul shrieking and spitting and bleeding set us off—
the smell of nice clean grass confused us.
It is the eyes, it is the old sweet eyes showing just a little fear.
It is the simple mouth full of honest juices.
It is the little legs crossed at the bony joints.
—It is not greed—it can't be greed—it is fasting;
it is not divorce—it is custody;
it is not blood—it is supineness.

This Is Lord Herbert Moaning

This is Lord Herbert moaning and sighing over his lost manuscripts.
This is meek old Blake wandering down the street with his wolf's face on.
Lamb, Lamb is a master—Marvell, Sidney, beautiful, beautiful.
A whole world of lucid and suffering poets talking to themselves.
I dream almost steadily now of interpenetration,
but not with beasts—I have had that for twenty years—
I begin with sanity now, I always begin with sanity.
—After a period of time the old lobster crawls back into his cave;
after a period of time the wise Indian puts on female clothes.
I watch them with love;
my own poor ghost would like to smash everything,
woods and all, cave and all;
I have to smother him with kisses,
I have to carry him from the room,
I have to show him what darkness is, what brightness is.
For twenty years, without knowing the name, I fought against beasts,
but my whole life is centered now in my lips
and their irruptions.
   It is beautiful watching the sun slip through the bent fingers.
   It is beautiful letting the brain move in and out of its own cloudbank.

In Kovalchick's Garden

It is dusk, the drive-ins are opening, the balloon is coming to rest.
Out of the east, so fitting, the cardinal moves into the light.
It is the female, almost too small and shabby for its splendor.
Her crest opens out—I watch it blaze up.
She is exploring the dead pear tree.
She moves quickly in and out of the dry branches.
Her cry is part wistful, part mordant.
She is getting rid of corpses.

The Blessed

He who destroys, he who reigns, he who meditates;
now, more than ever before, these are the three.
It is life simplifying itself,
the head cut off and the face lifted.
It is the brown rabbit dying of its fever;
it is the gray one surviving.
It is the little house of justice.
It is the dead picking flowers, dancing and eating corn.
It is the new one waving his sheaf.
It is the old one wiping his eye.
It is the Eagle Knight shaking the whole desert with his passion.
It is the strange pity of Rimbaud.
It is the strange pity of Browning. It is the towers meeting.
It is the soul of Whitehead moving into its last obscurity.
It is Walter Savage Landor's dream of entablature.
It is Walter Savage Landor in the eighteenth century.
It is Landor's hatred of kings. It is Landor's mind.
It is Landor's ceremony. It is Landor's violence.
It is the life. It is the vile reduction.
It is the new one picking flowers.
It is the old one wiping his nose, waving his eye.
It is the terror of criticism.
It is the torment of money.
It is the weariness of work.
It is the gravity of love. It is the dignity of isolation.

The Unity

How strange it is to walk alone,
the one leg never growing tired of the other;

the ears still beautiful but the sound
falling in new places;

all that I formerly believed in
explained and sweetened.

I have to concoct my own past now
out of old inhalations.

I have to live in two lives
with the same blood.

I have to separate the thirsts
without hatred.

It is a good desert—
snakes and horses—

cooks, whores, doctors—
ghosts, vistas,

women and men of all sizes and all ages
living together, without satire.

His Animal Is Finally a Kind of Ape

His animal is finally a kind of ape—after all—and not an elephant,
a release for him, but more than that for the two exhausted beasts.
For years he struggled between them
and it was either the violence of the one or the obscurity of the
    other,
either way, as it seemed to him then, a concealment,
but now that the choice was made
they could move back into a simple relationship with him, and with
    each other.

What is amazing is the choice itself.
You would expect him to move from elephants into owls
or into the seal-like creatures or into pelicans,
or at least—if he had to go back—back now into hares—
or shrews and weasels, if what he needed was viciousness.
At least you would never expect him to choose the ape again,
not after three hundred years of greed and malice,
but what he was after was not the choosing of new animals
but another collaboration with the old ones,
and for this purpose the ape now more than the elephant
would suit his fever, or what there was left of it.

I remember sitting and talking for hours about the elephant.
I remember the room trembling with belief
and I hesitate, out of loyalty, to do any harm to that beast.
But it is he who will be free at last of *my* compulsion,
and able to graze, and able to panic,
without my interference.
The ape is different—it will be years before he is free;

in the meantime, when we rise we will rise for each other
and when we howl it will be in each other's faces.

There is nothing degrading or cynical in this.
We had to go back again for the sake of all three.
Otherwise we would mix our disgust forever with our dream.
What the ape does is separate once and for all the one from the
     other.
What he does is illuminate the distance.
What he does is make it bearable.
The leaves sticking out of his mouth, the puffed-out belly, the dirt
     on his lips,
this I pity;
the muzzled face, the musk-like odor,
this I pity.
I lived and I lived constantly on the verge of a true destruction.
Because of these animals I was able to break away.
I am in their debt.

The Goons Are Leaving

The goons are leaving, and the Hawaiians, and the taffy-pullers,
and the charred wives, and the blackmailers:
this is their Labor Day, the feast of wages.
Only the insolvents are left, and the waifs, and the vagrants.
For one more week we will move through the loose sand
in simple luxury.
We will walk into the sanctuaries and turn the signs;
we will pick our way through the wreckage;
we will start fires;
we will lie in the sun.
At night we will walk the 127 miles in peace.
We will shake the bones of the Unamis and the Presbyterians.
We will sit in the Mansion of Health.
We will rid ourselves of the consining insects.
We will smell the old meadows.
We will undress in the cedars.
We will meet raven on the beach.
Only money and luck have made us different from the others.
We live in grief and ecstasy.
It is our justice.

Bird Cursing

for King Hoban Topatrapanning

I want to watch my sweet body go out again into the beach plums
and hang again with all that luxury
between the marsh islands of Stone Harbor
and the monkey gardens of Anglesea.

I want to see my dark shoulders rise and fall
in oblique reference to the cry of hunger
and the large shadow slipping over the lawns.

I want to hear the great grasses hiss with delight
as Wildwood drops back again into the sand.

I Will Be a Romantic

To the wild grape vine, the wild hop vine, the honeysuckle and the
    Virginia creeper
I sing my song.

When I die I will not hang under the loose pipe
or in the cellar beside the broken screens
or in the YMCA or at the Greenwich.

A gull will carry my bulging eye to a clean and brilliant place
in the fields of guano.
I will be enriched.

On the Far Edge of Kilmer

I am sitting again on the steps of the burned out barrack.
I come here, like Proust or Adam Kadmon, every night to watch the
    sun leave.
I like the broken cinder blocks and the bicycle tires.
I like the exposed fuse system.
I like the color the char takes in the clear light.
I climb over everything and stop before every grotesque relic.
I walk through the tar paper and glass.
I lean against the lilacs.
In my left hand is a bottle of Tango.
In my right hand are the old weeds and power lines.
I am watching the glory go down.
I am taking the thing seriously.
I am standing between the wall and the white sky.
I am holding open the burnt door.

By Coming to New Jersey

By coming to New Jersey I have discovered the third world
that hangs between Woodbridge Avenue and Victory Bridge.
It is a temporary world,
full of construction and water holes,
full of barriers and isolated hydrants,
a world given over to Humble,
no place to live, no place to walk,
not even in hatred.
But wherever I am it has nothing anymore to *do* with hatred,
anymore than it has to do with haggling wisdom.
I live in weird equipoise, all the time now,
like a banded turkey, one foot on top of the other,
my heart jumping between two weights,
my ruined tongue reminiscing, my brain wandering.

Going North on 202

Going north on 202 I have to wait for hours
for the American lambs to pass by.
Thousands, thousands, crossing the great circle at Flemington,
more thousands coming up the road from Frenchtown,
the meat juices running down their lips,
their undersides stained with excrement,
their hooves bloody from fighting.

On route 78 I pass Columbus
going the other way, looking for the Hudson.
His boat rocks on the empty highway
as he struggles through New Jersey.
In the back seat the cross
rattles against the window
and the frightened chickens scream.
In one more hour he will enter the last tunnel
before his departure.

With its small people standing in the rain,
with its bishops smiling happily,
with its daydreaming kings scratching their stomachs,
with its donkey races, and its monsters, and its bells,
tiny Europe waits for him,
tiny Europe, smelling of camphor.

The Poem of Life

Why should our nation, into whose purses of charity are poured countless
dollars, permit the birds of her land, her poets, to suffer
scorn and privation?

—*Robert Summers,* My Poem of Life

For three days now I have been watching the blue jay take over—
my soul there, shrieking and squalling,
nodding and jerking its head, fluting its tail.
All day Friday it moved nervously between the two maples.
All day Saturday it hopped through the garbage collecting wisdom.
Today it is Sunday, June 4, 1968—I have *marked* it.
My wife and Bob Summer's wife and the little stoned dancer
have driven to New York to look at Martha Graham's old age.
Summers and I are sitting under the honeysuckles
smoking parodis and discussing the poem of life.
Once he had it down to thirteen words—
the Napoleonics, the logic, the letters of pride,
the six demonstrations, the five assumptions,
all his anger and irony, all his honesty,
his dream of the theatre, his terror, his acts of power—
reduced to thirteen words.
—The blue jay is youth, right?—
clawing his chin, stuffing his belly, fighting the dove, fighting the owl,
filling the lawns and woods with his violent sounds.
By eight o'clock everything will be quiet here.
The miserable family upstairs will slam their back door,
the jays will disappear into the maples
and we will have the yard to ourselves.
We will go on for hours,
moving our lips, waving our parodis,
seizing and judging everything that comes
into the range of our brutal memories,

two delectable Jews,
spending our happy and cunning lives
in the honeysuckles.

The Weeds

I love the weeds—I dream about them—
grass clogging the ditches, mustard sleeping in the ground—
I love their stubbornness and secrecy.
Five years ago I thought only about a war
and like a greedy Czar
my mind was fixed on the inhuman heaven of the west;
now almost for the first time I am free of that sickness
and able to live without a constant slaughter.

The mother of violence goes in dirt and water.
She dreams of irrigation and her mouth opens at the sight of dams.
She stands like Charlemagne among the delphiniums,
crushing the Saxons and feeding the poor.
She reads the lecture on smothering to the little sons and daughters
    of grass.
She divides the good from the damned.

I want a king to go easily into the trees.
I want his sticks to break without horror.
I want the wind to lengthen his muscles.
I want him to despise mortification.
I want him to make a final choice between regulation and affection.
I want the water to come from his own eyes.
I want him to be carried with aplomb.
I want him to be alive.

Wind is the last master.
It blows the crazy fire, it splits the rain,
it pulls at the mind.

What is pernicious? Here in New Brunswick the dead are
    gluttonous.
They crowd the river. They move against the bridge.
They cross the parkway. They circle the missions. I sing
to myself like a lost Tzaddik in front of the First
Dutch Church on Neilson Street, for that is my nature;
and I walk down Little Carthage dreaming of ungoverned bodies,
for that is my nature too;
and I crowd the river myself in order to feel
the greed at its source, for that is my nature too.
Life on the earth is not a sickness. For years
I hung—like a German—between two wildernesses.
Now there is a third. I cross it with relief.

The Supreme Subject

Pittsburgh, 1967

At an unexpected turn in the Kiskiminetas
I suddenly saw again what the valley looked like
before the Scotchman came with his bitter stick.
—It is what we spent our youth arguing over:
the beauty of the rivers before the settlement
and the horror after.
The supreme subject! Contracted in our lives!
   We talked through smoke—in Hell—like fiery puddlers,
rubbing the cinders out of our hair and spitting out clinkers.
   It was sad, really—
we couldn't even enjoy the dreams of the Tortured,
our Hell was so literal.
Not that we were advanced. God! God!
We were just getting into the sensitive
when everyone else was moving on to the vile,
and when we looked up
our eyes were red with poverty as well as grime.

Gilbert went to Provence;
I went to Batsto;
and Hazley went to the mountain.
But what I write about—
and I think what we all write about—
is someway connected with the memory of that darkness
and our escape.

For the rest, I have no heart:
Thomas Mellon howling among the Presbyters.
Frick bleeding.
Berkman raging.
The reconciliation. The conversion.

Entelechy? The Soul?

Well, we do have interesting place names in western Pennsylvania.
Everybody knows Blueball and Intercourse down there in the East,
but we have irony, our cities are named after trees,
trees and animals, and of course millionaires, and of course
    Indians.
—Kiss, kiss Mamma for me. Say hello to your Mary.
Goombye, Hunkies. Goombye, goombye, Hunkies.

When I Have Reached the Point of Suffocation

When I have reached the point of suffocation,
then I go back to the railroad ties

and the mound of refuse.
Then I can have sorrow and repentance,

I can relax in the broken glass
and the old pile of chair legs;

I am brought back to my senses
and soothed a little.

It is really the only place I can go
for relief.

The streets, the houses, the institutions,
and the voices that occupy them,

are too hard and ugly
for any happiness

and the big woods outside
too full of its own death—

I go to the stone wall,
and the dirty ashes,

and the old shoes,
and the daisies.

It takes years to learn how to look at the destruction
of beautiful things;

to learn how to leave the place
of oppression;

and how to make your own regeneration
out of nothing.

My Flow: His Stoppage

In the next booth over the hairless white
With the shivering legs and rotten shoes
Is straining and grieving, the pain of stoppage
Acute, the pain of blockage frenzied;

His feet curling, his breath coming
In intervals, his shanks hammering
The blazed puny wooden walls
Of all three booths, in his stoppage one empty;

While I in alternate vegetable coldness
And vegetable heat and vegetable sorrow—
A vague distressing sense of sickness,
Dolor, weakness, regret, suspicion—
Am frightened more by my flow than his stoppage.

No Mercy, No Irony

This is the hawk I love.
His weight is determined precisely by the distance of his fall.
He sticks to his decisions.

Lost with Lieutenant Pike

How was I to know—in 1938—that anyone but
Zebulon Pike could be the master of my imagination

or that the one book belonging to my dead sister—*Alice in
Wonderland*—did not have to lie for twenty years, hidden
on a closet shelf

or that I was allowed to throw out my stupid molds, my
set, that never once, with all my pouring, managed to make
one soldier without a leg missing or without an incredible
wound in the side of his neck.

Slowly I became a man, and as I did I looked back with
shame, which was the lawful payment for my ignorance and meekness.

Whatever I have to do now to outlive my string of errors I will do,
and I will live as divided as I have to, and as loose and as senseless.

In another life it will be all masted vessels and sugar houses
and tea-pouring and little men running down their lanes;
this time around there will be no government for anyone.

I have to live on the lid of Hell, poor friend;
I have to leave the woods and the Shul and the chicken
standing on its wings and the white silk scarf
and the visit from Mars and the long journey to Harrisburg, P.A.

It is something to stand on a hill in the middle of November, 9,000 miles from Jerusalem, with the ice forming inside your nostrils, and to feel your own widsom.

Goodbye, Morbid Bear

Goodbye, morbid bear; you will be waving your morbid arm forever, forcing your way into the nursery rhymes.

Immanuel Kant and the Hopi

There was a time
when the only friends I had were trees
and the only pleasure I had
was with my crippled soldiers and my glue.
I don't say this aloud
out of any sickening desire to bring back the sensitive years,
like little Lord Christ
over in the Blue House,
but only because I am spending more and more of my time
    remembering
as my eyes change.
I guess you should weep for me because I am thinking,
like the silk merchants of Easton in their meditation rooms,
and the dead barbers in their chairs,
and the gorillas on their stone seats.
I could spend about ten good years
bringing the things together
that go into my brain,
ten good years on the river
watching the spars and the starved deer and the bathtubs float by.
    Up the street McCormick lies in wait for me,
hoping to help me with my tires and my trees
and down the street Repsher senior burns and burns,
an abused man, living on anger.
I go in and out of this road every day now
as you do on an island.
My house, with its nine white pillars,
sits peacefully on the ground
and I am the strange man

who has moved into the ruin.
From now on I am going to have something to think about
when I drive into the parking lots;
I am going to be refreshed when I walk over the asphalt;
I am going to live on two levels, like a weasel.

It is spring; 1971.
I am looking through my open windows at the Delaware River.
I am looking through the locust trees that grow here like weeds.
This summer I am going to strip some of the delicate leaves from
    their stems;
I am going to swim over to Carpentersville;
I am going to write twenty poems about my ruined country.
   Please forgive me, my old friends!
I am walking in the direction of the Hopi!
I am walking in the direction of Immanuel Kant!
I am learning to save my thoughts—like
one of the Dravidians—so that nothing will
be lost, nothing I tramp upon, nothing I
chew, nothing I remember.

Pleistocene

I wasn't sure—when I reached 45—
whether I would grow less and less interested in the densities
and move, like Samadryad, into the unobstructed
or whether I would begin, finally, to accept them all
one by one, in their time and at their own bidding.
To the left is the way of Lear, the penniless old man of the library,
struggling with his water;
to the right is the way of Gurion, grandfather of all Zion,
standing on his cunning old head.
You grow more and more rich as you move in that direction;
you leave yourself and go to live with the diseases;
you become a river, and a house, as well as a man.
    Poor rat of 35—
you were so encumbered you couldn't begin to imagine
what a little rest could bring.
Life, the trap, it could have missed you, you could have slipped by.

I go back and forth every day now over a bridge that separates
    Riegelsville, New Jersey from Riegelsville, P.A.
The two sleepy guards barely lift their arms as they see me drive by.
In my mind are the mammoths
and the sheets of cold ice
and the men who moved up and down with the great snow.
Over there, in a swamp, the bearded Carnegie is dancing in front of
    his new library;
the workmen leave their fires and lift him up on their shoulders,
    singing in Latin;
I am already sitting there, beside the iron frog and the fountain.

The Anger of Age

The anger of age—I'll love it!
Broken teeth! Screaming
at the young!
My liver rotting
over the Talmud—
cursing the sperm wasted
on miserable dreams.

I Called the Wolf Josephus

I called the wolf Josephus,
rotting in his cage,
thoughtful, greedy,
the dogs' Jew.

The Heat Rises in Gusts

The heat rises in unpredictable gusts
Shaking the cords and lifting the valances.

The sofa lies against the swollen wall
Only an arm away from the window.

All this time it was not being that was a problem but tenderness.
All our talking in German was a waste, all our languages.

In the center of the room, where the weight is, stands Nietzsche the
     chopping block.
He is strapped together with unbreakable rods and locked in by bolts.

He is a monster of energy out of the nineteenth century
Redeemed by a just world.

Burst of Wind Between Broadway and the River

Between the eighth and the seventh avenue
I am hit in the face by a burst of wild air—
it is Nietzsche again, disguised as dust.
Twenty seconds we slap each other's faces,
grip hands and break each other's backs.
I sort of trot up thirty-eighth past Lerner and Bear's
looking for the dairy restaurant in which my brain was stranded.
There at the little chairs and the round tables
the rebbes read and eat.
I walk between them like a learned soul,
nodding my head and smiling,
doing the secret steps and making the signs,
following the path of authority and silence,
I and the dust, in the black soup and the herring.

Top Rock

This is just what I expected, the roots above the ground,
the rocks crowding out the soil, the whole universe popping in my head.
That is the heart over there
between the old leaves and the bottle,
and that is the broken neck,
and those are the shoulders reaching down to the small terrace.
 Behind the pine, through the starved needles,
Nietzsche is there preaching against redemption.
He is scolding the cripple, the hunchback and the mute;
I drag him one step at a time from his eyrie;
whatever I touch comes to pieces in my hands.
 Down below the generators are burning up the river.
The inspectors are sneaking through the weeds, disguised as fishermen.
My perverse heart is helping out, giving a little aid to the managers,
a little to the police.
My hands float on top of the water, like the fog.
I am living in both places at once.

Going down I am more like an animal
and I go sideways around the berries and the poison ivy.
After five minutes I am through the brush and practically running.
For just one second at the bottom of the hill I disappear altogether
and re-appear twenty feet away in a different clearing.
The straight hemlocks, the simple ascent,
whatever it was that made me take the one path up,
are now—for me—indistinguishable from the rest.
I will see them in the future only as a part of the general luxury
at the foot of a mountain.

Columbia the Gem

I know that body standing in the Low Library,
the right shoulder lower than the left one, the lotion sea lotion—
his hold is ended.
Now the mouths can slash away in memory
of his kisses and his stupefying lies.
Now the old Reds can walk with a little spring
in and around the beloved sarcophagi.
Now the Puerto Ricans can work up another funny America
and the frightened Germans can open their heavy doors a little.
Now the River can soften its huge heart
and move, for the first time, almost like the others,
without silence.

Delaware West

I walk now along the mule path between the first and second locks
and come to rest in my own front yard on the Delaware River.
I am tearing one world apart and building another.
I have left the Swedes to their own dark spittle and the Poles to
      theirs.
I have discovered tires and bedsprings richer than anything in
      Björnstrom or Polanski.
I lift one finger to store the crazy ruins of four lifetimes
and one foot to the accumulated ash of half a century.
Under the stove, beside the broken window,
I have found the complete collection of *Orgy*.
While the light dies and the river rises
I will push the wasps aside and live in the dark
with the pregnant grandmothers, the rampant dogs
and the paralyzed strippers—
in tearful brotherhood with the grim sots
and the noisy oracles—
two long hours away from the downtown freaks
and the uptown rabbis.

Planting Strawberries

If this is a thing of the past,
planting strawberries on the Delaware River
and eating zucchini from my own garden,
then I will have to be buried too,
along with the beer-hall musicians
and the "startlingly beautiful sunset"
and the giant Swiss pansies,
in the ruins of Pennsylvania.
  I put the strawberries in one by one.
They look like octopuses and their feet dance in the water
as I cover them up to their necks.
They take up so much room
that I could eat an acre of them for breakfast
sitting in the dirt.
What I like best is having a garden this close to
the factories and stores of Easton.
It is like carrying a knife in my pocket!
It is like kissing in the streets!
  I would like to convert all the new spaces
back into trees and rocks.
I would like to turn the earth up after the bulldozers
have gone and plant corn and tomatoes.
I would like to guard our new property—with helmets and dogs.
I would like us to feed ourselves in the middle of their civilization.

Look at Us Play with Our Meat

Look at us play with our meat,
turning it over in the juices,
pecking at the carrot pieces.
Look at us fight for forks,
desperately looking for new silver,
the clean untarnished tines.
What a horror civilization is!
I remember walking on top of three layers,
sinking down through bed after bed,
reaching into the flint.
I remember the lopped femur,
the artistic grooves at the handle,
the club side still stained and splintered.
I remember Harry Truman signing orders,
the sun shining on his steel glasses,
the pens lined up on the velvet;
I remember him at Howard Johnsons
wolfing down the clams,
on the walls mermaids without nipples
floating in dead little pools
for the older women of America—I remember
the German mind at its peak,
rays of charity spreading in all directions,
old men in the Gobi reading Hegel,
Bushmen weeping over the sad pages of Heine,
Argentinians unpacking heavy wooden boxes of Dresden,
Japanese turning gently to the new instruments,

the winds of Leipzig and Vienna
blowing lovingly over Fuji,
the violins appearing everywhere,
the air shrieking and sighing with the new harmony.

Two American Haikus

1. *Mao Tse-tung*

The loose poems falling like blossoms
and the rain drops hitting the water like heads
dropping into the waste basket.

2. *W. C. Fields*

Gloves, gloves, and a tubular hat,
and a white carnation, and a queen of spades
and the cheeks of a president.

The Stick of Wrath

The love of concrete objects
led me into this deadfall.
Queen Nofret
in the sitting position.
King Zoser in water.
Virgil in wax.
—The marbles of Abu.
The kneeling woman of Baluba.
The demon Humbaba.

> I dream of the cave where Naz
> and his lovers beat their wings
> in the fire.

> I dream of the marsh where Liz
> turns her bright teeth
> on the ferns.

In the great mock spring
Lincoln comes out of the mud
like a prurient rhubarb
feeling the heat;
the banks close,
the Republicans thunder
and the hyacinths die
in their own tears.

I quit everything
at the first sign of the thaw

and worked back
to the waste places.
I thought of the bulging eyes
of the sorcerer
and like an ithyphallic
I raced along the ground,
cursing the two preposterous
images of our life,
the philosopher picking his nose
and the ape bearing a crucifix.
I drifted up to my knees
in burdocks.
I sang and breathed
in the upright position,
and with my open hands
I moved easily
through the lace and nettle.
—The sun freed me—
this I know—
the sun freed me,
drawing out poisons,
converting the ice into pools,
and laying bare our
secret tortured connections.
My head was full of light
and my blood turned,
only out of some crazy past,
some deadfall,
I kept my strange feelings

even from myself.
I bore the full guilt
of my affections—my fate,
bearing the guilt,
going round (as I do)
like a man with a weight
interested in justice.
I fought for balance and gravity—
even against the lips—
I fought for old equity,
in ignorance and nostalgia;
I fought against violence, against weakness, against perversion—
my ears rang
as I swayed with the excitement
of conflict
and my hands shook
as I moved to the points of contact.

That great love needs
good government
is the theory of Ruskin.

That loveliness
can be restored
is the theory of the sorcerer.

The Bite

I didn't start taking myself seriously as a poet
until the white began to appear in my cheek.
All before was amusement and affection—
now, like a hare, like a hare, like a hare,
I watch the turtle lift one horrible leg
over the last remaining stile and head
for home, practically roaring with virtue.
    Everything, suddenly everything is up there in the mind,
    all the beauty of the race gone
    and my life merely an allegory.

Two Birds

When I first saw this twittering thing
I knew I was in for another seige of forgiveness.
I never saw such watery eyes,
such a corrupted mouth.
God, how I am attracted to the diseased and fallen—
my house is like a hospital.
—I remember one that struck like a jay
and taught you to beware of birds.
His heart pounded with hatred—there was no pity—
and his neck jerked with a warning.
But later, much later,
he dipped his face in water, he gurgled, he preened,
and gazed at the paralyzed world with a softened eye.

They are all alike, the birds.
Rain fattens them, hunger sets them on, love dements them.
—This one lives in the dark
dreaming of its sanctuary.
Its eye follows the least light
and its mind moves in meshes.
Even its escape is weak.
Only its ecstasy, its uncontrollable fit on the singing ground,
something florid, something convulsive rolling through its wild brain
releases it.

The clumsiness and the disconnectedness are the things I stay away
        from.
What I like is the respect for distance and the attitude to light.
What I revere is the evening madness, the entelechy.

It Is Not Berenson's Blood

It is not Berenson's blood, it is not Cramer's,
it is not Carleson's. It is not Searle's.
It is not Merk's, it is not Priff's. It is not Harper's.

That delight is ended.

The waters are theirs, the bridges,
the cunning, the intimacy, even the peace;
but not the blood.

I am dividing my life up.
I am separating pleasure from disease and kindness from
    humiliation.
I am becoming a prince of ashes.
I have learned to nourish fire, to love oxygen, to live with the
    shovel.
I have come to respect the smoke, to honor the chain.
Day after day I free the living coals.
And shake away the dross. And feed the flame.
It is my life.

Dog in the House

On Long Island in 1951 I fought against bats for hours
and ended up with a little pile of bodies on the dining-room table,

and I have killed spiders inside the house so large
they bleed to death from their wounds like mammals,

and I lived for a whole year once
with a parasitical fox under my back porch,

and I have been horrified enough by baby birds in the attic
and live squirrels in the wall,

and I have had to slam the front door against dogs
and wait like a prisoner in my own living room,

so when it snows I look very carefully at the tracks
to see which ones hang back and which come close,
knowing what exhaustion does to animals.

In humans when it comes there is no control in the heart;
we spend our time in remorse
and weep at the sight of our frozen clothes
and look at our feet with pity.

We lose our thoughts,
we turn to phantasy and contortion,
we walk without leverage
and fall down from confusion.

The rest of our lives we spend in front of a fire
remembering our cold bodies
and the frightening steps we took to save them.

In Carpenter's Woods

This is a corner of heaven here,
the moss growing under the leaves,
the rocks cropping up like small graves under the trees,
the old giants rotting in the shade.
I used to come here every Sunday
to stand on the bridge and look at the bird-watchers.
Once I made love in the dead brush
and slept impaled on the thorns, too tired to move;
once I gave myself up to the *New York Times*
and buried myself in sections a whole afternoon;
once I played football with the radicals
while the sun and the rain fought for control.
   At the bottom of the hill where the trees give way to grass
a creek runs through a silent picnic ground
almost a mile away from any access.
Here the neighborhood dogs broke into their runs
at the first threat of authority.
Here the exhibitionists came out in the open
after the long morning with the squirrels and flickers.
Here the Jehovah's Witnesses lay down their arms
and gathered quietly around the tables.
—Without knowing the name or the reason
I gave myself up to vertigo;
I lay for hours with my eyes closed listening to the great sounds
coming in from Germantown;
I loved the ground so much that I had to hold on to the grass for
      balance.
   I can tell you that where those two girls go carefully over the stones,
and where that civilized man and his son

pick up loose wood for the fireplace
was, for three years, my refuge.
I can tell you that I have spent half a lifetime hunting for relief,
that in the simplest locations, in libraries,
in drug stores, in bus stations—
as well as under stone bridges and on hillsides—
I have found places to wait and think.
I tell you that world is as large as the one you sigh and tremble over;
that it is also invulnerable and intricate and pleasurable;
that it has a serious history;
that it was always there, from the beginning.

Eroica

Forgive me for being alone.
I'm breaking skulls like I used to
to get at the brain.
Now I am drinking fragments of memory,
now I am sucking on idle nerve cells.
This is Haydn here, who belonged to Carl Rosenbaum,
he is full of holes;
and that is Emmanuel Swedenborg
under the eighteenth century wig.
    There used to be dozens of us here;
now, beside myself, there are only a few others.
We're crazy, aren't we?
What gives us away?
I watch the president's party
wave goodbye;
I watch learned men and women
sit down on dirty little rugs
and I go back to my skulls in peace.
    "A jet of fire, a rain of stars in the night. . ."
Old Rolland and I are paying tribute to Beethoven.
". . . the voice of Death is drowned in the roars of Joy,
in the rush of the Revolution mob
demolishing the Bastilles and leaping over the tombs."
He was a skull-master too, Beethoven.
He knew how to widen the opening,
he knew how to lift the juices to his lips,
he knew all the highways and byways.
True, he was a bastard.
True, the screams of the poor reached his ears in a strange way.

True, he made a fetish of morality.
—Ah, we would differ on pity,
and I could never beat my breast like he did,
but I would give something to walk round the ramparts with him,
even to argue with him about Klopstock *und* Goethe.
I would love to reason with him about the *ubermensch*.
I would love to swap tales about our covenants with injustice.
I would love to fight with him over the soul.

  I'd like to hear him thunder,
with all his opaqueness;
I would be still, sometimes, for that one.
For that one I would drag out my discarded rug, and listen.

From the Pennsylvania Side

The weeds are out,
the flowering heads, the prickles,
I can walk with safety again.
I study the roadsides and fences
with secret pleasure;
all the stragglers and drifters
are blooming peacefully;
no one in the whole county will disturb them.

It isn't daytime yet for the chained dogs
and I am able to sneak past them for the first time
without a sound.
I smile at the floating hair
taking me seriously as a hillside
and the sticky barbs mistaking me for a sheep.
Like a loyal friend
I shift my leg to let the small teeth
get a good grip on my socks and shoe laces
and kick my toes in the mud
to liberate the sleepers.

At 6 A.M. I wash my eyes with dew
as Dante did at the foot of Purgatory
and fill my lungs with a little morning air
to clear my brain of Hell.
The Riegel Paper Company
is all I can see from where I sit.
Its stone chimneys and rusted machinery
belie its subtle connection

with Chase Manhattan and New England Life.
Inside hatchet men from International
are forcing the career men out
and the whole valley is trembling with bankruptcy.
Down the road the People's Dump
still takes whatever the rich Hog rejects.
There is enough free paper there
for the artists on both sides of the river.

I put my head on the ground
and lie there thinking.
For years I have been trying to figure out which I hate the most,
the House Beautiful with microwave ovens and high-heat incinerators
or the House Ugly with leaky stoves
and plastic bags spilling out over the sidewalk.
Across the river the milk run from Trenton
works its way up to Riegelsville, New Jersey.
It will take a whole morning
to maneuver four boxcars onto the siding
and three full days to unload them.
I will pass them once in the morning and once in the afternoon
on my own run into New Jersey.
I will slow down to look at the faded symbols
and read the signs.
Overhead the birds will pass obscure seeds
through their stomachs
and whatever the birds don't take the wind will.

At 8 o'clock I will go into the Cup and Saucer for breakfast.
The moody owner will stare resentfully into his television set,
the tired women will fall asleep over their coffee
and the heavy men will bend quietly over their eggs and bread.
The struggle for air and water will be forgotten
at the little tables;
no one in the room will have to fight for sunlight
or search for space;
they will be able to rest themselves—for thirty minutes—
before they go back again to their small trucks and their houses.

Turning into a Pond

All I need is one foot in the mud
to keep my sanity.
That way the water snakes can swim through my blood
and the greedy pickerel can hide
under my leaves.
All I have to do is fall asleep in the water
and let the yellow lights turn from gold to brown
as I sink to the bottom.
When it rains I can lie face down in the lilies
and let the naked couples rest their tired legs on my back.
When it gets dark I can sing to them about insanity
and compare my community to theirs.
I will release information softly,
using a deep voice for emphasis,
telling them one thing at a time.
At night I will slow down
and drift with the zooplankton.
I will dream about Voltaire and his white feet,
about Mozart and his hands.
The large mammals will waddle down to the shore
and drop their heads into the water.
The dragonfly will pull in its murderous lip
and the fisher spider will rest on its line.
In a century or two the beavers will turn me into a meadow
and my muddy wife will walk over my chest listening for cattails.
We will be so far apart it will take us weeks to reach each other.
Going by road you will be able to point me out when you get to Two
    Bridges,

in back of Penn Run, in Indiana County.
The weeds and grasses are beginning to struggle for attention;
the water is turning warm; we are going into April.

Lucky Life

The Power of Maples

If you want to live in the country you have to understand the power
    of maples.
You have to see them sink their teeth into the roots of the old
    locusts.
You have to see them force the sycamores to gasp for air.
You have to see them move their thick hairs into the cellar.
  And when you cut your great green shad pole
you have to be ready for it to start sprouting in your hands;
you have to stick it in the ground like a piece of willow;
you have to plant your table under its leaves and begin eating.

The Last Self-Portrait

Now I know why I have kept this orange flower wrapped up in tissue
and this faded picture and this rotting telephone number;
and now I know why I hang on to this wool jacket
when the threads are already showing and the lining is ruined;
and now I know why I empty my pockets
before I go to sleep and stare at my face in the mirror
like a white-haired painter going back to England
with four old suitcases and a leather trunk
full of ancient sketchbooks and stiff brushes,
holding my chin up for the last self-portrait.

At Bickford's

You should understand that I use my body now for everything
whereas formerly I kept it away from higher regions.
My clothes are in a stack over against the orange pine cupboard
and my hair is lying in little piles on the kitchen floor.
I am finally ready for the happiness I spent my youth arguing and
    fighting against.
    Twenty years ago—walking on Broadway—
I crashed into Shaddai and his eagles.
My great specialty was darkness then
and radiant sexual energy.
Now when light drips on me I walk around without tears.
—Before long I am going to live again on four dollars a day
in the little blocks between 96th and 116th.
I am going to follow the thin line of obedience
between George's Restaurant and Salter's Books.
There is just so much feeling left in me for my old ghost
and I will spend it all in one last outburst of charity.
I will give him money; I will listen to his poems;
I will pity his marriage.
—After that I will drift off again to Bickford's
and spend my life in the cracked cups and the corn muffins.
I will lose half my hatred
at the round tables
and let any beliefs that want to overtake me.
On lucky afternoons the sun will break through the thick glass
and rest like a hand on my forehead.
I will sit and read in my chair;
I will wave from my window.

One Foot in the River

Living on the river I am able to dip my feet in darkness
whenever I want to and touch the bottom with my with my white
     hands.

I am able to live for days in a cold state
besides the catfish and the bony shad.

Going to New York I carry the river in my head
and match it with the flow on 72nd Street and the flow on Broadway.

I always know where I am when the struggle begins
and a butchered face goes by me in the water.

I walk down as far as I can without sinking
and make my bed in the black sand and the bottles.

I lie there for hours watching the blood come,
one foot on 72nd Street, one foot in the river.

Straus Park

If you know about the Babylonian Jews
coming back to their stone houses in Jerusalem,
and if you know how Ben Franklin fretted
after the fire on Arch Street,
and if you yourself go crazy when you walk through the old shell
on Stout's Valley Road,
then you must know how I felt when I saw Stanley's Cafeteria
boarded up and the sale sign out;
and if you yourself mourned when you saw the back wall settling
and the first floor gone and the stairway gutted
then you must know how I felt when I saw the iron fence
and the scaffold and the plastic sheets in the windows.
—Don't go to California yet!
Come with me to Stanley's and spend your life
weeping in the small park on 106th Street.
Stay with me all night! I will give you
breast of lamb with the fat dripping over the edges;
I will give you the prophet of Baal
making the blood come.
Don't go to California with its big rotting sun
and its oleanders;
I will give you Sappho
preparing herself for the wind;
I will give you Mussolini
sleeping in his chair;
I will give you Voltaire
walking in the snow.
—This is the dark green bench
where I read Yeats,

and that is the fountain where the Deuteronomist sat
with his eyes on the nymph's stomach.
I want you to come here one more time
before you go to California;
I want you to see the Hotel Regent again
and the Edison Theater
and the Cleopatra Fruit Market.
Take the iron fence with you
when you go into the desert.
Take Voltaire and the Deuteronomist
and the luscious nymph.
Do not burn again for nothing.
Do not cry out again in clumsiness and shame.

Let Me Please Look into My Window

Let me please look into my window on 103rd Street one more time—
without crying, without tearing the satin, without touching
the white face, without straightening the tie or crumpling the flower.

Let me walk up Broadway past Zak's, past the Melody Fruit Store,
past Stein's Eyes, past the New Moon Inn, past the Olympia.

Let me leave quietly by gate 29
and fall asleep as we pull away from the ramp
into the tunnel.

Let me wake up happy, let me know where I am, let me lie still,
as we turn left, as we cross the water, as we leave the light.

I Need Help from the Philosophers

I need help from the philosophers, I am still attacked by memory;
I am losing Blake and his action, I'm losing his carved line;
I am haggling over my youth like a tender dealer.
    Let me close my eyes for one second and I see Bobby
Wiseman stuttering through his father's old jokes;
I see Olive Oyl sobbing behind a fence in Bluto's thick arms;
I see Geezil trying to keep his dignity in the azaleas;
I see my lapels carrying me over the reservoir, across the river;
I see my neck fresh from the barber, my chest bursting.
Oh I need help from Spinoza.
I don't want to grab Dante by the finger and ask him about my lost
    woods.
I don't want to hang around like Proust in the damp privies.
    My car rattles as I drive through the outskirts of Trenton looking
    for 539.
One more time I am going to Long Beach Island to lie down with the
    sand dollars.
I go there to watch the gulls and the pigeons struggle in their
    corridors.
I go there to encounter the jellyfish and the fleas.
    Up and down the strip the Philadelphians are lying in rows breast
    side up.
They are convalescing.
I go into the sea wrack itself to get as close as possible to the
    trenches.
I lie in the middle of the egg capsules and the lettuce.
I fish through the skeletons.
    With all my heart I study the crab's thin shell—

like a prostrate rabbi studying his own small markings—
so I can rise for one good hour like him
into a second existence, old and unchanging.

I Am So Exhausted

I am so exhausted I can barely lift my arms over my head to pull the
    vines down.
I try to pick up the soaked logs but my fingers slide over the bark
and my knees get wet from falling into the hillside.
    My wife is across the road glorying in her winter aconites.
Spring to her is setting out the onions
and moving the straw and resting on the wall.
We meet in the mud, like two crayfish;
I tip my ax, she tips her forsythia.
    It will take us time to learn to live together again,
to learn what to do with each other in the daylight,
to learn to talk again, without doors.
It will take us time to remember each other's secrets,
where the lilies are buried, where the moles are.
It will take us time to find our sadness,
and scrape the stones from our tongues,
and turn the dirt up for our slippery hearts.

On the Island

After cheating each other for eighteen years
this husband and this wife are trying to do something with the three
days they still have left before they go back to the city;
and after cheating the world for fifty years these two old men
touch the rosy skin under their white hair and try to remember
the days of solid brass and real wood
before the Jews came onto the island.
They are worried about the trees in India
and the corruption in the Boy Scouts
and the climbing interest rate,
but most of all they spend their time remembering
the beach the way it was in the early thirties
when all the big hotels here were shaped like Greek churches.

Me, I think about salt
and how my life will one day be clean and simple
if only I can reduce it all to salt,
how I will no longer lie down like a tired dog,
whispering and sighing before I go to sleep,
how I will be able to talk to someone
without going from pure joy to silence
and touch someone
without going from truth to concealment.

Salt is the only thing that lasts on this island.
It gets into the hair, into the eyes, into the clothes,
into the wood, into the metal.
Everything is going to disappear here but the salt.
The flags will go, the piers,

the gift shops, the golf courses, the clam bars,
and the telephone poles and the rows of houses and the string of cars.

I like to think of myself turned to salt
and all that I love turned to salt;
I like to think of coating whatever is left
with my own tongue and fingers.
I like to think of floating again in my first home,
still remembering the warm rock
and its slow destruction,
still remembering the first conversion to blood
and the forcing of the sea into those cramped vessels.

County Line Road

for Elmer Litschauer

You should hear the German farmers swearing in the underbrush
as they drag out another heavy stone and drop it in the cart.
They wish they were back in Germany,
thousands of miles away from this glacier,
sitting in their clean yards.
You should hear them still twittering in the sky,
arguing over peas and potatoes;
you should see their cows spread out in the grass
and their pigs drifting under the trees.
You should see their wives at the windows
taking a quick look at Hexenkopf Rock
and fixing the little buds on their nightgowns;
you should hear the iron beds creaking
before they fall asleep.
Oh you should come to these old fields and woods
to hear their voices move along the ground
and feel their fingers touch you as you bow down
to grapple with the blue stones, your head bent over steel,
your eyes bulging from the weight, your painful cries
floating through the wild flowers and the weeds.

Margie Moser's Garden

1 *Afternoon: Margie's American Revolution*

Thousands of ajugas marching down the hillside
in their pretty blue uniforms;
a few red blossoms gathering together for their last stand.

2 *Evening: Margie's Clothesline*

One end of Margie's clothesline is attached
to an English walnut.
She has five children and she spends the day
running and slaving for social agencies.
She sits on her wooden bench
as beautiful as either the small white duchess of Goya
or the golden sisters of Gauguin.

3 *Night: Margie's Peach Trees*

At midnight I walk up and down the white stone steps
that Russ Moser has constructed for the convenience of the Dunlap sisters
when they go to pick violets in the upper woods.
I feel like King David rising from his bed to give thanks
for being brought into the Garden.
Everything here is stone—stone walls,
stone bridges, stone walks—a paradise of stone,
and the air is filled with the odor of wild phlox and locust.
I lie on the grass beside the peach trees

looking at the moon and trying to figure out a just price
for the black walnut.
Down below the mimosa has closed up for the night
and the courtly tulips have rested a little from their constant bending
in the direction of the sun.
The rest of the night I will lie here listening to the dogs bark
and watching the tiny shadows on the peach trees.
I will look at my face drifting through the dark clouds
and dream about my life on the river.

When It Gets Cold

When it gets cold I put my body in the sun
and let the heat go through my clothes.
I develop small pockets of air
for my icy hands and fingers
and lie in my envelope
dreaming of fire.

I live in the brain,
drinking its water,
eating its rich food,
waiting for it to send out its small pulses
and find good furrows for the threads to root in,
waiting for it to search through the wet patches
and bring back fresh mud, and flowers, to my bed.

The Days of Nietzsche

I have moved so far into my own thought
I have almost forgotten the days of Nietzsche,
when he was my guide.

Now when I land in the steam
I walk between the Saints without anger,
leaving them to their own fires.

And when I drink my juice
I get as close as I can to the orange cooler
without getting wet.

And when I cross into Switzerland
I stay on the side of Schwarz's and Gubelin's
so I can see the dust shining.

And when I buy my tie
I let the blue hang out like a silk shawl
so I can lean a little before going back.

And when I receive my torn tongue in the mail
I put it between my teeth like a dead mouse
and let the blood run down my chin.

And when I stop to think
I know I am where I should be—I let the old restaurants
fill my soul—I let my feelings take over.

Burying an Animal on the Way to New York

Don't flinch when you come across a dead animal lying on the road;
you are being shown the secret of life.
Drive slowly over the brown flesh;
you are helping to bury it.
If you are the last mourner there will be no caress
at all from the crushed limbs
and you will have to slide over the dark spot imagining
the first suffering all by yourself.
Shreds of spirit and little ghost fragments will be spread out
for two miles above the white highway.
Slow down with your radio off and your window open
to hear the twittering as you go by.

The Sensitive Knife

Every day the dark blue sky of brother Van Gogh
gets closer and closer,
and every day the blue gentians of brother Lawrence
darken my eyes.
It is blue wherever I go,
walking the towpath,
climbing the stone island,
swimming the river,
and everywhere I sit or kneel
the blue goes through me like a sensitive knife.

I am following my own conception now
and during the night I flap my two-foot wings
in the black locusts.
I move thoughtfully from branch to branch,
always loving the stiffness and shyness
of the old giants.
I think of my own legs as breaking off
or my wings coming loose in the wind
or my blossoms dropping onto the ground.

Across the river the sticks are coming to life
and Mithras and Moses and Jesus are swaying and bowing
in all directions.
I swim carefully through the blood
and land on my feet on the side of Carpenter's Hill.
There on a flat rock

my father is placing the shank bone
and the roasted egg on a white napkin.
I climb over the rhododendrons and the dead trees to meet him.

The One Thing in Life

Wherever I go now I lie down on my own bed of straw
and bury my face in my own pillow.
I can stop in any city I want to
and pull the stiff blanket up to my chin.
It's easy now, walking up a flight of carpeted stairs
and down a hall past the painted fire doors.
It's easy bumping my knees on a rickety table
and bending down to a tiny sink.
There is a sweetness buried in my mind;
there is water with a small cave behind it;
there's a mouth speaking Greek.
It is what I keep to myself; what I return to;
the one thing that no one else wanted.

Four Sad Poems on the Delaware

1 *The Flowering Dogwood*

This is an old tuxedo shirt
gone a little yellow with age.
I open it up
and its petals fall into the grass.

2 *The Wild Columbine*

This is one of the flower animals.
Its head hangs down like a horse's
and its snout waves patiently in the wind.
It moves on the rock like the slowest of mollusks,
an inch every hundred years.

3 *The Mayapple*

This is a mayapple, living like a socialist
in the shade of the towpath.
It is one of the machines for living
that Le Corbusier designed in the old days.

4 *The Black Locust*

This is a locust tree, dying of love,
waiting one more time for its flowers to come,
regretting its life on the stupid river,
growing more and more Jewish as its limbs weaken.

On My Poor Road

On my poor road there is nothing but opossum and groundhog,
the two vegetables of the animal kingdom;
no skunk, no deer, no beaver—not even a small snake
to ruin the balance;
only easy digging, and soft chewing, and staring at the sky.

On my poor road a man lives like a slug;
he rides along the soil like an old wheel,
leaving a trail of silver,
and makes his home in the wet grass and the flowers.
He is finally free of all the other mysteries
he had accepted
and sees himself suddenly lying there warm and happy.

At night he drinks his water by the dark stove
while the small radio moans
and the heart breaks in two to the words of old songs
and the memory of other small radios in other gardens.

Blue Skies, White Breasts, Green Trees

What I took to be a man in a white beard
turned out to be a woman in a silk babushka
weeping in the front seat of her car;
and what I took to be a seven-branched candelabrum
with the wax dripping over the edges
turned out to be a horse's skull
with its teeth sticking out of the sockets.
It was my brain fooling me,
sending me false images,
turning crows into leaves
and corpses into bottles,
and it was my brain that betrayed me completely,
sending me entirely uncoded material,
for what I thought was a soggy newspaper
turned out to be the first Book of Concealment, written in English,
and what I thought was a grasshopper on the windshield
turned out to be the Faithful Shepherd chewing blood,
and what I thought was, finally, the real hand of God
turned out to be only a guy wire and a
pair of broken sunglasses.
I used to believe the brain did its work
through faithful charges and I lived in sweet surroundings for the brain.
I thought it needed blue skies, white breasts, green trees,
to excite and absorb it,
and I wandered through the golf courses dreaming of pleasure
and struggled through the pool dreaming of happiness.
Now if I close my eyes I can see the uncontrolled waves
closing and opening of their own accord
and I can see the pins sticking out in unbelievable places,

and I can see the two lobes floating like two old barrels on the Hudson.
I am ready to reverse everything now
for the sake of the brain.
I am ready to take the woman with the white scarf
in my arms and stop her moaning,
and I am ready to light the horse's teeth,
and I am ready to stroke the dry leaves.
For it was kisses, and only kisses,
and not a stone knife in the neck that ruined me,
and it was my right arm, full of power and judgment,
and not my left arm twisted backwards to express vagrancy,
and it was the separation that *I* made,
and not the rain on the window
or the pubic hairs sticking out of my mouth,
and it was not really New York falling into the sea,
and it was not Nietzsche choking on an ice cream cone,
and it was not the president lying dead again on the floor,
and it was not the sand covering me up to my chin,
and it was not my thick arms ripping apart an old floor,
and it was not my charm, breaking up an entire room.
It was my delicacy, my stupid delicacy,
and my sorrow.
It was my ghost, my old exhausted ghost,
that I dressed in white, and sent across the river,
weeping and weeping and weeping
inside his torn sheet.

The Sounds

After it rains you should sigh a little for the spongy world.
You should listen to the fish gasping in the underbrush
and the duck's heart beating twenty yards away.
When the music arrives you should let it take you back across the river
into the kitchens where the clean hands are linked.
You should lie on the stones underneath the cold waterfall
and let your fingers drift hopelessly through the foam.
You should float slowly past the row of barking dogs
and visit the silent opossum in his grotto.
You should go to sleep between the sobs of the 9 o'clock local on the
    Jersey side
and the whines of Sea-Land and Roadway on the Pennsylvania.

Sometimes When I Close My Eyes

Sometimes when I close my eyes in the late afternoon
another eye is looking at me in the center of my lid.
It is a bird's eye, with its special flap of skin
pulled up and over its great bulge of vision,
and I look in curiosity, and peace, at my enemy.
    But sometimes, when I stare, it also blinks and waters
and turns away with such shyness I am almost frightened,
finding weakness and sensitivity reflected in that eye.
Then I get up, put on my clothes, and walk outside
to stand watch by the cold river,
hoping I don't have to spend the rest of my life out there
staring through the trees,
hoping that my odd mind will keep me going
if nothing else does
and hoping my lips alone can carry me from place to place
and tremble when they have to, and sing when they have to,
without help, or interference.

The Blue Tie

With the cry of the duck in my ears
I go out every morning
to fish for keys, to hunt for brushes,
to untwist cables.

More and more I go into the dark
sighing for what I leave behind me
instead of caring for what lies ahead.

Some days my car stands still
on the bridge that separates two states
and my hand drops over the iron rail like a tired bird.

That is when my mind disappears
on the first bend up the river
and hangs between the two concealed shores.

That is when I struggle back and forth
like a leather wing looking for wisdom
in the cold schools and the empty gas stations.

That is when I wear my old blue necktie
and fly low like a frozen jay looking for happiness
in the slippery roads and the silent covered faces.

Mentioning of the Souls

If I get up one more time in the dark
you will have to cover me up completely
I will be shaking so much from the cold.
And if my voice trembles as I go from room to room
you will have to leave your own luxury
to see if I am just moaning or already talking to the dead.
If you come into the kitchen
you will see how painful it is
to cross over to the dark stove;
if you sit with me one whole night
you will see how slow the hours go
in front of the hanging plants.
Stand by the crowded window for five minutes
and watch the light come in through the crippled birch.
You can laugh a little
at my wolfish soul staring at the moon;
you can close your eyes
as I say the names,
and remember, with your own lips,
as I go over the victories and the failures.

Self-Portrait

When I turn the ceiling light on
the sky turns purple and the bathroom window is filled
with a mountain of crooked limbs like a huge Van Gogh.
When I turn it off the details change,
the trunks appear, the ducks walk up the grass
and the candles begin to shine in the dark canal.
In either case I am looking at two large gum trees
sweetly shaped by years of care and now
left alone to live or die slowly and peacefully.
I will think about them all day and dream about staying here
like a secret body at the window while they change in the light
from snarled twig to violent branch to limb with shadow;
and I will dream about standing out there on the towpath
staring back at myself in this large empty house.
      Others will go to Paris, sit at the tables,
and do the River, and do the Boulevard;
I will stand at the window dressed like a prisoner
in old corduroys and Brown's Beach vest and jacket
fingering the stamped buttons and testing the pockets.
I will look at my greenish eyes in the mirror
and touch my graying hair and twist my hat.
I will think of Van Gogh in Brussels raging
against the bourgeois world, I will think of him
working all day in the sun, I'll think of him in shock;
and I will think of myself sitting in Raubsville,
the only Jew on the river, counting my poems
and—finally—counting my years; and I will think of
Van Gogh when he headed south, I will think of him giving his
life to the art of the future, I will think of his poverty,

I will think of his depressions and exaltations;
I will think of him with yellow straw hat and pipe;
I will think of him with fur cap and bandaged ear;
I will think of him against the whirling lines,
small and powerful in the hands of the blue God;
and I will think of myself walking down my road
between the rows of dogs—so familiar now
that only one still barks, the horrible Schoene,
clawing her concrete and biting her twisted fence,
and I will think of the weeds and watery places
where I can go to rest between the scourges,
and I will think of New York just two hours away
still rotting and gleaming in the golden dust.
—I will think of myself in my rabbi's suit
walking across the marshland to my car;
I will think of myself in black beard and corncob
dragging the hay or leaning against a locust;
and I will think of the mad existence of all artists
as they lean against trees, and doors, and I will look with
horror at the vile ones, the bugs eating up our leaves,
and I will dream of another artistic life for
the fiftieth time, of a small decayed city
half buried in sand, surrounded by trees and water,
with artists living together, with old newspapers lying
piled up under the porches, with that whole race
of mothers and carpenters and gardeners
living inside their houses and in their yards.
    For the sake of Van Gogh I will dream it, for the sake of his
        olive trees,

for the sake of his empty chair, for the sake of his Bible,
for the sake of his inflamed eyes, for the sake of his wild mind;
and for the sake of his black Belgians retching and gasping for air
and for the sake of his Londoners stumbling over the greasy cobbles
and for the sake of his exhausted farmers stabbing at their potatoes
and for the sake of all the lunatics of God, for the sake of the flesh-
eaters gathering after work at the Authority, for the sake of
the wagons and baby carriages lined up outside the Armory, for the
    sake of
the frozen Armenians going back into their empty towns, for the
    sake of
the Jews of Vilna waiting inside their synagogues and for the sake of
the naked boys moving between the numbered tables and for the sake
of the slowly moving bodies under Lexington Avenue and for
the sake of the horses that labored quietly for three thousand
years and for the sake of the unassimilated wolves who lay trapped
inside their own forests; and in memory of the first stones we dragged
out of the mountain and in memory of the Fire
out of which the burned doves flew looking for water
and in memory of the long life that stretches back now
almost a million years and in memory of the cold rain
that saved our lives and in memory of the leaves
that helped us breathe and in pleasant memory
of the grass that clung to our slippery arms and legs
and in memory of the nourishing sand in which we lay like dead fishes
slowly mastering the sky. In honor of Albert Einstein.
In honor of Eugene Debs. In honor of Emma Goldman.

Lobelia

I have to be somewhere inside those flats
stretching my roots out and reaching down for water.

I have to be living in that black world
swallowing whatever I can that is soft and fluid.

I have to be growing so quietly
the smoke goes over me and the wet claws pass me by.

I have to be lying there in globes of dirt
sharing justice with the thin blades of grass.

Three Tears

1

If you have seen a single yellow iris
standing watch beside the garden,
then you have seen the Major General weeping
at four in the morning in his mother's Bible;
and if you have seen the rows and rows of onions,
then you have seen the army with its shoes half off
and its rifles half stacked and half scattered in the witch hazel.
But you who have seen the half-eaten leaves of the hackberry
have seen the saddest sight of all,
a nest inside a ruined building,
a father hugging his child,
a Jew in Vilna.

2

You would have to sit at my bedroom window
to see the dog of hay guarding the strawberries.
He is twice the size of an Irish wolfhound
and heavier than a bear.
He belongs to the hairy species with the sheepdog
and the long-nosed collie.
He lies there day after day in the middle of the garden
with his paws crossed under his chin and his eyes watching the road.
He is so clean-smelling and so peaceful
that we forget the strength in his huge body
and the malice in his jaws.

3

I have to lie on my back for two hours
before a certain cloud comes by;
then I only have three or four good seconds
before it disappears again for another day.
What would it have been like
if there had been no maples and no viburnum
to cut off my vision,
if I could have lived all year in the sand
with nothing to stop me but my own thoughts,
if I could have let my eye go freely down the line
choosing its own movement and its own light?

Climbing This Hill Again

This is a feast, climbing this hill again,
snapping thorns, rubbing a little blood on my ankle.
I know every tree on the hillside,
every stump and runner.
I lie on my back again as I always do,
stretching my legs out and entering the blue world.
Over my head a 30,000 pound stone sits
supported by a lump of grass and a few flowers.
I draw little figures in the flat spaces
with my round eye, as I always do,
and make the shadows out of the sun's roots.
This year I do it in memory of Emma Goldman
and the immigration officer who gave her a bouquet of white lilacs
for her trip back to Russia,
and I do it in memory of her fight against property
and I do it in memory of her unprinted speeches.
It doesn't really matter;
I could do it for Pablo Casals just as well
and the lost Republic,
or Simone de Beauvoir waving goodbye to a deranged America,
the woods are so rich here and the stone so smooth.
I will probably be able to come back ten more years
before it gives way and falls into the river.
Next year I will know for sure if I have to change my mountain;
in the meantime I will learn how to lie down without pain
and I will learn how to let my mind go more and more astray.
    Tonight I am going into Philadelphia to hear two
New York poets sing about the wilderness.
If I grow a little arrogant, or a little sleepy,

it is because of the stone I am lying under
and the river I always drag around behind me.
I reach into my pocket for the small Barlow
I carry with me to remind myself of my own
hatred of captivity
and cut a little at the thick vines that are choking
the life out of these trees.
It is a quiet act which I do out of memory,
having little to do with the injustices of nature
and even less to do with the slaughters—and stupidities—of history.
—Their wilderness is good too, the rat smells
behind the Jewish bakery, the Norwegian birches in the hallway,
the seashells floating in the windows.
   It is good to have a high place to come back to.
It is good to be able to separate yourself
from the man sleeping beside the dogwoods
and the ladies with buckets digging up jack-in-the-pulpit
and pulling wild columbine out of the rock face.
This has to be the last week the poison
will let me lie here on the ground
without running violently through my skin.
I throw a tender look at Emma Goldman
bending over my face to show mercy.
I reach up with long horrified fingers
to touch the strings of the sainted cello
and start my slide down the soft dangerous hillside.

Lucky Life

Lucky life isn't one long string of horrors
and there are moments of peace, and pleasure, as I lie in between
    the blows.
Lucky I don't have to wake up in Phillipsburg, New Jersey,
on the hill overlooking Union Square or the hill overlooking
Kuebler Brewery or the hill overlooking Saints Philip and James
but have my own hills and my own vistas to come back to.

Each year I go down to the island I add
one more year to the darkness;
and though I sit up with my dear friends
trying to separate the one year from the other,
this one from the last, that one from the former,
another from another,
after a while they all get lumped together,
the year we walked to Holgate,
the year our shoes got washed away,
the year it rained,
the year my tooth brought misery to us all.

This year was a crisis. I knew it when we pulled
the car onto the sand and looked for the key.
I knew it when we walked up the outside steps
and opened the hot icebox and began the struggle
with swollen drawers and I knew it when we laid out
the sheets and separated the clothes into piles
and I knew it when we made our first rush onto
the beach and I knew it when we finally sat
on the porch with coffee cups shaking in our hands.

My dream is I'm walking through Phillipsburg, New Jersey,
and I'm lost on South Main Street. I am trying to tell,
by memory, which statue of Christopher Columbus
I have to look for, the one with him slumped over
and lost in weariness or the one with him
vaguely guiding the way with a cross and globe in
one hand and a compass in the other.
My dream is I'm in the Eagle Hotel on Chamber Street
sitting at the oak bar, listening to two
obese veterans discussing Hawaii in 1942,
and reading the funny signs over the bottles.
My dream is I sleep upstairs over the honey locust
and sit on the side porch overlooking the stone culvert
with a whole new set of friends, mostly old and humorless.

Dear waves, what will you do for me this year?
Will you drown out my scream?
Will you let me rise through the fog?
Will you fill me with that old salt feeling?
Will you let me take my long steps in the cold sand?
Will you let me lie on the white bedspread and study
the black clouds with the blue holes in them?
Will you let me see the rusty trees and the old monoplanes one more
        year?
Will you still let me draw my sacred figures
and move the kites and the birds around with my dark mind?

Lucky life is like this. Lucky there is an ocean to come to.
Lucky you can judge yourself in this water.

Lucky the waves are cold enough to wash out the meanness.
Lucky you can be purified over and over again.
Lucky there is the same cleanliness for everyone.
Lucky life is like that. Lucky life. Oh lucky life.
Oh lucky lucky life. Lucky life.

Malagueña

With a dead turtle floating down my canal
and a stone pillar in my river
and wild jewels growing outside my door,
all I have to do is reach up
and I am back again, living with shadows.

I come from such an odd place
that the slightest wind ignites me
and the smallest tremor makes me weep or lie down.

Tonight, in the dark living room, my daughter is
playing "Malagueña" on her warped piano.
After two weeks of dampness the moist notes
float across the road trying to find brotherhood
with anything that is crooked or twisted or smiling.

I am over here in the garage
letting the mold take over;
I am getting ready for my own
darkness;
I am letting the sound of the islands
go through my veins again, like water.

Pile of Feathers

This time there was no beak,
no little bloody head, no bony
claw, no loose wing—only a small
pile of feathers without substance or center.

Our cats dig through the leaves, they
stare at each other in surprise,
they look carefully over their shoulders,
they touch the same feathers over and over.

They have been totally cheated of the body.
The body with its veins and its fat
and its red bones has escaped them.
Like weak giants
they try to turn elsewhere.
Like Americans on the Ganges,
their long legs twisted in embarrassment,
their knees scraping the stones,
they begin crawling after the spirit.

Feeding Prisoners

The weeds give up suddenly after a small struggle
and fall into your hands like German prisoners.
Suddenly you are surrounded by a whole division of undressed men
who are looking to you for wisdom and shelter.
Now you have to grow food again.
You have to put stakes in the ground
to mark the boundaries
and tie little rags
to the invisible wires.
You have to start moving the rusted tanks out
and stack the oil drums up behind the latrines.
You have to think up a plan for getting out food and water.
Suddenly you are back again in a crowded city
full of corruption and loneliness
after your quick and easy victory.

Gold Flower

This is the season for chrysanthemums,
the gold flower of Japan.
Everything else is already spotted and dry and crumbled.
I am holding five varieties in my hand,
the quill, the daisy, the spoon, the spider, the button.
I am putting them in clean jars and glasses.
I didn't begin my new worship
until the last sun of the year
brought me face to face with the shiny clusters.
I had never seen them before.
I had walked through gardens all my life without seeing them.
How ignorant I was;
and what I lost through anger and impatience.
Dear ladies, how gravely you stand there in your wool suits and your
        jewelry;
what strength there is in your fingers;
how you have come to resemble each other after forty years.
Dear old man, how your great nose and your pouches took over at last;
how your hand hangs limply over its pipe;
how you smile in the middle of your bright giants
remembering your dead wife.
Dear world of strangers!
Dear life I half missed!
Dear hidden rules. Dear men and women
carrying the sunlight down into the soft dirt with you.

Honey Locust

Here are about seventy snakes waiting to come to life,
each one about a foot long,
with noisy seeds inside them like little coffee beans.

They are curled up for the winter,
some in the leaves, some on the grass walk,
some lying face down or face up in the snow.

I put about twenty in my pocket so I can look at them
when I get home and tear them apart slowly
and shake them like old rattles in my ear.

I read and study all night trying to understand their cries
as they pull themselves loose and dance around in their beds
and sing about their lives like old musicians
singing about theirs.

Proverbs

It is when there is not one leather jacket left with
the rivets crawling up and down the arms like civilized lice
and not one wrinkled hand or one tired forehead
carrying the creases in both directions
and not one pair of eyes that hates light
the way a starling hates wisdom
that I will be able to live again in a chair
with my feet propped up in the window
and know there is a future for my sanity.

Gert's Gifts

There were two jokes played on me on my first long walk in Florida
    this winter,
the English muffin joke and the foam rubber joke.
Nothing else fooled me, none of the grotesqueries and combinations,
not even the driftwood tree growing fresh purple flowers on its
    green tips.
It's good to be back in Florida where the dead things bloom,
where the sea grapes drop leather leaves in the sand
and the saw grass grows through the cracked cement
and the sweet honeys walk by on silk platforms
promising luxury and renewal in the green darkness.

Stepping Out of Poetry

What would you give for one of the old yellow streetcars
rocking toward you again through the thick snow?

What would you give for the feeling of joy as you climbed
up the three iron steps and took your place by the cold window?

Oh, what would you give to pick up your stack of books
and walk down the icy path in front of the library?

What would you give for your dream
to be as clear and simple as it was then
in the dark afternoons, at the old scarred tables?

Behaving Like a Jew

When I got there the dead opossum looked like
an enormous baby sleeping on the road.
It took me only a few seconds—just
seeing him there—with the hole in his back
and the wind blowing through his hair
to get back again into my animal sorrow.
I am sick of the country, the bloodstained
bumpers, the stiff hairs sticking out of the grilles,
the slimy highways, the heavy birds
refusing to move;
I am sick of the spirit of Lindbergh over everything,
that joy in death, that philosophical
understanding of carnage, that
concentration on the species.
—I am going to be unappeased at the opossum's death.
I am going to behave like a Jew
and touch his face, and stare into his eyes,
and pull him off the road.
I am not going to stand in a wet ditch
with the Toyotas and the Chevies passing over me
at sixty miles an hour
and praise the beauty and the balance
and lose myself in the immortal lifestream
when my hands are still a little shaky
from his stiffness and his bulk
and my eyes are still weak and misty
from his round belly and his curved fingers
and his black whiskers and his little dancing feet.

Love for the Dog

Bob Summers

Before he opened his eyes, as he lay there under the window,
he was convinced he would be able to speak this time and sort
    things out
clearly as he did when his tongue was still a hammer;
a half hour later he was once again on the chair
with all these keepers staring at him in pity and fear
and giving him milk and cocoa and white napkins.
In the middle of his exhausted brain there rose a metaphor
of an animal, a dog, with a broken spine, sliding around
helplessly in the center of the slippery floor
with loving owners all around encouraging him
and the dog trying desperately to please them.
He sat there proud of his metaphor, tears of mercy in his eyes,
unable in his dumbness to explain his pleasure,
unable now even to rise because of the spine.
He felt only love for the dog,
all different from the ugly muscular cat
which had leaped the day before on his bony thigh
as if it were a tree limb or an empty chair,
as if he could not run again if he had to,
as if there was not life still pouring out voluptuously
like wild water through all his troubled veins.

Psalms

When I drove through the little bald hills of Tennessee
I thought of the rabbis of Brooklyn bent over their psalms.
I thought of the tufts of hair and the bones and ridges
and the small cows eating peacefully
out on the open slope or in the shadows
while the forehead wrinkled and the gigantic lips moved
through the five books of ecstasy, grief and anger.

This Is It
1974

It is my emotions that carry me through Lambertville, New Jersey,
sheer feeling—and an obscure detour—that brings me to a coffee
    shop
called "This Is It" and a small New Jersey clapboard
with a charming fake sign announcing it to be
the first condemned building in the United States
and an old obese collie sitting on the cement steps
of the front porch begging forgiveness with his red eyes.
I talk to the coughing lady for five minutes,
admire her sign, her antique flag, her dog,
and share her grief over the loss of the house next door,
boarded up forever, tied up in estates,
surrounded by grass, doomed to an early fire.

Everyone is into my myth! The whole countryside
is studying weeds, collecting sadness, dreaming
of odd connections and no place more than Lambertville
will do for ghosts to go through your body
or people to live out their lives with a blurred vision.
The old woman is still talking. She tells me
about her youth, she tells me about her mother's ganglia
and how the doctor slammed a heavy Bible down
on her watery wrist, scattering spoons and bread crumbs
and turning over little tin containers
of alyssum and snapdragon. She tells me about the
curved green glass that is gone forever. She tells me
about her dog and its monotonous existence.

Ah, but for sadness there are very few towns like Lambertville.
It drips with grief, it almost sags from the weight.
I know Frackville, P.A., and Sandusky, Ohio,
and I know coal chutes, empty stores and rusty rivers
but Lambertville is special, it is a wooden stage set,
a dream ridden carcass where people live out serious lives
with other peoples' secrets, trying to touch with their hands
and eat with their cold forks, and open houses with their keys;
and sometimes, on a damp Sunday, they leave the papers on the front
      porch
to walk down York Street or Buttonwood Street
past abandoned factories and wooden garages,
past the cannon with balls and the new band shell,
past the downtown churches and the antique shops,
and even across the metal plates on the Delaware River
to stinking New Hope, where all their deep longing
is reduced to an hour and a half of greedy buying.

I crawl across the street to have my coffee at the low counter,
to listen to the noise of the saws drifting through the open window
and to study the strange spirit of this tar paper cafe
stuck on a residential street three or four blocks
from Main and Bridge where except for the sudden windfall
of the looping detour it would be relegated forever
to the quiet company of three or four close friends
and the unexpected attention of a bored crossing guard
or exhausted meter man or truck driver.
I listen to the plans of the three teen-age businessmen
about to make their fortune in this rotting shack

and walk—periodically—past the stainless steel sink
to take my piss in the misplaced men's room.
I watch the bright happy girls organize their futures
over and around the silent muscular boys
and I wait, like a peaceful man, hours on end,
for the truck out back to start, for the collie to die,
for the flies to come, for the summer to bring its reckoning.

The Cemetery of Orange Trees in Crete

In Crete the old orange trees are cut back until they are stumps,
with little leaves coming out again from the butchered arms.
They are painted white and stand there in long straight rows
like the white gravestones at Gettysburg and Manassas.
    I first came across them on the bus ride to Omalos
as we began our climb through the empty mountains,
thinking of the beauty and exhaustion that lay ahead.
They are mementos of my journey south, the renewal
of my youth, green leaves growing out of my neck,
my shoulders flowering again with small blossoms,
my body painted white, my hands joining
the other hands on the hill, my white heart remembering
the violence and sorrow that gave us our life again.

96 Vandam

I am going to carry my bed into New York City tonight
complete with dangling sheets and ripped blankets;
I am going to push it across three dark highways
or coast along under 600,000 faint stars.
I want to have it with me so I don't have to beg
for too much shelter from my weak and exhausted friends.
I want to be as close as possible to my pillow
in case a dream or a fantasy should pass by.
I want to fall asleep on my own fire escape
and wake up dazed and hungry
to the sound of garbage grinding in the street below
and the smell of coffee cooking in the window above.

If You Forget the Germans

If you forget the Germans climbing up and down the Acropolis,
then I will forget the poet falling through his rotten floor in New
    Brunswick;
and if you stop telling me about your civilization in 1400 B.C.,
then I will stop telling you about mine in 1750 and 1820 and 1935;
and if you stop throwing your old walls and your stone stairs at me,
then I will drop my overstuffed chairs and my rusty scooters.
—Here is an old leather shoe to look at;
give me anything, a pebble from the Agora, a tile from Phaistos;
and here is a perfectly intact bottle of Bollo;
give me a delicate red poppy or a purple thistle growing beside the
    Parthenon.
Here are the photographs, myself crawling out on the charred beam,
a carton of Salems, a crib with mattress, a pigeon feather,
a plywood door, a piece of the blue sky,
a bottle of Smirnoff's, a bottle of Seagram's,
a bottle of Night Train Express.
Show me yours, the oldest theater in Europe,
a woman playing the harp, a marble foot,
a bronze frying pan, a fish swimming in crystal,
a boar's tusk helmet, a god screaming, a painted eyelid.
Here are the thoughts I have had;
here are the people I have talked to and worn out;
here are the stops in my throat;
here is the ocean throwing up dead crabs and card tables.
—If you go by bus, take the Suburban Transit
and get off if you can before the Highland Park Bridge.
If you go by car, take route 18 east
past the Riverview Bar and try to park

on either Peace or Church.
If you walk, go north on Church past the old Gramercy
and the health food store and God's Deliverance Center
to the mound of dirt and the broken telephone booth.
Do not bury yourself outright in the litter;
walk gently over the broken glass;
admire the pictures on the upstairs rear wall.
Sing and cry and kiss in the ruined dining room
in front of the mirror, in the plush car seat,
a 1949 or '50, still clean and perfect
under the black dust and the newspapers,
as it was when we cruised back and forth all night looking for
    happiness;
as it was when we lay down and loved in the old darkness.

The Hungarian

If I waited till September
I could no longer walk on the bottom of the river.
I would be up to my waist in water,
fighting off gnats
and trying to find the stones with my soggy shoes.
By then the Hungarian would already be back in Europe,
telling his friends about the man he met in Pennsylvania
who spoke to him in German and told him about the
glaciers and the violent American poison.
—I could have kissed him goodbye, I knew him so well.
We walked up and down the mule path for two hours
with our hands behind us.
We bent down to pick up fish hooks and cigarette packs
as if we were walking through our own park.
We touched in each other one last loving time
the dream of justice we both had buried in our own rivers
like two gnostics who buried their city's statues
twenty feet down in the thick mud and the shadows
to keep them from greed and hatred,
to save them for the serious souls to come.

Bob Summers: The Final Poem

There are two men I know who wander around all winter as I do,
half listening and half falling over rocks and curbs.
One is a bicyclist who pedals all day on
an old balloon-tire bike through Upper Black Eddy;
the other is a bridge-walker who wears a long army
overcoat with "P.O.W." still faintly printed across the back.
There was a third who walked down the streets of Philadelphia,
touching base at the Chess Club and Frank's and the Greek's
like a farmer, or beggar, doing the daily round.
If you saw just the back of his head
and his hands waving you would know he was leading you
through one of his darker arguments;
if you followed him further
you would be dragged to a place where every connection was smashed
and the brain had trouble sorting out its own riches.
I last saw him concentrating with all his power
on the problem of simple existence,
trying to match words with places
and blurred thoughts with things,
reducing everyone who knew him or came near him
to a state of either pity or shame
because of his strangeness and clumsiness.
I remember the rope he carried
and the knot of terror he fingered as he daydreamed,
the knot of release, hanging slack like a crown
over the back of his neck,
always ready to guide him through his weakness,
ready to give him back his health and wisdom.

God of Rain, God of Water

Each spring the long-nosed god of rain,
when it's his turn, rises from the gang of old men
sitting day and night in the dirt in front of the fire
and makes the monotonous noises and does the slow
crawling steps and little bows that are his stock in trade.
Tears pour from his eyes, rheum from his nose,
saliva from his mouth and clean colorless water
in an endless cascade from his swollen tube.

I see him in various conventional shapes in the clouds,
long arms slowly shifting through the light and dark,
or sometimes in the leaves of the two trees,
waving his head and shoulders in the sky
and dropping mist on everything that passes,
or sometimes as an all-night and all-day rain
filling the whole house with dread and sorrow,
or sometimes just as a dirty runnel sweeping
relentlessly through stones and leaves and paper
and down the storm sewers to the river,
singing wildly in the underground passages.

What I do is go around the countryside looking for mosses
or wait for the geese to come back up the river
or stare at the strange red blossoms in my front yard
that are either old seedpods or new leaves on the old maples.
There is a line of sticks I look at on the Jersey side
that I can just see from my bedroom window before my own
trees turn green and blot out the view.
When these sticks grow soft, when there's a slight blur on everything,

then I know the bees are circling the dead logs,
the vines are taking hold in the new dirt
and the first flowers are starting to use the light.

Then I remember other springs
when, in a sudden fit of violence, my own life was changed
in the very middle of its flowering.
I am able to zero in on those years with more clarity now
as each new one passes, so that not one detail is lost;
as if the clarity illuminated the pain;
as if the pain decreased where the clarity took over;
as if the clarity were taking the place of the pain.
—The old man when he goes back into the circle is still weeping
and War and Procreation and Music, three of the oldest and saddest,
slap him on his soaking back, shouting above the roar of the fire
and the constant din of the unorganized gods chattering,
"Nice show, good show, good show," but he, the rain god,
is sobbing uncontrollably, thick drops are coming from his eyes,
and he is gasping and finally his arms alone are moving,
and he is in the center of the huge circle on his hands and knees
pounding the earth, dry gasps are coming from his throat
and a trickle of thin water from his mouth,
while all around him violets are springing up in the dirty cinders,
and giant thistles and strings of chicory and daisies,
to pay him for his tears, to pay the old god for his tears,
apart from everything else, to pay him for his tears.

Home from Greece

You can have the Old Causeway Inn on a Saturday night
with two hundred people waiting to get at the fish platters;
I will walk down the road to Stewart's
and sit at the counter with my watery root beer.
And you can have the future home of the Frenchtown Roller Rink
if I can have the field with cows grazing on silk and alfalfa;
and you can take Memory Town, U.S.A.,
and Land of Make Believe and Story Book Forest
if you give me an old bathtub on legs,
if you give me Nate's Pub buried in Spotswood;
and you can have the seven-headed beast or the nine-,
rising from the waves,
if you give me a dog whining on his foul croppers
by way of a man-faced leopard or a four-horned goat.

If the horses did come they would pick Stewart's.
That is where the sun and moon would be darkened.
That is where the grass would be burnt.

I have been crying this out for years.
I have been standing on the upper highway
above the salt beds and the mosquito ditches;
I have been sitting inside the miniature golf course
beside the plywood castles and windmills;
I have been leaning against the wire fence,
surrounded by bread and seashells,
counting beasts in the moonlight.

Long Nose

It is this Mexican lying on his back with his
face in the air that gives me my new distance.

It is the way he stares at the ceiling, the way he listens,
the way he expresses himself with only a head.

It is his thick painted lips and his high cheekbones.

It is his two noses and the old conflict between them,
the two cultures fighting against each other,
a strip of wood and some rusty nails hiding
his rich knowledge,
the eyebrows and the mustache making a joke
of the longing in his close-set eyes,
the holes in the temples finishing the job,
string hanging down over the wine bottles,
the wooden chin coming back to life
with memories of sweat in the old sunlight
and memories of pleasure in the silent afternoons.

If You Saw Me Walking

If you saw me walking one more time on the island
you would know how much the end of August meant to me;

and if you saw me singing as I slid over the wet stones
you would know I was carrying the secret of life in my hip pocket.

If my lips moved too much
you would follow one step behind to protect me;

if I fell asleep too soon
you would cover me in light catalpa or dry willow.

Oh if I wore a brace you would help me, if I stuttered
you would hold my arm, if my heart beat with fear

you would throw a board across the channel, you would put
out a hand to catch me, you would carry me on your back.

If you saw me swim back and forth through the algae
you would know how much I love the trees floating under me;

and if you saw me hold my leaf up to the sun
you would know I was still looking for my roots;

and if you saw me burning wood
you would know I was trying to remember the smell of maple.

If I rushed down the road buttoning my blue shirt—
if I left without coffee—if I forgot my chewed-up pen—

you would know there was one more day of happiness
before the water rose again for another year.

The Thaw

1 *Coleus*

Here's a blue flower to keep me company,
a piece of the tropics, in the middle of my bedroom.
It is exactly like my mind, a blue spike
surrounded by thick red leaves and shiny branches.
I will come up here every hour to watch it grow,
to watch it push itself against the leaves
and finally bend, as it must, under the pressure
and scatter its dust in the white dirt;
and I will watch the new minds coming,
mostly green at first, more like awkward leaves themselves
with only touches of the great blue in them,
like touches of madness in the colored forest,
new clusters of joy and anger and sorrow
pulling down again on the overworked branches.

2 *Night-blooming Cereus*

This one has wings and sends out aerial roots
like a leafy insect sending out feelers.
One night a year, when darkness and light work out
their secret balance, it makes its large white flower.
I will dream of it while I call my weary friends
for the third year in a row to help me drag
my books and furniture out of the dirty water,
and I will think of its flat green curled branches
while the ice floats on the river and the blunt-backed starling

slides on the glazes of the black birch,
dreaming of its own darkness and its all-night flowering.

3 *Curly Ivy*

This is a plant I almost didn't move
when my line of workers began climbing the stairs,
dragging lamps and chairs and heavy rugs with them.
There is no part of my body it matches, no stringy
organs, no starved liver or withered heart,
and nothing in me that reaches out
to its dryness or its deadness by way of identity.
It is what it is, a brittle curly ivy
ruined by extreme cold and extreme heat.
I touch it once, I almost pet it, and then I
leave it in its white saucer and its red pot
with the jades and spiders, waiting to be saved.

Morning Harvest

　　　　Pennsylvania spiders
not only stretch their silk between the limbs
of our great trees but hang between our houses
and pull their sheets across the frantic eyes
of cats and the soft chests of men.
Some are so huge they move around like mammals,
waddling slowly over the rough cement
and into the bushes to nurse their young or feed
on berries and crunch on bones.
But it is the ones that live on the iron bridge
going across to Riegelsville, New Jersey,
that are the most artistic and luxurious.
They make their webs between the iron uprights
and hang them out in the dew above the river
like a series of new designs on display,
waiting for you to choose the one most delicate,
waiting for you just to touch the sticky threads
as you look at their soft silk, as you love them.

If your mind is already on business,
even if your mind is still into your dream,
you will be shocked by their beauty and you will sit there
two minutes, two hours, a half a century you will sit there
until the guards begin to shout, until they rush up in confusion
and bang on your window and look at you in fear.
You will point with your left finger at the sun
and draw a tracery in the cold air,
a dragline from door handle to door handle,
foundation lines inside the windows,

long radials from the panel to the headrest
and gluey spirals turning on the radials;
and you will sit in the center of your web
like a rolled-up leaf or a piece of silent dirt,
pulling gently on your loose trapline.
They will scream in your ear,
they will tear desperately at the sheets,
they will beg for air
before you finally relieve them by starting your engine
and moving reluctantly over the small bridge.

Do not regret your little bout with life in the morning.
If you drive slowly you can have almost one minute
to study the drops of silver hanging in the sun
before you turn the corner past the gatehouse
and down the road beside the railroad cars
and finally over the tracks and up the hill
to the morning that lies in front of you like one more design.
It is the morning I live in and travel through,
the morning of children standing in the driveways,
of mothers wrapping their quilted coats around them
and yellow buses flashing their lights like berserk police cars.
It is lights that save us, lights that light the way,
blue lights rushing in to help the wretched,
red lights carrying twenty pounds of oxygen down the highway,
white lights entering the old Phoenician channels
bringing language and mathematics and religion into the darkness.

Peddler's Village

The small gray bird that fit inside the hand
of a nine-year-old girl is himself a grandfather
with a tear stuck to the side of his round face;

but he hopped on the red bricks and absentmindedly
pecked at her hand as if he were still young and blue,
with oily wings and a stomach full of seeds.

If she could see his heart she would know how terrified he was.
She would take off her colored handkerchief and stop being his
    grandmother;
she would take away his paper bed and stop being his sister and his
    bride.

If she knew how old he was she would bow down
and kiss his loose feathers
and listen carefully to his song.

There had to be wisdom with all that age,
something he could give her,
something she could remember him by and love him for;

there had to be some honor, some revelation,
some loveliness before he died;
before the lice robbed him,
before the bitter wire snapped him in two,
before a thousand tragedies took away his warmth and happiness.

The Sweetness of Life

After the heavy rain we were able to tell about the mushrooms,
which ones made us sick, which ones had the dry bitterness,
which ones caused stomach pains and dizziness and hallucinations.

It was the beginning of religion again—on the river—
all the battles and ecstasies and persecutions
taking place beside the hackberries and the fallen locust.

I sat there like a lunatic,
weeping, raving, standing on my head, living
in three and four and five places at once.

I sat there letting the wild and domestic combine,
finally accepting the sweetness of life,
on my own mushy log,
in the white and spotted moonlight.

Too Much, Too Much

No matter what anyone says it is I who
have found a dead spider inside the pages of the
Philadelphia Inquirer and it is I who have held it up
to the light and it's I who have waved it back and forth,
holding on to its gluey leg, and I who have turned
it over to study its dark stripes and its beads and I
who have finally discovered its eyes hanging useless
like two black bulges from its flattened brain.
I turn the pages with dread; no matter where I go
I return to the tales of Turk Mendelsohn and Samuel Rappaport;
no matter what I do I am the subject of their humor;
no matter where I look I am the victim of their weight.

I dream about Turk Mendelsohn all morning
while the ice completely covers up the storm windows
and we are locked in our frozen bedroom drinking coffee
and listening to frightened voices describe the new chill factor.
He was lucky to die before the ground froze
so he could have the benefit of a soft digging
and he was lucky to have fifty cars follow him down Broad Street
and Mayor Rizzo cry for him in his new Chrysler.
It was the mayor who converted the Turk in the old days
when he was a bagman and wore a pinstripe suit
and it was the mayor who got him a decent job
driving a truck for the Philadelphia Inquirer.
It was in the desert of South Philadelphia that Rizzo
first felled him and made him give up the rackets
and put away his coat and his white fedora
and it was Rizzo who taught him to love cops and firemen

and give them comfort at wife beatings and holocausts
by bringing in boiling soup and tea and sandwiches.
Because of this he had no fear but died
a happy man on the subway platform on Broad Street
and had, for his last reward, a statesman's funeral.

Samuel Rappaport is a scavenger himself
who spins his threads over the run-down buildings
of old Philadelphia, cleans them up a little,
and fills them with amusement arcades and peep shows.
His empire includes a whole string of rotten monuments
with leaking pipes and bulging walls and ceilings
which he rules from a basement office on lower Market Street.
Now he has leased the Reading Terminal Market,
famous for its sausage and cheese and ice cream,
and plans to bring the building up to code
by raising the rents and adding a few new vendors.
—I see the two of them in years to come
in the kitchens, or bathrooms, of the old Jewish Valhalla,
two great hustlers, sharing space with the socialists—
who will look at them both with hatred—with the old-time
poets and actors, with doctors and violinists and lawyers
and arrogant waiters, our only royalty, the
last of our kings, who will find them all weak and wanting.

I have put the spider down on my small brass table,
I have rid myself of all my other obligations
and it's only he and I, or she and I, left in this freezing world.
I am light and weightless from being a vegetarian and she is

that way from being dead; we are both bloodless
from having been sucked dry; we are both exhausted from
too many loves and too much wasted silk.
It's Sunday night and I am thinking of my walk.
I've put the spider inside my left breast pocket
and the two of us are getting ready to face the cold.
Her little legs are curled up for safety
and she is probably thinking of all the dark places she has lived in
and all the insane chances she has taken.
We whisper together a little—she alone of all
living things—of all dead things—knows what it is I want.
The road takes us down to the locks and the new bridge
and the road brings us back to the white door and the pillars.
I wish she could see the sky and the river and the black birch.
I wish she could feel the dead leaves through the snow.
I wish she could hear the dogs and know what the water sounds like
when it drops off the huge spillway and know what the ducks sound
        like
when they leave their bushes in the morning to begin their
        preening
in the bright sunlight, on the cold and empty towpath.

Underground Dancing

There's a bird pecking at the fat;
there's a dead tree covered with snow;
there's a truck dropping cinders on the slippery highway.

There's life in my backyard—
black wings beating on the branches,
greedy eyes watching,
mouths screaming and fighting over the greasy ball.

There's a mole singing hallelujah.
Close the rotten doors!
Let everyone go blind!
Let everyone be buried in his own litter.

Something New

This year I sat with women, gathering up
wet sand between my legs and making Byzantine
castles with my gritty hands. It was the first time
in four years I didn't dream up
a new encounter with a black cloud or a ruined building
to describe the state of my mind. I sat there
discussing the simple pleasures, beekeeping
and massage, poker and ice-cream making,
as well as the more serious matters
such as divorce and bladder infection, and I thought
only of the harmony between us and the love
that would last forever by the boring sea.
Forgive me ten times, but this is what I did, and
except for the brutal argument over middle-income housing
between myself and the fat stomach sitting next to me
there was nothing but peace and affection in our little community.
Yes, on the third day, at three o'clock,
I noticed that the sky dropped and the ground lost its weight,
but that was only because a storm was coming up and
the air currents seemed to make the earth move more quickly.
Everybody got cold and began shaking out sheets
or started climbing the hill toward the houses
but nobody saw any sudden warning or important anniversary out
     there.
For that matter we all returned the next day
and began another castle and buried combs and love notes
in the sand and drank Diet Pepsi and
ate pieces of raw cauliflower with sand giblets in them.
Next summer is the charm and already

I am getting ready for it; I am waiting
for the shore and the ocean to stop their sloppy maneuvering
for one minute; I am waiting for my body
to slow down and my mind to stop falling apart
every other year like a cheap clock; I am imagining
what the waves will look like this time when I am finally standing
on the black rocks with another whole year behind me,
and I am imagining myself whispering words of greeting—
"Kalimera, kalimera"—to the little Greek genius
inside the hill of sand that used to be our castle
and her looking up with unforgiving eyes,
daring me to give myself up to the waves as she did,
daring me to simplify my twisted feelings
and throw away this and throw away that and live
as she does under the buried notes and the combs,
singing and humming and sleeping by the sea she loves.

The Red Coal

The Faces I Love

Once and for all I will lie down here like a dead man,
letting the socialists walk over my face, letting the fascists
crawl through my veins, letting the Krishnas
poison me with their terrible saffron.

Once and for all I will lie here helpless and exhausted.
I will let dishonor rise from me like steam
and tears fall down on me like oily rain.

In the end my stillness will save me;
in the end the leopard will walk away from me in boredom
and trot after something living, something violent
and warm to excite him before his death.

In the end I will have my own chair.
I will pull the blinds down and watch my nose and mouth
in the blistered glass.
I will look back in amazement at what I did
and cry aloud for two more years, for four more years,
just to remember the faces, just to recall the names,
to put them back together—
the names I can't forget, the faces I love.

Little White Sister

It was in Philadelphia that I first lived a life of deferment,
putting everything off until I could be at ease.
There, more than in New York and more than in Paris,
I lay for hours in bed, forgetting to eat, forgetting
to swim, dying of imperfection and loneliness.
It was in Vienna that I learned what it would be like
to live in two lives, and learned to wander between them;
and it was in the rotten underbelly
of western Pennsylvania that I was saved twice by a pear tree,
one time living and one time dead, and enslaved
once and for all by a patented iron grate
carrying words of terror through the yellow air.
    My ear betrayed me, my little white sister
glued to the side of my head, a shiny snail
twisted everywhere to catch the slightest
murmur of love, the smallest sobbing and breathing.
It wasn't the heart, stuck inside the chest
like a bloody bird, and it wasn't the brain,
dying itself from love; it was that messenger,
laughing as she whispered the soft words,
making kissing sounds with her red lips,
moaning with pleasure for the last indignity.

Swan Song

A bunch of old snakeheads down by the pond
carrying on the swan tradition—hissing
inside their white bodies, raising and lowering their heads
like ostriches, regretting only the sad ritual
that forced them to waddle back into the water
after their life under the rocks, wishing they could slither again
as they did in the old days, wishing they could lie again in the sun
and dream of spreading their terrifying wings;
wishing, this time, they could sail through the sky like horses,
their tails rigid, their white manes fluttering,
their mouths open, their sharp teeth flashing,
drops of mercy pouring from their eyes,
bolts of wisdom from their foreheads.

Immensity

Nothing is too small for my sarcasm. I know
a tiny moth that crawls over the rug
like an English spy sneaking through the Blue Forest,
and I know a Frenchman that hangs on the closet door
singing *chanson* after *chanson* with his smashed thighs.
I will examine my life through curled threads
and short straws and little drops of food.
I will crawl around with my tongue out, growing
more and more used to the dirty webs hanging
between the ridges of my radiator and the huge
smudges in that distant sky up there, beginning
more and more to take on the shape of some great design.
    This is the way to achieve immensity, and this is the
only way to get ready for death, no matter what Immanuel Kant
and the English philosophers say about the mind,
no matter what the gnostics say, crawling
through their vile blue, sneezing madly in the midst of that
life of theirs, weighed down by madness and sorrow.

Rotten Angel

My friends, still of this world, follow me to the bottom of the river
tripping over roots and cutting themselves on the dry grass.
They are all over on the left side, drinking beer and crying,
and I am there by myself waiting for the rotten angel.
For my sake it hasn't rained for twenty days
and all the old jetties are showing up again in the water.
I can reach my arms up into the second row of branches
and pull down clumps of dead leaves and barrel hoops.
I finally find my clearing and fall down in the dirt,
exhausted from thirty minutes of fighting for air.
I put an *x* on the ground and start marking off
a place for the gravel, the rhododendron and the iron bird.
My friends stand above me, a little bored by my death
and a little tired of the flies and the sad ritual.
—How I would love it if I could really be buried here,
a mile away from my house in this soft soil.
I think the state could do this for me—they could give me
a few feet of earth—they could make an exception.
I tell you it really matters and all that talk
about so many cents worth of fat and so many grams
of water is really just fake humility.
I would hate being dusted on the ocean or put in a drawer
for perpetuity—I want to be connected
with life as long as possible, I want to disappear slowly,
as gruesome as that sounds, so there is time
for those who want to see me in my own light
and get an idea of how I made my connections
and what I looked at and dreamed about
and what the river smelled like from this island

and how the grackles sounded when they landed
in the polished trees and how the trucks sounded
charging up 611 carrying the culture
of Philadelphia into the mountains
and how the angel must have gasped as he swam
back to the shore and how he must have dipped
his head in the green water to escape the gnats
swarming after him in the dirty sunlight
a million miles from his New York and his Baltimore and his
    Boston.

Dangerous Cooks

I am serving my own head on a platter, as Ensor did.
I am a plucked chicken hanging in the air.
I am lying on the floor with a pig's body and a pince-nez.
I am dropping tears in a frying pan.
    Always I am in the middle of everything.
My voice is in the woods;
my hands are in the water;
my face is in the clouds, like a hot sun.

Good Friday, 1977

Suddenly there are hundreds of fishermen on the road,
wearing hats and waders and thick shirts and badges.
Their cars and trucks are lined up on the lawns and ditches.
Dozens are in the water already,
side by side, casting and reeling in the foam,
ending Christianity once and for all on this small river.

Pick and Poke

I began this fall by watching a thin red squirrel
sneak out of my neighbor's wrecked Simca and run over
a pile of bricks into one of its small forests.
Then and there I set up my watch
so I could follow that thin redness
in and out of our civilization.
    It would have been so easy with the old English taxi
at Pick and Poke. It stands six feet high,
like a small coach waiting for its shabby prince
to walk through his porch posts and his barrels
and mount the leather seat in two short steps,
whereas the Simca is practically buried in the leaves,
its glass is gone, and half its insides are rotted.
But it isn't size, and it isn't even location;
it has something to do with character, and something
to do with ideas, and something, even, to do
with the secret history of France, and of England.
After two weeks I saw everything
as clearly as a squirrel does—a Simca
is part of nature, lying halfway between
the wet maples and the field of tarpaulin,
the armrest is a perch, the back seat is a warehouse,
and the gearshift is a small dangerous limb.
But my loyalty is mostly to England,
so I found myself wandering down
day after day to the big yard at Pick and Poke.
There I studied the square wheelbarrow
and the lawn furniture—I walked around the taxi,
measuring the giant wheels and fancy tool box,

and I sat in the back and rapped on the glass partition
over the jump seats, ordering my driver to carry me
down the river to New Hope and Philadelphia.
After just a few hours I understood the English spirit,
and after a day I even understood the English garden
from watching the scattered shutters and old storm windows.
    We here in France salute the English.
We admire them for their tolerance and shyness.
We love them for their geography and their music,
their hatred of theory and their bad food,
their optimism and love of animals.
We in America are more like red squirrels: we live
from roof to roof, our minds are fixed on the great
store of the future, our bodies are worn out from leaping;
we are weary of each other's faces, each other's dreams.
We sigh for some understanding, some surcease,
some permanence, as we move from tree to tree,
from wire to wire, from empty hole to empty hole,
singing, singing, always singing, of that amorous summer.

Royal Manor Road

It would be worth it to go ninety miles out of your way
to see these cows eat and sleep and nuzzle in the mud.
It would be worth it to leave the tables at Grand Ticino
and walk down Thompson Street talking about the eyes—
"Are they the eyes of Kora, are they soft and slanted;
are they the eyes of Juno and drunken Hathor?"
All my reading, all my difficult reading
would be worth it as I stood in the weeds
watching them run up like kittens, watching them
crowd each other for little tastes of clover and hepatica.
To reach my hand inside
and touch the bony forehead and the stiff hair
would be worth it.

Modern Love

In a month all these frozen waterfalls
will be replaced by Dutchman's breeches
and I will drive down the road
trying to remember what it was like
in late February and early March.
It will be 72 degrees on March 24th
and I will see my first robin
on the roof of the Indian Rock Inn.
My wife and I will go in to stare at the chandelier
and eat, like starved birds, in front of the fireplace.
I know now that what I'll do
all through supper is plan my walk
from Bristol, P.A. to the canal museum.
I will exhaust her with questions about old hotels
and how much water I should carry
and what shoes I should wear,
and she will meet me with sweetness and logic
before we break up over money and grammar and lost love.
Later the full moon will shine through our windshield
as we zigzag up the river
dragging our tired brains, and our hearts, after us.
I will go to bed thinking of George Meredith
lying beside a red sword
and I will try to remember how his brain smoked
as he talked to his wife in her sleep and twisted her words.
—Where I will go in the six hours before I wake up freezing
I don't know, but I do know
I will finally lie there with my twelve organs in place,
wishing I were in a tea palace, wishing

I were in a museum in France, wishing
I were in a Moorish movie house in Los Angeles.
I will walk downstairs singing because it is March 25th
and I will walk outside to drink my coffee on the stone wall.
There will still be drops of snow on the side of the hill
as we plant our peas and sweep away the birdseed.
Watch me dig and you will see me
dream about justice, and you will see me
dream about small animals, and you will see me
dream about warm strawberries.
From time to time I will look over
and watch her dragging sticks and broken branches
across the road. We are getting ready
for summer. We are working in the cold
getting ready. Only thirty more days and the moon
will shine on us again as we drive to Hellertown
to see Jane Fonda grimace, and drive back
after midnight through the white fields,
looking for foxes in the stubble,
looking for their wild eyes, burning with fear and shyness,
in the stunted remains of last summer's silk forest.

Little Did the Junco Know

Little did the junco know who he was keeping company with this
    Christmas,
he and the nuthatch and the chickadee and the red sparrow,
racing back and forth between the bag of fat
and the pan of birdseed under the dead vine.

Little did those sweethearts know who was in their midst,
with his round eye and his small head and his plump body
rolling after the neck like a mop keeping up with its tiny handle.

And little did he know himself why people fought over him
and waved him in the air and sent him out
morning after morning in the first light—
that soft gray one with the long tail
and the monotonous voice,
gorging himself at the battered aluminum pan.

Lord, Forgive a Spirit

So what shall we do about this angel,
growing dizzy every time he climbs a ladder,
crying over his old poems.
I walk out into the garden and there he is,
watering the lilies and studying the digitalis.
He is talking to his own invisible heart;
he is leaking blood.
    The sun shines on him all day long
as he wanders from bush to bush.
His eyes flash with fire, his eyelashes blaze and
his skin shines like brass,
but he trips in the dirt just like any gardener, or grieving poet.
    I watch him walk beside the cactus;
I watch him kneel in front of the wet horsetails;
I touch his lips.
I write all day. I sit beside him all
day long and write the garbled words.
I sit in the sun and fill a whole new book
with scrawls and symbols.
I watch the sky as he talks about the gold leaf
and the half-forgotten ruins; I watch the words
drift from his mouth like clouds.
I watch the colors change from orange to red
to pink as he tries to remember his old words—
his old songs, his first human songs—
lost somewhere in the broken glass and the cinders,
a foot below the soft nails and the hinges.

Elaine Comparone

I love to sit down
in front of my lilac fence
and watch the wind blow through the pointed leaves.

If I could do exactly what I wanted
I would move a harpsichord into my back yard
and ask Elaine Comparone to play for me all morning.

My friend Barbara Dazzle said she would move
her dining-room furniture out and put the long red box
in the middle of the gardenias and the hanging ivy.

Either way I would listen to the steel bird sing
and watch Elaine shift back and forth on her chair,
torn between my love of Domenico Scarlatti
and my desire to lay my head down on her flowery lap.

My joy begins as I dream of a woman blushing
beside her stone wall, and my pain begins
when she turns into a shadow, with notes falling
around her like blossoms on the wet grass.

I run through the garden shouting kiss me, kiss me!
In one more day the petals will be curled and brown,
they will lie piled up like dead leaves—
smeared on the walk like blood;

O in one hour the great tree will stand there shaking
and the box will be carried out like a heavy coffin

and Elaine Comparone will sit with her hands in her lap,
in the cold air, rushing back to the city,
remembering the notes falling on the ground
and the red spikes inside the creamy blossoms
and the new leaves making their way like tiny crescendos
in the drawing rooms of Petrograd and Stockholm,
dreaming of sunlight and rain and endless dancing.

Ice, Ice

When I woke up this morning I knew there was horror, I
remembered the rain last night and I knew the ice had
come. I knew the doves would be dragging their stiff tails and
I knew the yard would be filled with broken branches. I sing
this for Hubert Humphrey, dead last night, and I sing it
for the silent birds, and I sing it
for the frozen trees and the bouquet of frozen buds,
and the tiny puffs of smoke now rising from our chimneys
like the smoke of cave men rising from their fissures,
their faces red with wisdom, their dirty hands scraping
grease from the stones and shaking ashes from their beds,
their black eyes weeping over the chunks of fire,
their tears turning to ice as they leave the circle.

One More Time the Lambs

One more time the hard green daffodils are growing
in clumps beside the stone wall and the cesspool.
They go with the melancholy and the cold rain,
with the black tree and the frozen seedpods.
I resist every effort at exhaustion
and walk by all the traps as if nothing were happening.
I am going to go through it with ease,
no bitterness and no indecision this time.
Again the river rises and again the logs
and oil drums float by;
again we are sleeping, again we wait
for the sun to make our lives more pleasant.
One more time the lamb rests his soft head
on the stone culvert, one more time he lies there
cool and thoughtful, one more time he drops his red blood
on the dirty ice. I study the thin green trees
and the blue water hanging in the air;
I stay awake for two long days and start my
sleep at four in the evening. The wind is my love,
the rain is my love, the torn lamb is my love.
The sun goes off and on like a white eye
watching. I wake up floating—and singing—
inside my shelter.

The Sacred Spine

It will always be invisible, it will
have hair on it, but that will be false,
and skin, but that will be stretched over
the branches like a sweater dipped in alum.
It will hang from the mouth
like a piece of paper or a large caterpillar.
It will twist over doubly
like a ravenous birch.
It will lie rigid.
It will scream out,
trying to find a position.
It will turn in pain,
trying to escape, trying to release
itself, trying to live again
without fear and exhaustion,
trying to float once more, trying to rest, trying to rise
in the fine dust and the feathers,
in the wet leaves and the grass and the flowers,
on the bleached wood and the pillows and the warm air
and the weeds and the water.

I Remember Galileo

I remember Galileo describing the mind
as a piece of paper blown around by the wind,
and I loved the sight of it sticking to a tree
or jumping into the back seat of a car,
and for years I watched paper leap through my cities;
but yesterday I saw the mind was a squirrel caught crossing
Route 80 between the wheels of a giant truck,
dancing back and forth like a thin leaf,
or a frightened string, for only two seconds living
on the white concrete before he got away,
his life shortened by all that terror, his head
jerking, his yellow teeth ground down to dust.

It was the speed of the squirrel and his lowness to the ground,
his great purpose and the alertness of his dancing,
that showed me the difference between him and paper.
Paper will do in theory, when there is time
to sit back in a metal chair and study shadows;
but for this life I need a squirrel,
his clawed feet spread, his whole soul quivering,
the hot wind rushing through his hair,
the loud noise shaking him from head to tail.
    O philosophical mind, O mind of paper, I need a squirrel
finishing his wild dash across the highway,
rushing up his green ungoverned hillside.

Potpourri

I see my wife struggling in the dirt
with her roses and her iris and I watch her
domesticate every mountain within ten miles,
but I know it is the delicate spring things,
the bloodroot and the columbine, that move her.
I think of the great space between her and
the wild domestic poets I hear reading at the Moat
and the Lavender Gate and I understand
exactly the difference between them;
and when I watch her on the flowered sheets,
with her eyes finally closed
and her purple T-shirt already wet with sleep,
I understand a delicacy and a mournfulness
that neither Nietzsche my one love
nor Van Gogh my other
could help me with, for all their knowledge and purity.
    Tonight a huge black rose
sits on the oak chest
beside the silver candlesticks,
dominating the small room with
its size and odor.
I am sitting down eating strawberries
and turning the rose on its thick stem.
Across the room a potpourri waits,
like a rich grave full of herbs and spices,
for the moist petals;
and under the light a bouquet of wild daisies
with three round thistles on the outer edges
is half buried inside a tin pitcher.

—What I will do after a minute is walk outside
to pluck the strings
and I will feel pleasure in the darkness
that will unite me forever with the sleepless Italians
and the waterless Greeks beside their stone jars.
In the morning we will sit on the metal chairs
and drink coffee and exchange dreams;
tonight I will sit there alone, listening to trucks
go up the highway and getting small glimpses
of the sky between the eaves and the black maples.
I will do two things before I go upstairs:
I will see if the thorn tree is still living
and I will put a blue trumpet in my shirt pocket.
On my way in I will practice a little
breathing, a little emptiness,
and I will listen to the crazy night bird
with my hand against the pillar and my head bowed
so I can lie down in wisdom and luxury.

Magritte Dancing

Every night I have to go to bed twice,
once by myself, suddenly tired and angry,
and once when my wife turns the weak light on
and stumbles over my shoes into the bathroom.
Some nights there is a third time—the phone
is ringing and I rush out into the hall;
my heart is pounding but nobody is there
and I have to go back to bed empty-handed
just as my brain was beginning to pick up signals.
This time it takes me all night to get back to sleep.
I don't sink again into the heavy pillow
but lie there breathing, trying to push
everything back into its own channel.
For hours I watch the dark and then gradually
I begin watching the light; by that time
I am thinking again about snow tires and I am thinking
about downtown Pittsburgh and I am thinking
about the turtles swimming inside their brown willows.
I look at the morning with relief, with something close
to pleasure that I still have one more day,
and I dance the dance of brotherliness and courtliness
as first my neighbor the postman, pocked and pitted,
goes crawling off in his early morning bitterness
and then my neighbor the body man goes bouncing away,
his own car rusty and chromeless, his T-shirt torn,
his eyes already happy from his first soothing beer.
—The dance I dance is to the tune of Magritte
banging his bedposts on a square mountain,
and Oskar Schlemmer floating up a stairway,

and Pablo Picasso looking inside a woman's head.
I dance on the road and on the river and
in the wet garden, all the time living in Crete
and pre-war Poland and outer Zimbabwe,
as through my fingers and my sparkling hair
the morning passes, first the three loud calls
of the bluejay, then the white door slamming,
then the voices rising and falling in sudden harmony.

The Shirt Poem

It is ten years since I have seen these shirts
screaming from their hangers, crying for blood and money.
They shake their empty arms
and grow stiff as they wait for the light to come.
I open the door an inch at a time to let them out
and start candles all over the room to soothe them.
—Gone is sweetness in that closet, gone is the dream
of brotherhood, the affectionate meeting
of thinkers and workers inside a rented hall.
Gone are the folding chairs, gone forever
the sacred locking of elbows under the two flags.

On Sunday night they used to sing for hours
before the speeches. Once the rabbis joined them
and religion and economics were finally combined in exile.
"Death is a defect," they sang, and threw their hats
on the floor. "We will save nature from death,"
they shouted, and ended up dancing on the small stage,
the dark crows and the speckled doves finally arm in arm.

They will never come back—in a thousand years;
it is not like bringing a forest back, putting a truckload
of nitrogen in the soil, burning some brush,
planting seedlings, measuring distance—
these are people, whose secret habits we no longer know,
how they tore their bread and what designs they made on the
    tablecloth,
what they thought about as they stared through the warped glass,
what the melting ice meant to them.

Poor dead ones! Forgive me for the peace I feel as I walk out
to the mailbox. Forgive me for the rich life I lead.
Forgive me for the enormous budget and the bureaucracy and the
    permanent army.
When I come home from New York City I stand outside
for twenty minutes and look out at the lights.
Upstairs the shirts are howling and snapping,
marching back and forth in front of the silver radiator.
In a minute I will be up there closing doors
and turning on lamps.
I will take the papers out of my coat pocket
and put them in their slots.
I will think of you with your own papers and your rubber bands.
What is my life if not a substitute for yours,
and my dream a substitute for your dream?
Lord, how it has changed, how we have
made ourselves strange, how embarrassing the words
sound to us, how clumsy and half-hearted we are.

I want to write it down before it's forgotten,
how we lived, what we believed in;
most of all to remember the giants
and how they walked, always with white hair,
always with long white hair hanging down over their collars,
always with red faces, always bowing and listening,
their heads floating as they moved through the small crowd.

Outside the wind is blowing
and the snow is piling up against the pillars.

I could go back in a minute to the synagogue in Beechview
or the Carnegie Library on the North Side.
I could turn and shake hands with the tiny man
sitting beside me and wish him peace.
I could stand in front and watch the stained-glass
window rattle in its frame and the guest speaker
climb into the back seat of his car.

I am writing about the past because there was
still affection left then, and other sorrows;
because I believed my white silk scarf could save me,
and my all-day walks;
because when I opened my window the smell
of snow made me tremble with pleasure;
because I was a head taller than the tiny man sitting next to me;
because I was always the youngest;
because I believed in Shelley;
because I carried my entire memory along with me in the summer;
because I stared at the old men with loving eyes;
because I studied their fallen shoulders and their huge hands;
because I found relief only in my drawings;
because I knew the color and texture of every rug and every chair
and every lampshade in my first house.

Give this to Rabbi Kook who always arrived
with his clothes on fire and stood between the mourners,
singing songs against death in all three languages
at the crowded wall, in the dark sunlight.

And give this to Malatesta who believed in
the perfect world and lived in it as he moved
from country to country, for sixty years, tasting the
bread, tasting the meat, always working,
cursing the Church, cursing the State,
seeing through everything, always seeing the heart
and what it wanted, the beautiful cramped heart.

My shirts are fine. They dance
by themselves along the river
and bleed a little as they fall down on the dirty glass.
If they had knees they would try to
crawl back up the hill and stop the trucks
or march back and forth singing their swamp songs.
They see me coming and fly up to the roof;
they are like prehistoric birds,
half leaping, half sailing by.
They scream with cold, they break through the hall window
and knock over baskets and push open doors
until they stand there in place, in back of the neckties,
beside the cold plaster, in the dust
above the abandoned shoes, weeping in silence,
moaning in exhaustion,
getting ready again to live in darkness.

June First

for Abigail Thomas

Some blossoms are so white and luscious, when they
hold their long thin hands up you strip them for love
and scatter them on the ground as you walk;

and some birds look at you as if there were no
great line drawn between their lives and yours,
as if you drank together from the same cement;

and some pods spin in the wind as if you would not pick
them up gingerly to see if they had wings
and then would not break them open to see what made them
fall, to study their visceras.

I touch you as I would the sawdust in the eaves
or the crazy buttercups in the middle of the mulepath
or the frightening foil
jumping and leaping in front of the oily grackles;

and I touch you as I touch the grass, my body falls down on the
        ground
and I pull at the roots as I watch you in the limbs
bending down to avoid the red blossoms,
hiding in the leaves,
reaching up like the tallest dryad,
your curved arms and your jeweled fingers
waving slowly again in the hot sun.

Thinking About Shelley

Arm over arm I swam out into the rain,
across from the cedars and the rickety conveyor.
I had the quarry all to myself again,
even the path down to the muddy bank.
Every poet in the world was dead but me.
Yeats was dead, Victor Hugo was dead,
Cavafy was dead—with every kick I shot
a jet of water into the air—you could see
me coming a mile away, my shoulders rolling
the way my father's did. I started moving
out into the open between the two islands,
thinking about Shelley and his milky body.
No one had been here before—I was the first
poet to swim in this water—I would be the
mystery, I would be the source
for all the others to come. The rivers of China
were full of poets, the lakes of Finland, the ponds
of southern France, but no one in Pennsylvania
had swum like this across an empty quarry.
I remember at the end I turned on my back
to give my neck a rest; I remember floating
into the weeds and letting my shoulders touch
the greasy stones; I remember lying
on the coarse sand reaching up for air.

This happened in June before the berries were out,
before the loosestrife covered the hills, before
the local sinners took off their clothes and waded
like huge birds in the cold water.

It was the first warm day and I was
laboring in this small sea.
I remember how I hoped my luck would last;
I remember the terror of the middle
and how I suddenly relaxed after passing the islands;
I remember it was because of Shelley
that I changed my innocent swim
into such a struggle,
that it was because of Shelley
I dragged my body up, tired and alive,
to the small landing under the flowering highway,
full of silence now and clarity.

Cow Worship

I love the cows best when they are a few feet away
from my dining-room window and my pine floor,
when they reach in to kiss me with their wet
mouths and their white noses.
I love them when they walk over the garbage cans
and across the cellar doors,
over the sidewalk and through the metal chairs
and the birdseed.
—Let me reach out through the thin curtains
and feel the warm air of May.
It is the temperature of the whole galaxy,
all the bright clouds and clusters,
beasts and heroes,
glittering singers and isolated thinkers
at pasture.

Joseph Pockets

Have you ever lived through seven fat years and grown soft
from eating lamb and bulgur? I remember lawyers
standing in line for doughnuts and geniuses painting
the walls of Idlewild Airport. Two things happened
to make me remember: one was a film about the 30's,
put together to show the times as primitive
in the Eisenstein style; the other was my invasion
of Kaufmann's department store to buy a suit
from the crowd of salesmen dressed up in plaids and stripes,
to go with my new dignity and ferocity.

In *The Hunger March* thousands of lean men converge
on Washington in sheepskin coats and fedoras.
Already the cap was dead; already the workingmen
had started to move out of their small houses.
The joy was watching them go through city after city.
The joy was watching the camera catch their happiness
as they half ran down the old highways,
singing of empty stomachs and freezing rain.

In *The Ford Massacre* the figures move
in a rush across the screen; they either are buried
down the tracks in puffs of smoke or stand
on top of you, screaming for justice in silent voices.

The seven lean years came first—they lasted seven years;
the seven fat years lasted over twenty-five.
Joseph comes later. He turns the past into a dream
and shows us how we lived and what disappeared

as we left the 40's and went into the 50's.
I'm back in Pittsburgh now; it's only here
and maybe Detroit and maybe a little Chicago
that there are Joseph pockets where you can see
the dream turned around and the darkness illuminated,
some of the joy explained, some of the madness—
Chicago, St. Louis, Minneapolis, Boston, Buffalo.

When I walked into the lobby I felt like a visitor.
I sat beside a black-haired woman with a shawl
who knew what I was radiating and touched me
on the little wooden arm. I lived in a Joseph
pocket there and when I left she touched me
again as if to say, "Well, wait for me. The marches
will be over in fifteen minutes and we can walk
through Father Demo Square past our brick mansion
where we could imagine living in half-dark rooms,
drinking tea from flowered cups and sleeping
in modern anarchy under the blue skylight."

When I walked into Kaufmann's I carried the past
with me like a colored stone in my pocket.
Two diplomats walked over, their eyes showing
almost no pity, their voices cold and resentful
as they abandoned me in front of the hooded sweaters.
I had to look at suits myself; I had to learn
about European cuts and what vents did for my body
and what my sloping shoulders needed and where the

sleeves should end and where the collar should be,
without a sucking salesman hanging on
and dragging me around from rack to rack.

I will be living in Pittsburgh one more month.
All the time I am here I will move between
my hatred of Frick and my love of the forty bridges.
Over and over again I will walk downtown
through Market Square and past the Oyster House,
or I will drive through South Side and Mt. Washington,
wishing the Japanese could see these hills.
This is the city where art was brought in by the trainload
and Mellon money is wasted to bring Grace Kelly
on stage to read poems about birds and their transcendence.
This is the city where Iron is our drink, we say, "Iron,"
we say, "Give me Iron," we say, "Piss on watery Miller's."
This is the city where I lay down like a twisted
poppy to read my Marlowe and my Pound.

I can look down the river from my back room.
I can see the lights hanging from broomsticks
and the cars bouncing up and down on the crooked boulevard.
But the best view is ten o'clock in the morning;
the sun is behind me then and I can see
the light shining down on the whole city.
I want to float on that river—what dark legs
will push me, what silk hand will carry me
across the plain to the first row of mountains,

or drop me, singing, into the other river
beside a coal barge or a sleek cruiser?

My sister is buried in Carrick in the Jewish cemetery
three miles from the Liberty Tubes, beside my grandmother,
Libby Barach, and my grandfather, B. Barach,
both of them resting above her like two old friends.
For once I feel cut off and except for the presence
of the blue Nova in front of the service building
I might be in a Jewish graveyard in Poland,
crowded with souls, everyone a stranger.

I borrow a book from the bleak office and open
to the page to be read at the graveside of a sister.
I ask her first to remember her shocking death
and all the clumsiness and sadness of her leaving.
I ask her to describe—as she remembers it—
how I stood in front of her white coffin
and stared at the mourners in our small living room.
I ask her to think again about the two peach trees,
how close together they were, how tiny their fruit was,
forty years ago in the light rain,
wherever she is, whatever wing she was under.

This is my last Joseph pocket. I am going
back to New York City. O Japanese,
you will love this place; you will spend a week
visiting junk stores and eating steaks and buying

boots and dishes to take with you back to Asia.
What I'll do is talk to the glass buildings
and explain myself. I think I'll stand in one place
to say good-by. I think I'll leave in the snow
with the wind blowing down the alley and the cars
going ten miles an hour up the Parkway, the cinder trucks
moving along in convoys, big clouds of steam
rising up from the river, all the sorrows
of life disappearing like drops of snow
as we pick up speed going east on the empty turnpike.

Phipps Conservatory

Pittsburgh, 1978

Whoever wants to can live a lifetime in this herb garden,
rubbing leaves and sighing,
making choices among the mints and the scented geraniums.
He can listen to the flute and watch the girls
come one at a time into the arms of the shrill satyr.
He can walk through the borders and bend down like a stiff king
over the yellow marigolds.
He can sit on the lover's plank
and wail with joy
in his newfound misery
or talk to the Pole walking lightly away
with seeds in his pocket, wrapped in tissue paper,
ready to burst with life on his rich hillside.

Days of 1978

This is the only thing that clarifies my life,
this beautiful old living room
with the pink walls and the mohair sofa.
I walk out every night singing
a little song from Gus Williams or W. C. Handy.
I throw my yellow scarf around my neck
and pull my cap down over my eyes.
Even here I am dressed up,
walking through the light flakes and the ice puddles.
—Tonight I will think about Cavafy
and the way he wept on his satin pillow,
remembering the days of 1903.
I will compare my life to his:
the sorrows of Alexandria,
the lights on the river;
the dead kings returning to Syria,
the soap in my bath.
—Later I will lie on my own pillow
with the window open and the blinds up,
smiling a little myself at the thick blankets
and the smoking candles
and the stack of books,
the new clarity beginning
to monopolize my own memory.

No Wind

Today I am sitting outside the Dutch Castle
on Route 30 near Bird in Hand and Blue Ball,
watching the Amish snap their suspenders at the sunglasses.
I am dreaming of my black suit again
and the store in Paradise where I will be fitted out for life.
   A small girl and I recognize each other
from our former life together in Córdoba.
We weep over the plastic tote bags, the apple combs and the
      laughing harmonicas,
and fall down on the hot carpet
remembering the marble forest
of the Great Mosque
and the milky walls
of the Jewish quarter.
   I will see her again in 800 years
when all this is sorted out.
I give it that much time,
based on the slack mind,
the dirty drinking water and the slow decay.
I give it at least that much time
before we lie down again in the tiny lilacs
and paper love houses of the next age.

June Fourth

Today as I ride down Twenty-fifth Street I smell honeysuckle
rising from Shell and Victor Balata and K-Diner.
The goddess of sweet memory is there
staggering over fruit and drinking old blossoms.
A man in white socks and a blue T-shirt
is sitting on the grass outside Bethlehem Steel
eating lunch and dreaming.
Before he walks back inside he will be changed.
He will remember when he stands again under the dirty windows
a moment of great misgiving and puzzlement
just before sweetness ruined him and thinking
tore him apart. He will remember lying
on his left elbow studying the sky,
and the loss he felt, and the sudden freedom,
the mixture of pain and pleasure—terror and hope—
what he calls "honeysuckle."

The Angel Poem

My broken wing is on the left near the large joint
that separates me so crazily from half the others.
I think of trees and how they break apart
in the wind, how sometimes a huge branch
will hang in strips, what would be skin
in humans or angels, and how the flesh
is like pulp, and almost blood-red where the break is.

I tend to drag the wing because the pain
in lifting it is too much for me to stand.
That part of me that is still human recalls
what pain in the shoulder can be, and I remember
not only the sharp stabs when I had to turn
but the stiffness that made me keep my arm at my side
and forced me to plan my eating and my painful sleeping.

As far as birds, I am more like a pigeon than a hawk.
I think I am one of those snow-white pigeons with gold
eyes and a candy-corn beak, with a ruffled
neck—a huge white hood—and ruffled
legs, like flowers or long white pantaloons,
shamelessly exposed under my white dress
and hopelessly drooping when I run in
fear and slip and fall on the dirty newspapers.
I fly with shame, when I fly, but mostly I sit
quietly or rise with effort to do my dance,
my head moving back and forth like a loose pendulum.

My main thought is how I can translate pain
into a form that I can understand,
so I break a wing or bruise my foot; but the wound
is more like panic, more like flying
without a shadow or flying in darkness,
something like the human dream when fear
makes them rise out of a sound sleep
and move without control above their bodies,
along the ceiling or through the closed windows,
pushing and yelling as they fall through the glass.
Either way we both have bloody feathers and
wake up groggy, sitting on the foot of the bed
listening to the birds slow down and the day start,
thinking about the dream and its double meaning.

I have looked myself up in the Jefferson Market Library,
in the pink basement where the ghosts of hundreds
of coiners and draft dodgers are still standing
under the arches, waiting to be dragged away.
Sometimes I sit there for hours reading about winged
servants and the mountains of justice and
the hierarchies of the Moors and the Akkadians.
I know—if anything—I am one of the million
Enoch encountered on his first trip to Heaven.
I sit against a freezing wall—my place is
forever against a freezing wall—my hands
hanging loosely down from my knees, a black cat
with wings rubbing up against my leg.
I know I am also the dark part of the leaf,

that I walk upright, that I am half snow, half fire,
that I can move like light from one end of the house to the other,
that I have something in common with Tammuz, and with Shelley.

I am wearing my long gray coat so I can hide
whatever I have to inside like stiff parchment.
I walk upstairs to look at the stained-glass windows
and touch the yellow stars and ruby petals
or move along the shelves, reaching at random
for the literature that will change my life.
I love this library above all others—I love
the two stone heads and the huge painted doors,
and I love standing outside underneath the pillars
and the great carved seal of New York City,
with all that Bavarian madness above me,
the clock and the chimneys and the turrets and the gargoyles,
a step away from the drowned lion on
one side and the fenced-in Greening on the other.
I wait for fifteen minutes, helping couples
move their heavy strollers, telling time
to Temple blonds dragging their sacred books,
and talking sweetly to Vichians and Spinozists.
Across the street is Balducci's where lamb chops go
for thirty dollars a pound and salmon is guarded
by Cuban soldiers; and just up Sixth is the flower
store, loaded with carnations and chrysanthemums,
where I was taken for a city inspector
with my yellow tablet and my blue jacket.

I start my walk at seven o'clock. Maybe
I'll reach the Port Authority by eight-thirty or nine.
All those who live in pain go on fixed walks
between two stations and mark the passage with drops
of blood. They push against each other, bruising
their delicate shoulders and legs—who would know
that one man's stomach is gone, that one has ankles
the size of balloons, that one is in terror
of impotence, that one has blood in her throat.
Dreiser is there pitying the dying poor,
Dostoevsky is studying the black sky,
Balzac is making new souls out of the dust.
They wear wings over their leather coats
and walk through mud as I walk over cement
and shout at the horses blocking their narrow paths.
When I reach Fourteenth I am practically running—past
the Greenwich Savings Bank and Corby's Bar,
past the dead pigeon and the Vitamin Quota.
I start to sing at Eighteenth Street across
from Wanamaker's lost department store—a kind
of Parthenon in the heart of the old soft goods—
and make my turn at Twenty-third past the empty
Paradise Cafeteria. I stop, lovingly
and longingly, in the lobby of the Chelsea
to look at the marble and dream about my life
as a man of letters, coming down the elevator
and standing outside in front of the bronze plaques
before I go to the nearest Blarney Stone
to eat my stew and think about my future.

St. Patrick's Day, 1979

I'm dreaming of the dahlias up there on the radiator,
starting to grow leaves,
and the jade plant getting a little fatter
and a little thicker every day.
I am the man with the rake, bent over with
emotional neck pains, standing in my yard getting
ready to be a garden adviser and a river prophet.

It's freezing—which is what peas like—and every
bird within half a mile is grating its beak
and foolishly chirping and coughing and whistling, half off key.
I have to make up my mind whether to look
back upstairs at the jade plant and the thick
white rag pulling it back in place or at the
sparkling river carrying everything—good and bad—
with it downhill to Trenton and Philadelphia,
fifty miles beyond my graveyard and my roaring spillway.

This spring song is for the drunks in New York,
and the Chinese witch hazel,
and the crow in New Jersey,
and the dying maple,
and the trellis and the rake and the shovel
and the small packet of new snap peas.
It is for the loud wind, and the clear shadows,
and the white cardboard and the red pen.

It is for the poet bent over his rows,
digging up huge chunks of dirt,
bowing and dancing like a white pigeon on Spring Street,
singing again about buried love and crazy renewal.

Visiting Florida Again

At Eleventh and Euclid I stood in front of an air
conditioner and listened to it whir. For just a second
I thought it was an insect screaming in anger
before it sucked up its enemy or ran into the hibiscus
to brood. For the first time
I gave thanks to my brother the machine,
my little friend, so out of place in the tropics,
so close now, compared to the hideous ichneumon
waving its long needle
or the velvet ant
searching for babies—
so misunderstood and abused.
—Shivering in the heat, I wanted to touch
some great yellow steam shovel or biplane,
something so oily and awkward
that it coughed and groaned for hours
before it moved its huge body
into position.
I felt as pure as Mayakovski
climbing into his aluminum vest,
as dear as Pico della Mirandola
watching his Jewish soul rise.
I joined the Shakers at their amorous stations,
the Anarchists
resting in the sun.
For just one second I was in London again
in the iron palace,

I was in Pittsburgh,
sitting in the old reference room,
reading Thomas Paine and William Blake and Peter Kropotkin,
creating my first dreams.

Hanging Scroll

I have come back to Princeton three days in a row
to look at the brown sparrow in the apple branch.
That way I can get back in touch with the Chinese
after thirty years of silence and paranoid reproach.
It was painted seven hundred years ago by a Southerner
who was struggling to combine imitation and expression,
but nowhere is there a sense that calligraphy
has won the day, or anything lifeless or abstract.
I carry it around with me on a post card,
the bird in the center, the giant green leaves
surrounding the bird, the apples almost invisible,
their color and position chosen for obscurity—
somehow the sizes all out of whack, the leaves
too large, the bird too small, too rigid,
too enshrined for such a natural setting,
although this only comes slowly to mind
after many hours of concentration.

On my tree there are six starlings sitting and watching
with their heads in the air and their short tails under the twigs.
They are just faint shapes against a background of fog,
moving in and out of my small windows
as endless versions of the state of darkness.
The tree they are in is practically dead,
making it difficult for me to make plans
for my own seven hundred years
as far as critical position, or permanence.
—If the hanging scroll signifies a state
of balance, a state almost of tension

between a man and nature or a man and his dream,
then my starlings signify the tremendous
delicacy of life and the tenuousness of attachment.
This may sound too literary—too German—
but, for me, everything hangs in the balance
in the movement of those birds,
just as, in my painter,
his life may have been hanging from the invisible apple
or the stiff tail feathers or the minuscule feet.
I don't mean to say that my survival
depends upon the artistic rendering;
I mean that my one chance for happiness
depends on wind and strange loyalty and a little bark,
which I think about and watch and agonize over
day and night,
like a worried spirit
waiting for love.

A Hundred Years from Now

A hundred years from now nobody will know who Zane Grey was
nor what the ten-cent pulp smelled like
nor what it was like to carry *Liberty* magazines on your back.
If you are bored to death by this then think of Wallace Stevens
when he first walked into the University of Pennsylvania library
and the memories he had of certain leather chairs,
or think of Ts'ai Yen in the land of frost and snow,
remembering his young mother.

I myself am searching for the purple sage that I can share
for all time with the poets of Akkadia and Sumeria.
I am starting with my river bottom, the twisted
sycamores and the big-leaved catalpas, making the connections
that will put Zane Grey in the right channel. I am
watching a very ancient Babylonian who looks something
like me or Allen Ginsberg before he shaved his beard off
pick up *The Border Legion* and *The Riders of the Trail*
from the dust. I am explaining him the spirit
of America behind our banality, our devotion
to the ugly and our suicidal urges;
how Zane Grey, once he saw the desert,
could not stop giving his life to it,
in spite of his dull imagination and stilted prose;
how the eternal is also here,
only the way to it is brutal.
O Babylonian, I am swimming in the deep off the island
of my own death and birth. Stay with me!

The Poem of Liberation

The smell of piss is what we have in the city
to remind us of the country and its dark ammonia.
In the subway it's like a patch of new lilac
or viburnum in the air or like that pocket
of cold water you swim in at Batsto
or that other pocket of water at Amagansett.
In the telephones it sinks in the metal plates
like the smell in a rug or a rotten sofa,
a stain you run away from in grief and anger.

Sometimes I walk in the East Side past the brownstones
on Fifty-second Street or the long sleek canopies
that almost cover the sidewalks from Fifth to Madison.
Then it's like remembering the stone walls in Italy
or the tiny alleys behind the bazaars in Africa.
Then I know, walking in front of Park East
or the Hampton House or the Penguin,
that New York will be the first city to go,
and we will no longer live like English,
hating the sight of sweet bananas and thick-armed
women smashing dice against the boards.

Across the street from St. John's there is a large
vegetable garden planted in the rubble
of a wrecked apartment house, as if to claim
the spirit back before it could be buried
in another investment of glass and cement.
There are thin maples and pieces of orange brick
and weeds and garbage as well as little rows

of beans and lettuce and hills of squash and melons.
It is a confused garden but I think the
soul of New York is there in the vague balance
of shape against shape and in the lush presence
of objects, from the blue cement fish pond
to the curved brick walk to the outdoor grille and chair;
a boxed-in mulch pit, iron candelabra, deep
irrigation ditches, delicate flower beds,
everything crowded into the smallest space.

I stand on the steps in front of the straining prophet,
looking across at the other two buildings, saved
by the squatters in 1970. I look at the splintered
doors and the pile of rubbish outside the windows
and make my own philosophical connections.
Behind the church, totally hidden from the street,
is another garden, planted by the women
of St. John's, this one a biblical
fantasy of trees and herbs and flowers,
from Matthew and John and Samuel, laid out in perfect
clusters, poplar from Genesis, reeds from Kings,
nettles from Job, lovely carob from Luke,
completely different from the other garden,
but not a mirror image of it
and not a sacred version of the profane,
one a vile parody of the other,
although these ideas flooded through my mind.

I fall asleep under the olive trees
thinking of Jezebel and Elijah.
I want to like one garden and hate the other
but I find myself loving both, both ideas,
both deeply thought out, both passionate.
I talk to the fat Englishman—the curator
of the church museum—about the two gardens
and the squatters and the church's benign role
and get his views on property, and mercy,
and study his tiny feet and row of books.
Finally I walk across the street again
to look at the People's Garden and plan my
little corner next to the climbing roses,
maybe a hosta or a bleeding heart.

My last hour is spent reading the poem
of liberation—in Spanish and English—
nailed up on the wire fence
and walking through the Plaza Caribe
under the slogans and the brown faces.
—At first I think it's hope again, hope played out
on a two-stringed instrument or a soggy drum,
Hebrew melancholy and Moorish wailing
under a fringed lamp, in a ruined chair,
but then I realize it's hope mixed in with memory
and not that other bitter stupid dream again,
stuck to the face like a drop of baby dew.
I love memory too, the weeping mouth
that will not let you go, the wet smell drifting

through the alleys, the hum at the high window;
and I love the fact that, this time, no one will stand
with his straw hat in his hand in the marble courtroom
singing, "I love you, Kate Smith. I love you, I love you,
I love you, *presidente,* I love you, *señor* mayor."
I dig a hole in the ground
and pour in my mixture of meal and water.
I spread the roots out in three directions
and pack them in with dirt.
I leave by the southern gate
across the street from the Hungarian pastry
and walk down 111th like a Bedouin farmer,
like a Polish shepherd,
like a Korean rope master,
my small steel shovel
humming and singing in the blue dust.

Acacia

In locust trees the roots run along the ground
and bury themselves in the sides of hills for survival.
They grow in roses and strawberries
and come from little sticks humbly and touchingly.
In three counties I am the only one who loves them;
I am the only one who reads about them in Ilick;
I am the only one who grieves when they turn brown and
die, or lie bent and broken in the rain.

Three summers ago I walked through the streets of Albi
with my friend Dave Burrows—who has since become
        Das Anudas—
and a French parasite and his little American wife.
We saw the locusts from the river not far from the brick
cathedral—made out of Protestant blood—not far from the huge
Toulouse-Lautrec collection housed in a palace,
something, it seemed to me then, like housing hundreds
of baby lambs or tons of fresh flowers
in the lobby or restaurant of a Howard Johnson's.

We argued for half an hour about the locust.
He told me it was now French but originally
it grew in southern China and India.
I told him it came from western Pennsylvania
and was brought to Europe in the nineteenth century.
He told me it was planted on the side of streets and in parks
because of its shade and its ornamental qualities.
I told him it was practically a weed in America,
that farmers valued it mainly for fence posts.

I remember his wife—she was displaced;
her eyes were round, her skin almost transparent.
We ate a late supper in the square near the railroad
station and her voice had already assumed that
flat ungoverned tone I have heard in dozens
of museums and restaurants from London to Heraklion.
When she and I talked English her vile husband
frowned and barked at her in his southern French,
and when I shook hands with her to say good-by
and kissed her on the side of her small mouth
it was like stripping those tiny leaves from their stems
or smelling again the sweetest of all blossoms,
like being again in the Allegheny mountains
where locusts first started, four million years ago.

And that, my love, is a continent and a half away
from Albi, where the northern French descended
on the southern French and in the name of Jesus
destroyed their culture and their strange religion
and made them build a tributary cathedral
where Das Anudas and I walked all morning,
noting every detail of the pink fortress,
fainting from the beauty,
growing hungry from the climb,
changed forever halfway through our lives.

Your Animal

The final end of all but purified souls
is to be swallowed up by Leviathan,
or to be bound with fiery chains and flogged
with 70 stripes of fire.
I walk along the mule path dreaming of my weaknesses
and praying to the ducks for forgiveness.
Oh there is so much shit in the universe
and my walks, like yours,
are more and more slippery and dangerous.
I love a duck for being almost like a vegetable.
I love him because his whole body can be consumed,
because there is no distance between him and his watery offal.
Your animal is almost human,
distant from his waste,
struggling to overcome the hated matter,
looking up with horrified white eyes,
eternally hunting for space in the little islands of Riverside Drive
and the fenced-in parks of the Village.

I love duck and potatoes, duck and red beets,
duck and orange juice.
I love the head of duck dipped in sugar,
I love chocolate duck with chipolota sausages,
fragrant crisp duck mixed with shrimp and pork.
I love the webs and the heart; I love the eggs
preserved in lime and potash, completely boned duck
filled with ham and chestnuts, fried duck with pineapple
and canned red cherries or sections of tangerine.

This is a poem against gnosticism;
it is a poem against the hatred of the flesh
and all the vicious twists and turns we take
to calm our frightened souls.
It is a poem celebrating the eating of duck
and all that goes with it.
It is a poem I am able to write after walking every day
through the flocks, and loving the babies, and watching them slip
down the mud sides and float into the current.
It is a poem about shooting galleries and cardboard heads,
about hunters and their checkered hats and frozen fingers,
about snow-white cloths and steaming laced-up birds
and waiters standing in little regiments
getting ready to run in among the tables and start carving.
—It is my poem against the starving heart.
It is my victory over meanness.

The Rose Warehouse

Ah tunnel cows,
watching over my goings out
and my comings in,
you preside, like me, over your own butchery.

I always look for you
when I go back to Pennsylvania,
driving under the rusty piers
and up Fortieth Street.

All of New York must be laid out for you up there,
the slope on Park Avenue,
the moon on the river,
the roof of the Port Authority.

I feel like putting up my own head,
the head of Gerald Stern,
on the side of the Rose Warehouse, his glasses slipping off,
his tears dropping one by one on Eleventh Avenue.

I want to see if he will sing
or if he will stare out at the blue sky forever and forever.
I want to see if he's a god
and feels like murmuring a little in the lost tongue

or if he's one of those black humans,
still mourning after thirty years—
some German Jew
talking about Berlin,

the town that had everything;
some man of love
who dug his own grave and entered there;
some sorrowful husband

refusing to wash, refusing to listen to music,
cutting his flesh, rubbing dust in his hair,
throwing in dirt, throwing in flowers,
kissing the shovel good-by, kissing the small shovel.

The Red Coal

Sometimes I sit in my blue chair trying to remember
what it was like in the spring of 1950
before the burning coal entered my life.

I study my red hand under the faucet, the left one
below the grease line consisting of four feminine angels
and one crooked broken masculine one

and the right one lying on top of the white porcelain
with skin wrinkled up like a chicken's
beside the razor and the silver tap.

I didn't live in Paris for nothing and walk
with Jack Gilbert down the wide sidewalks
thinking of Hart Crane and Apollinaire

and I didn't save the picture of the two of us
moving through a crowd of stiff Frenchmen
and put it beside the one of Pound and Williams

unless I wanted to see what coals had done
to their lives too. I say it with affection,
wanting desperately to know what the two of them

talked about when they lived in Pennsylvania
and what they talked about at St. Elizabeth's
fifty years later, looking into the sun,

40,000 wrinkles between them,
the suffering finally taking over their lives.
I think of Gilbert all the time now, what

we said on our long walks in Pittsburgh, how
lucky we were to live in New York, how strange
his new fame was and my obscurity,

how we now carry the future with us, knowing
every small vein and every elaboration.
The coal has taken over, the red coal

is burning between us and we are at its mercy—
as if a power is finally dominating
the two of us; as if we're huddled up

watching the black smoke and the ashes;
as if knowledge is what we needed and now
we have that knowledge. Now we have that knowledge.

The tears are different—though I hate to speak
for him—the tears are what we bring back to the
darkness, what we are left with after our

own escape, what, all along, the red coal
had in store for us as we moved softly,
either whistling or singing, either listening or reasoning,

on the gray sidewalks and the green ocean;
in the cars and the kitchens and the bookstores;
in the crowded restaurants, in the empty woods and libraries.

There Is Wind, There Are Matches

A thousand times I have sat in restaurant windows,
through mopping after mopping, letting the ammonia clear
my brain and the music from the kitchens
ruin my heart. I have sat there hiding
my feelings from my neighbors, blowing smoke
carefully into the ceiling, or after I gave
that up, smiling over my empty plate
like a tired wolf. Today I am sitting again
at the long marble table at Horn and Hardart's,
drinking my coffee and eating my burnt scrapple.
This is the last place left and everyone here
knows it; if the lights were turned down, if the
heat were turned off, if the banging of dishes stopped,
we would all go on, at least for a while, but then
we would drift off one by one toward Locust or Pine.
—I feel this place is like a birch forest
about to go; there is wind, there are matches, there is snow,
and it has been dark and dry for hundreds of years.
I look at the chandelier waving in the glass
and the sticky sugar and the wet spoon.
I take my handkerchief out for the sake of the seven
years we spent in Philadelphia and the
steps we sat on and the tiny patches of lawn.
I believe now more than I ever did before
in my first poems and more and more I feel
that nothing was wasted, that the freezing nights
were not a waste, that the long dull walks and
the boredom, and the secret pity, were
not a waste. I leave the paper sitting,

front page up, beside the cold coffee,
on top of the sugar, on top of the wet spoon,
on top of the grease. I was born for one thing,
and I can leave this place without bitterness
and start my walk down Broad Street past the churches
and the tiny parking lots and the thrift stores.
There was enough justice, and there was enough wisdom,
although it would take the rest of my life—the next
two hundred years—to understand and explain it;
and there was enough time and there was enough affection
even if I did tear my tongue
begging the world for one more empty room
and one more window with clean glass
to let the light in on my last frenzy.
—I do the crow walking clumsily over his meat,
I do the child sitting for his dessert,
I do the poet asleep at his table,
waiting for the sun to light up his forehead.
I suddenly remember every ruined life,
every betrayal, every desolation,
as I walk past Tasker toward the city of Baltimore,
banging my pencil on the iron fences,
whistling Bach and Muczynski through the closed blinds.

The-Way-We-Were Lounge

This is the kind of place I loved when I walked
across Italy looking every night for open
spaces. I would have lain on my back
staring up at the two rusty cedar trees
and the broken notes and the tilted cocktail glass.
I would have sung myself to sleep
thinking about Padua and little Verona with the rose walls.
I was like a gorilla, making a new
bed every night, digging a hole so I could
lie on the ground without breaking my bones.
I was a believer—the one time in my life—
traveling from town to town with my marble notebook
full of dark signs and incantations.
I would have loved the swaying pole
and the white sidewalk.
I would have waited for hours
to put my shoes on
and wash my face at the iron spigot.
I would have stood up like a devout shadow
to look at the moon again in the first daylight.

Waving Good-by

I wanted to know what it was like before we
had voices and before we had bare fingers and before we
had minds to move us through our actions
and tears to help us over our feelings,
so I drove my daughter through the snow to meet her friend
and filled her car with suitcases and hugged her
as an animal would, pressing my forehead against her,
walking in circles, moaning, touching her cheek,
and turned my head after them as an animal would,
watching helplessly as they drove over the ruts,
her smiling face and her small hand just visible
over the giant pillows and coat hangers
as they made their turn into the empty highway.

In These Shadows

All that I know about the rose
and the paper snowflake and the living goddess
is in these shadows—the rose's limpness,
the snowflake's fluorescence, the goddess's violent
anger. All that I ever learned
is suddenly altered
and all the cunning and pain is reduced
to a dark image where the body falls.

Oh sweetness, sweetness! I can walk the length
of my dying maple; I can live again
in its old arms; I can watch it reach
out to the river, or stand like the first man
for hours in the cold sun,
looking at the soft ice,
sliding over the leaves,
disappearing in the blue water.

Dear Mole

Dear mole, I have forgotten you!
Living under the dahlias, making highways
under the pines, coming up to sniff
blindly, like John Ruskin,
at the pink chrysanthemums and the red berries
hanging from the ruined viburnum.

Everything depends on your sponginess,
the world you created with your
shoulders and claws,
the long tunnels and the quiet rooms
where you can wander—like Ruskin—
dreaming of smooth floors and vaulted ceilings.

He was like you,
always cramming and ramming, spluttering in disgust,
hating repression, living apart from others,
adoring mountains, drifting with the vortices,
hemorrhaging a little,
loving high sounds, loving the crystal orders.

He was like you,
following the laws of the fourteenth century,
envious of the fish,
curiously breathless and obsessed with shadows,
loving small girls, living deep in Hell,
always beginning, always starting over,
his head down, his black soul warbling and wailing.

My Hand

I have put my hand in a baby shepherd's mouth
and watched him whine with pleasure.
I have seen him roll on his back
with his white stomach facing the sun
and paw helplessly.
I think he is full of some low form of love,
something that Dante would have pitied
as he moved from heaven to heaven,
something akin to the drowned buttercup
or the red woodpecker swinging on his bag of fat.
There would be a crease at the corner of Dante's eye,
a roundness in his cheek,
that is for that animal alone—
a tiny sign
interrupting his climbing and his falling,
his concentration on justice and liberation.

These Birds

These birds burst in and out of their shadows
as if they alone in all the world were breathing,
as if their violent heartbeats were the only hope,
as if the snow could withstand two more contradictions,
as if they could defy the life of all sanity.

They bring their bodies with them
and walk into the wires and through the trees
as if they could drink and eat with impunity,
as if their wings gave them the right to stand there,
as if there were not another life to think of,
as if one stillness were not overlying the other,
as if they had not already created the first darkness,
as if dreaming and not dreaming were the same,
as if the sky could save them,
as if they could depend again on their own savagery.

Arthur's Lily

I could never feel sorry for Arthur Vogelsang,
resting among his kafir-lilies and his phoenix tree.
I could never say there he is
in Los Angeles wiping his eyes from the smog
and leaping across the great crack in his sidewalk.
He has a whole desert to live in without poets;
he has the letter of Ezra Pound cursing jellyfish;
he has the city of Baltimore to remember.
—I could never drop a tear for him,
knowing he is standing by his crooked mailbox;
I could never lure him with our warm water
or touch him with our snow,
knowing he is buying a white Chrysler,
knowing he is throwing the grapefruit;
I could never drag him back,
knowing he is talking to the cement frog,
knowing he is practicing footprints,
knowing he is planning another ecstatic voyage.

The Picasso Poem

It was when the bridal wreaths were all out
and those smelly weeds, the graduation speakers,
were blooming on one green lawn after another
that I sat on my porch trying to make up my mind
about the Pablo Picasso I loved the most.
It was Sunday morning and the *New York Times*
was full of his glory; it was Sunday
and the skinny runners were out
and the iris were combing their tiny beards
and the lilacs were waving a dark good-by.
I wanted to drive a 1936 Pontiac
to New York City to see the exhibition.
I wanted to drive through New Jersey with the picnic
basket bumping my knee and the line of trees
keeping the sun out from Phillipsburg to Newark.
Over and over again I thought of him
in the 1930's and I thought of the paintings
he did and I thought of the France he loved,
all plump and modern and corrupt.
He was 55 in 1936 and slipping
through the silence before his next flowering;
he was moving from one hard place to another,
dipping his hand and smearing the white canvas.
—I think I'd have to choose between the woman
with a hat or the one with rope for a face
or the one reclining—with stars—or the one in a nightmare
ripping apart a handkerchief;
or maybe the goat; or maybe the bicycle handle.
    On June ninth I stood peacefully in line

waiting to crawl through the numbered rooms.
I was so quiet little birds were resting
on my soft shoulder and little leaves were growing
from my legs and arms.
Somewhere, inside my chest, a heart was pounding,
and I was listening again, a little thinner
and a little whiter than the last time.
I walked through the birches, I walked through the dry rain,
I bent down and ran my fingers
through the black dirt. Three hours from then
I would walk down that line from the other side,
dreaming—I think—of my own next darkness.
God save Fifth Avenue, God save New York
from my assault. God let me drive
across the Pulaski Skyway singing those great
songs; leaning out the little window
and staring down at the Jersey swamp;
smelling that sulphur; driving up into the sun
and looking back on those iron lamps; looking forward
over and over to the future, streets in the sky,
towers in the ground, dancing people, little
dogs for every family. I waver between
that world and this. I travel back and forth
between the two. I lose myself
and crawl off singing or come back crying,
my face wet with misery, my eyes deep holes
where the dream was lost, my hands up in their favorite
position, the two unbroken fingers
cutting the air,

thirty feet above the river,
beside the hostas and the mugho pine,
the dirty bottles and the stones
fixing the boundary for another summer.

The Roar

That was the last time I would walk up those five
flights with a woman in tow, standing
in the hall patiently trying my keys,
listening to my heart pounding from the climb.

And the last time I would sit in front of the
refrigerator, drinking white wine and asking
questions, and lecturing—like a spider—
and rubbing my hand through my hair—like a priest.

Look at me touch the burning candle
with my bare palm and press a rusty knife
against my left eyelid while she undresses.

Look at me rise through the cool airshaft
and snore at the foot of the bed with one hand
on her knee and one hand touching the white floor,

the red and blue beacon of Empire
just beyond those little houses
as familiar now as my crippled birch

and the endless roar out there
as sweet as my own roar
in my other dream, on the cold and empty river.

For Night to Come

I am giving instructions to my monkey
on how to plant a pine tree. I am telling
him to water the ground for hours before
he starts to dig and I am showing him
how to twist the roots so the limbs will bend
in the right direction.
                He is grieving
because of the wet air, and remembering
our canoe trip, and how we went swimming
on Mother's Day. And I am remembering
the holiness and how we stopped talking
after we left Route 30. I show him the tree
with the two forks and the one with the
stubs and the one with the orange moss
underneath, and we make our nest in a clearing
where the wind makes hissing noises and the sun
goes through our heavy clothes.
                      All morning we lie
on our backs, holding hands, listening to birds,
and making little ant hills in the sand.
He shakes a little, maybe from the cold,
maybe a little from memory,
maybe from dread. I think we are lost,
only a hundred yards from the highway,
and we will have to walk around in fear,
or separate and look for signs before
we find it again.
            We pick a small green tree,
thick with needles and cones and dangling roots,

and put it in the trunk on top of the blanket,
and straighten the branches out, and smooth the hairs.
All the way back we will be teary and helpless,
loving each other in the late afternoon,
and only when we have made the first cut
and done the dance
and poured in the two bushels of humus
and the four buckets of water
and mixed it in with dirt and tramped it all down
and arranged and rearranged the branches
will we lie back and listen to the chimes
and stop our shaking
and close our eyes a little
and wait for night to come
so we can watch the stars together,
like the good souls we are,
a hairy man and a beast
hugging each other in the white grass.

Here I Am Walking

Here I am walking between Ocean and Neptune,
sinking my feet in mile after mile of wet life.
I am practically invisible
in the face of all this clutter,
either straying near the benches over the buried T-shirts
or downhill in the graveyard
where the burned families are sleeping in the sun
or eating dry lunch among the corpses.
I will finish walking in two hours
and eat my sandwich in the little park
beside the iron Methodist.
This is the first step.
Tomorrow I will start again in Barnegat
and make my way toward Holgate or Ventnor.
This is something different
than it was even five years ago.
I have a second past to rake over
and search through—another thousand miles of seashore
to account for.
—I am still making my mind up
between one of those art deco hotels
in Miami Beach, a little back room on a court
where you could almost be in Cuba or
Costa Rica of the sweet flesh, and
a wooden shack in one of the mosquito marshes
in Manahawkin or the Outer Banks.
I am planning my cup of tea
and my burnt biscuit,
or my macaroni soup

and my can of sardines.
If I spent the morning washing shirts
I would read for two hours
before I slept through the afternoon.
If I walked first, or swam,
I might feel like writing down words
before I went in for coffee, or more hot water.
I will sit on the black rocks
to make my connections,
near the small basin of foam.
I will look at the footprints
going in and out of the water
and dream up a small blue god to talk to.
I will be just where I was
twenty-five years ago,
breathing in salt,
snorting like a prophet,
turning over the charred wood;
just where I was then,
getting rid of baggage,
living in dreams,
finding a way to change, or salvage, my clumsy life.

Paradise Poems

Orange Roses

I am letting two old roses stand for everything I believe in.
I am restricting the size of the world, keeping it inside that plastic pot.
This is like Greece, the roses sitting in the hot sun,
the leaves exhausted,
the blue sky surrounding them.

I reach my fingers inside the dirt
and slowly scrape the sides.
One more flower will bloom the rest of this month,
probably symbolizing the last breath left
after a lifetime of tearful singing.

The wall in back of me is no part of this.
It shows only a large shadow overcome with thought.
It shows him in ruins,
his body spread out in all directions,
his pencil uprooted, his own orange roses dark and hidden.

Later Today

Later today, when most of the ice is melted
and the water is black again, we'll sit for one minute
on the side porch and stare at the bright shadows.
We'll start talking about the wall
and the green pool beside the copper feeder
and how the birch could grow again
and how the door would look with roses on it.
We will live in the light
as if we were still in France,
as if the boats were there
and we were staring into space,
as if we were in Babylon,
walking beside the iron giants,
touching their black beards,
looking at their huge eyes,
going down to our clay houses and our tiny cafés
on the muddy river.

Rhododendron

Here I am again with one more flower,
more lavender than pink this time,
more rich and red than ever.
Here I am after walking back and forth through the grass
with an armful of straw
and a fistful of white dust.
—I bend down to drink
like a lover, my words half muffled
by the bird clack, my secret softened
by the light rain and the dark sunshine.
I smooth the leaves and pull the petals out
with that quick underhand motion.
I prepare for life or death by lying down
with my left arm under my head, by saying my last
words to the two trees, by closing my eyes
to everything else, the dirty woods, the river,
the green tomatoes, the yellow marigolds,
the bloody squirrel, the bitter universe.

Picking the Roses

I am picking the roses for next time,
Little Darlings for the side of the house,
Tiffany and Lilli Marlene for the hot slope
where the strawberries used to be.
I am doing this in early February
before the ice cracks and the island gets back its dignity.
There is a towel against the front door
to keep the wind out
and newspapers squeezed into the holes
so we can have good reading for the bright wasps.
If there is a boar, he is outside snorting.
We will need him for the bleeding and regeneration to come.

Soon the dead plants will arrive by mail,
the roses in corrugated paper, their roots packed
in excelsior and moss,
the lilies in plastic bags, *their* roots like radishes,
a leaf or two to signify the good life of the future.
When the time comes I will walk outside to hear my name
ring through the trees, or stop for a minute to hear the words skip
on the water or collect like mice behind the garbage cans.
I will tear the ground with my shovel
and bark with pain as I bend down over the roots
and get ready for the dirty water and the dust.

Then for two blocks up and two blocks down
my screams, and the screams of the boar,
will mix together.
There will be talking afterwards and sobbing

and touches of cynicism and histrionics
in the living rooms by the river,
and single voices wailing in the tradition
of the old Orient, and choruses of flies
boring everybody with their small details,
crash of bone against bone,
mixture of broken weapons and falling shadows.

I will clean up
like a ghost at my own funeral.
My poor left eye will be closed shut
behind its puffy hill
and my right thigh will be permanently twisted.
I will sleep my sleep
on top of the mohair sofa,
over the *Inquirer* and the white espresso.
In one month
the twigs will be shining
and I will be rocking in my metal chair
or sitting on my swing
in the little room on the side porch.
One arm I'll hold up in the snake position
above my head
and one arm I'll hold out like a hairy fox
waiting to spring.
I will collect all the stupidity and sorrow
of the universe in one place
and wait—like everyone else—
for the first good signs,

the stems to turn green,
the buds to swell and redden,
the clouds to fall, the trees to bend,
the tenors of all 3,000 counties
to tremble in the grass,
to beat their chests, to tear their shirts,
to stumble against the sopranos, to rise and fall
like birds in the muddy grass,
like heavy birds in last year's muddy grass.

Clay Dog

I'll never forget the small red dog in Mexico,
his two long ears and his bulging eyes.
All the passion and courtesy of the artist
are in that body
and all the sweetness of his race.
—I think of him, after a long nap with his wife,
staring up at the sky, and I think of his left hand
resting under her head while his right hand works
above the smoke. I think of him touching her cheek
before he goes back to the sand, maybe toying
all the way down with either a snarling lower lip
or drooping cougar shoulder, maybe putting
a corn cob in the mouth so the teeth will show,
maybe turning the face back like a horse's
or stiffening the legs or flattening the back
to build the tension up in front,
maybe dividing the head into lobes or raising
the nose to give a look of fear or disdain,
maybe scraping the skin until it shines
or adding a little white to the tiny nails—
getting him ready to live under the stars,
letting him join the others,
taking the leaves off, cooling the hot bricks,
saving him from the mud and from the fire.

In Memory of W. H. Auden

I am going over my early rages again,
my first laments and ecstasies,
my old indictments and spiritualities.
I am standing, like Schiller, in front of Auden's door
waiting for his carved face to let me in.
In my hand is *The Poem of My Heart* I dragged
from one ruined continent to the other,
all my feelings slipping out on the sidewalk.
It was warm and hopeful in his small cave
waiting for the right word to descend
but it was cold and brutal outside on Fourth Street
as I walked back to the Seventh Avenue subway,
knowing, as I reached the crowded stairway,
that I would have to wait for ten more years
or maybe twenty more years for the first riches
to come my way, and knowing that the stick
of that old Prospero would never rest
on my poor head, dear as he was with his robes
and his books of magic, good and wise as he was
in his wrinkled suit and his battered slippers.
—Oh good and wise, but not enough to comfort me,
so loving was he with his other souls.
I had to wait like clumsy Caliban,
a sucker for every vagueness and degeneration.
I had to find my own way back, I had to
free myself, I had to find my own pleasure
in my own sweet cave, with my own sweet music.
    Once a year, later even once a month,
I stood on the shores of Bleecker and Horatio

waving goodbye to that ship all tight and yare
and that great wizard, bobbing up and down
like a dreaming sailor out there, disappearing
just as he came, only this time his face more weary
and his spirit more grave than when he first arrived
to take us prisoner on our own small island,
that poet I now could talk to, that wrinkled priest
whose neck I'd hang on, that magician
who could release me now, whom I release and remember.

Steve Dunn's Spider

Down in the sweet pepper bushes,
down in the birches,
down by the manmade lake,
I walk across the causeway
avoiding Steve Dunn's spider,
the little recluse with the white violin on its back.

Down on the nudist's log,
down in the soggy water,
down by the fat girl's tried and true paradise,
I avoid the thin white threads
at any cost,
the week in bed,
the oozing ankle,
the convulsive tightening in the throat,
the year of remorse and burning tissue.

In the twenty-fourth circle,
in the twenty-fourth or twenty-fifth circle,
in the pool of warm blood,
in old *Pomona Real*,
I try to save myself,
I hold the slippery tree between my legs,
I talk to a frog,
I talk to a hairy German,
I get ready for earthly bliss,
I go to the furthest limit,
I sink down of my own free will,
I lie on the wavy rocks

and I rise up
one more time in the brilliant sunlight,
across from the pine trees,
across from the cedars,
king of the water,
lord of the greasy log,
lord of the lake.

Romania, Romania

I stand like some country crow across the street
from the Romanian Synagogue on Rivington Street
singing songs about Moldavia and Bukovina.
I am a walking violin, screeching
a little at the heights, vibrating a little
at the depths, plucking sadly on my rubber guts.
It's only music that saves me. Otherwise
I would be keeping the skulls forever, otherwise
I would be pulling red feathers from my bloody neck.
It's only music, otherwise I would be white
with anger or giving in to hatred
or turning back to logic and religion—
the Brahms Concerto, hills and valleys of gold,
the mighty Kreutzer, rubies piled over rubies,
a little Bartók, a little ancient Bach—
but more for the thin white tablecloths under the trees
than for Goga and his Christians,
and more for the red petticoats and the cold wine and the garlic
than the railroad station and the submachine guns,
and more for the little turn on Orchard Street
and the life of sweetness and more for the godly Spanish
and the godly Chinese lined up for morning prayers,
and much much more for the leather jackets on sticks
and the quiet smoke
and the plush fire escapes,
and much much more for the silk scarves in the windows
and the cars in the streets
and the dirty invisible stars—
Yehudi Menuhin

wandering through the hemlocks,
Jascha Heifetz
bending down over the tables,
the great Stern himself
dragging his heart from one ruined soul to another.

It's Nice to Think of Tears

It's nice to think of tears as polliwogs
rolling down your face,
lost on the cheekbones and the distant chin
before they drop on the oilcloth and the pine floor.

It's nice to think of you reaching your hand up
and wiping them away,
all that sadness
welling up, then disappearing.

It's just fantastic to think of sorrow
as water,
to think of it dripping through the leaves
or escaping in the sand,

to see it stretching from one salt island
to another,
or filling the cellar up
and the pools and ditches—

all that grief
where the eyes were,
all that sobbing
where the heart was,

all those rivers flowing
where the swelling had been,
and all those lakes and oceans
where the head was lying,

where the mouth was open,
where the shoulders were bent,
where the hands were hanging down,
where the dark old hands were helpless and hanging down.

Souls from Emerson

for Myrna Smith

This is a kind of sunflower,
only smaller and less demanding,
on a side street in Phillipsburg
faced away from the truck fumes and the air horns.

It replaces the dead beehives and tobacco leaves,
bowed over from exhaustion,
and crawls over the side of the bird house and the wire fence
like a morning glory or daisy.

I come back here twice,
once to climb the hill
and once to touch the old head
and break a leaf off at the stem.

And I come back to see if I can find
the whitewashed wall
and hear the wild dog again
and see his fenced-in garden, the souls outside

going up and down like souls from Emerson,
trying to find a home on Marshall Street
beside the clothes pins and the oil drum,
near the slush and the pink mimosa—

left on the Parkway just before Jacob's Auto Parts,
across from the green island separating
the cars rushing west to Cleveland and Ypsilanti
and the cars rushing east to Whitehouse and Coney Island.

Song

There's nothing in this gardenous world more delightful
than blossoms lying where they fall,
soldiers sprawled from one ravine to another,
lovers under a bloody window.

I look up through the branches
dreaming of fate.
My old enemy the blue sky is above me.
My old enemy the hawk
is moving slowly through the string of white clouds.

One day I will wake up at dawn
and philosophize about my state
as I get ready.
I will put on my heavy shirt
and think of the long and bitter day ahead.

It will take hours to know
whether I will live or die,
which car to get ready,
which woods to pass by,
which animal to ride over,
which bridge to cross on the way.

I love the sight of me
rolled over on the ground.
I love being pierced through the heart,
half a man, half a flower,
reaching my hand out, turning my palm away,

one of the many pink and white blossoms,
one of the many on the brutal lawn.

Weeping and Wailing

I like the way my little harp makes trees
leap, how putting the metal between my teeth
makes half the animals in my backyard quiver,
how plucking the sweet tongue makes the stars
live together in love and ecstasy.

I bend my face and cock my head. My eyes
are open wide listening to the sound.
My hand goes up and down like a hummingbird.
My mouth is opening and closing, I am singing
in harmony, I am weeping and wailing.

Hidden Justice

This is my forest now, this Christmas cactus,
stretching out leaf after leaf,
pink blossom after pink blossom.
This is where I'll go to breathe
and live in darkness
and sit like a frog, and sit like a salamander,
and this is where I'll find a tiny light
and have my vision
and start my school—
in this dry and airy place
beside these trunks
in this fragrant mixture.

I will put my small stage here
under a thick leaf
and I will eat and sleep and preach right here
and put my two dogs there
to keep my two guards busy
with prayer and feeding.
I will live completely for the flowering,
my neck like a swan's,
my fingers clawing the air
looking for justice;
year after year the same,
my fingers clawing the air for hidden justice.

Christmas Sticks

Before I leave I'll put two sticks on the porch
so they can talk to each other about poor Poland
and wrap themselves around each other the way sticks
do when most of life is gone. They will lie
a little about Walesa, one will dance
and shake his dried-out leaves as if to threaten
the other, one will lean against the wall
as if there were boots to give him courage, as if
there was a moustache somewhere there among the scars
and a thin sword and a thin tear. I'd make them flower
again, I'd make them drive through Warsaw
on the back of trucks, I'd have them reach their wooden
hands through the flimsy slats and take the gifts
and live out the dream of 1830 and the dream
of 1863, the Russians gone,
the Germans gone, the life remade, the flags
flying over the factories, workers dancing
above the trees, a wedding under a walnut,
the food amazing, the last memory the bride's
father in white showing his empty pockets,
his beard a little white to match his suit,
his eyes all wet, his shirt half open—
all that sweetness, all that golden fat—
the fat I love, the sweetness I love—and the two of them
walking home at night after the wedding
talking to each other again about Pulaski
and Casimir the Great and Copernicus
and what it could have been if only sticks
had ruled the vicious world, remembering again

the Jews arriving from Spain, the scholars of Europe
descending on Cracow, half the Italian painters
living in Poland, the gentry reading books,
the women drawing and playing flutes—
forgetting the dream-crushers out there in the swamps,
forgetting the liars, forgetting the murderers—
two sticks in the moonlight carrying on
after the wedding, lifting their empty bottles
for the last time, one of them heaving his over
a sycamore—a buttonwood tree—one of them
heaving his across a frozen river
and listening with his hands on his bent knees
for the old crash, slow in coming, the impact
a half a minute later than he expected,
both of them laughing at the stupidity,
both of them weeping for the huge carp
frozen in mud, and both of them toasting the bride
with broken hands, with nothing this time, with fingers
ruined and shredded, kissing the dear one goodbye
before they go off like wounded soldiers, home
from fighting the Turks at Vienna, home from fighting
the Deutschers a hundred times and the Rooskies two hundred,
home from fighting the Swedes and the Austrians,
two great masters of suffering and sadness
singing songs about love and regeneration.

The Same Moon Above Us

When I see a man sleeping over the grilles
trying to get some heat for his poor stomach
then I think he must be Ovid dreaming
again of Rome, getting ready to write
another letter to Caesar, his third that day,
his tenth or eleventh that week, keeping track
somewhere in those dirty sweaters and coats
of what they owe him now that his labor is over,
now that he's lying there with his hands all grimy
and his face all ruined—

Although I think he is sometimes caught by the horror
as if he had just come to, as if he could finally
let the bitterness take over and just sit there
with his coats wrapped around him, his stinking animal skins
dragging through ice and mud, his mind and body
finally alike, the pedant's dream come true,
the mystic's dream, the lover's dream, his brain
reduced to pulp, his heart surrounded,
his only desire a little warmth, a fire
for his poor fingers, a fire for his poor toes—

I think in his fifties he learned a new language
to go with the freezing rain; he would have done this
anyhow, he would have shouldered his riches
and stripped things down the way men in their fifties
do, only this way he found it easy,
he only had to lift his cold face
from his thin notebook, he only had to look

at the street full of garbage and there he was.
He did have to find another instrument
since flutes wouldn't do and reeds wouldn't do
and the rattle of pencils on the metal grates
wouldn't do—

I see him lying there watching the wind cleaning
the blue sky, pulling a piece of sock
over his raw ankle, asking himself
what he was punished for. Was it because
he sang too much? Was it because
he was too playful, too pathetic? No one could possibly
know him here in New York City outside
the Prince Hotel and the twenty-eight marble steps;
no one could see him with his paper cup
staring up at the dirty ceiling,
trying to remember Love's reception, the white
horses waiting for him, the golden plates
with purple dolphins on them, all that happiness
the one time in his life—

What he thinks he can do sometimes is find
a way to live in this world without rotting
from too much thought, and he thinks he can sometimes walk
past the galvanized soil pipe or the Sid Vicious sign
or even sit all night in his plastic chair
across from the amazing brass ash tray
without half dying; and he thinks he can be an eagle again
and talk to Caesar, and he thinks sometimes, if he's lucky,

he can have his muse back and eat
from her sweet fingers just as he did before
and listen to her song against his lips
as if he were holding the sea in his black hands,
as if, after first giving him all that power,
she now could give him pity and consolation,
now that he's living in horror,
now that his hair is white and his feet are frozen,
she who lives on the side of Helicon,
the muse of luscious sight and lovely sorrow,
he who lives at Third and Houston,
the genius of murdered love—

Although he knows that without this last voyage
he would be only another ruined poet,
and this is his glory—Prince Street is his glory.
The truth is he has become his own sad poem,
he walks and eats and sleeps in total sadness,
sadness is even what he calls his life, he
is the teacher of sadness, there are no limits
to his bitter song, he sits at the long bar
across the street from New York Kitchen
drinking sadness—mixed with wine—
and it is his own regret that moves him to tears
and his own sorrow that saves him—he is saved
by his own sorrow—it is his victory—

And it is his victory that though he lay
bored and oppressed for the last ten years

he sang like no one else before him did
about himself and his own suffering.
He was the first, and since he wrote
in innocence both the remorse and pity
are almost forgivable. It is hard to think
of Coleridge without an Ovid first or Pound
alive in the cage without him. I myself
feel almost happy that he came before me,
that my own wailing
found such a model in his book of sorrow.
In my lighter moments when my cheeks
are dry and my heart is not yet pounding
I like to compare his heaviness to mine—
or mine to his—to see whose chair is older,
whose rug is thinner, whose hands are colder,
although the world I live and wander in
is really not like his, at least not yet—

And when the color south of Cooper Union
settles into mauve or streaky violet
I leave him lecturing his loyal wife
or cursing his rotten enemies
and make my way to the broken-down subway stop
at Spring and Broadway, humming in both languages,
the white moon above me, the dirt somewhere beneath me,
the sidewalks crazy again, the lights in Jersey,
the lights in Manhattan, like the fires in Rome,
burning again without me, I on the edge
of Empire walking west in the snow, my neck

now raw, my feet now raw, my eyes gone blind,
the last one on the streets, the last poet left
who lives like this, the last one who does a dance
because of the dirty ice and the leather boots,
alone in the middle of nowhere, no one to see
his gorgeous retrieval, no one to shake the air
with loud applause and no one to turn and bow to
in the middle of his exile ten cold minutes
before he leaves the street for his soft pillow
and his other exile, far from Rome's domain,
and far from New York's domain, now silent and peaceful.

Leaving Another Kingdom

for Phil Levine

I think this year I'll wait for the white lilacs
before I get too sad.
I'll let the daffodils go, flower by flower,
and the blue squill, and the primroses.
Levine will be here by then,
waving fountain pens, carrying rolled-up posters
of Ike Williams and King Levinsky.
He will be reaching into his breast pocket
for maps of grim Toledo
showing the downtown grilles and the bus stations.
He and I together
will get on our hands and knees
on the warm ground
in the muddy roses
under the thorn tree.
We will walk the mile to my graveyard
without one word of regret,
two rich poets
going over the past a little,
changing a thing or two,
making a few connections,
doing it all with balance,
stopping along the way to pet a wolf,
slowing down at the locks,
giving each other lectures on early technology,
mentioning eels and snakes,
touching a little on our two cities,
cursing our Henrys a little,
his Ford, my Frick,

being almost human about it, almost decent,
sliding over the stones to reach the island,
throwing spears on the way,
staring for twenty minutes at two robins
starting a life together in rural Pennsylvania,
kicking a heavy tire, square and monstrous,
huge and soggy, maybe a '49 Hudson,
maybe a '40 Packard, maybe a Buick
with mohair seats and silken cords
and tiny panes of glass—both of us seeing
the same car, each of us on
his own dirt road, both of us whistling
the same idiotic songs, the tops of trees flying,
houses sailing along, the way they did then,
both of us walking down to the end of the island
so we could put our feet in the water, so I could
show him where the current starts, so we could
look for bottles and worn-out rubbers, Trojans
full of holes, the guarantee run out—
love gone slack and love gone flat—
a few feet away from New Jersey near the stones
that look like large white turtles guarding the entrance
to the dangerous channel where those lovers—Tristan
and his Isolt, Troilus and you know who,
came roaring by on inner tubes, their faces
wet with happiness, the shrieks and sighs
left up the river somewhere, now their fingers
trailing through the wake, now their arms out
to keep themselves from falling, now in the slow part

past the turtles and into the bend, we sitting there
putting on our shoes, he with Nikes,
me with Georgia loggers, standing up
and smelling the river, walking single file
until we reach the pebbles, singing in French
all the way back, losing the robins forever,
losing the Buick, walking into the water,
leaving another island, leaving another
retreat, leaving another kingdom.

Near Périgord

On the first day of viburnum
I followed a school bus for five miles
past the magnolias and the copper lions
to the shad-men rocking and sleeping in their bleached boats.
I had just read Pound again and I was thinking
of his brain floating by me in the universe
and his dead body lying face up at Rapallo.
I picked him some violets, for his bitter nose,
and one or two strands of dry forsythia
for his empty hands, something to wave and wave
as he did his bitter business with Kung and Jefferson.
Later that day as I was driving past
my silver cliffs I stopped to pick him some grass,
and thought, if he could wait, I'd get him radishes
or daisies, when they come. Dead poets like him
are all for flowers, they still like to sniff
and stare in the air—vaguely—like sensitive horses,
their eyes filled up with grief and yearning.
If I had the casket before me I would put
a sunflower in the paw—he wouldn't mind—
as if he were lying there waiting to jump up,
waiting to shout, "it's me, it's me, I live
for beauty, I live for justice," and then sink back
on the satin pillow, his hair falling over the edges,
the crimson gone from his face, the yellow back.
—Dear poets of Périgord, dear poets of New York,
I stopped at a small park on the way back
to think about the centaurs and the white oxen.
I thought we'd share the light between us, I thought

we'd talk about Flaubert and his contempt
for *la bêtise moderne*, or for that matter
we could talk about the Venice of dreams
or we could turn to American poetry
since World War II and the function of government
to dirty the water or we could just sit and rage
at the new mushiness and the new anemia.
For silence he could stand there staring at the trees
or look at me in the face without a word,
the way he did at the end—for my own silence
I could go back to his death in '72
and what has happened to me in the last ten years
or I'd go back to 1948
and what it was like to read *Personae*, to sit
on the stone benches and read, or I'd return,
as I always do, to the hatred of Jews, to Pound's
own home-grown vicious boring *bêtise*, but mostly
I think my mind would drift away and the humming
and the breathing would just take over, a concentration
on something bright and tender, some dear memory
of southern France, the road below Carcassonne,
the smell of dust and rain. My last flower
was sticking out of the ash tray,
a piece of honeysuckle or mock orange,
and I was driving *up* the river. I ended
snorting the honeysuckle—that's what it was—
and watching the seals go by. I was thinking
of Wyndham Lewis, I think, when Pound disappeared,
and when he sang his bitter song again,

a kind of whistling on the passenger's side,
I was already looking at the orange sky
and thinking of the frog's glass throat and the green light
that gives him his wisdom, and I was thinking again—
one last time—of the steps of San Salvatore
and the towers floating in the water—1982,
City of Easton, the iron railroad bridges,
the old stone houses, the first American flag,
Age of the Reagans, horrible and disastrous.

For Song

I am sitting thirty feet above the water
with my hand at my throat,
listening to the owls go through the maples
and the seaplanes go up and down like cracked buzzsaws.

I am finding my own place
in the scheme of things
between the nation of Reuben half drunk on twisted coneflowers
and the nation of Dan all crazy for weird veronica.

I am paying attention to providence,
the silver hordes this time,
the mud up to my knees,
the glass on my fingers.

I am studying paradise and the hereafter,
a life beyond compare,
a great log thrown up for my own pleasure,
an unbelievably large and cold and beneficent sun.

I am lifting a blade of grass to my wet lips
for music;
I am trying a dozen fruits and flowers
to get one sound;

I am twisting my head around, I am slowly clapping
for harmony;
I am raising my eyes, I am listening to the worms
for song.

My Swallows

For hours I sit here facing the white wall
and the dirty swallows. If I move too much,
I will lose everything, if I even breathe,
I'll lose the round chest and the forked tail
and the nest above the window, under the ceiling.

As far as shame, I think I have lived too long
with only the moonlight coming in to worry
too much about what it looks like. I have given
a part of my mind away, for what it's worth
I have traded half of what I have—

I'll call it half—so I can see these smudges
in the right light. I think I live in ruins
like no one else, I see myself as endlessly
staring at what I lost, I see me mourning
for hours, either worn away with grief

or touched with simple regret, but free this time
to give myself up to loss alone. I mourn
for the clumsy nest and I mourn for the two small birds
sitting up there above the curtains watching—
as long as I am there—and I mourn for the sky

that makes it clear and I mourn for my two eyes
that drag me over, that make me sit there singing,
or mumbling or murmuring, at the cost
of almost everything else, my two green eyes,
my brown—my hazel, flecked with green and brown—

and this is what I'll do for twenty more years,
if I am lucky—even if I'm not—I'll live
with the swallows and dip through the white shadows
and rest on the eaves and sail above the window.
This is the way I *have* lived, making a life

for more than twenty years—for more than forty—
out of this darkness; it was almost a joy,
almost a pleasure, not to be foolish or maudlin,
sitting against my wall, closing my eyes,
singing my dirges.

Berkeley

Today I saw the weird leg of Apollo
go in after Daphne—it was either cyprus
or Monterey pine, I am so blind and ignorant
of West Coast flora. I saw the wood waver
and the ground shake; I sat on my black briefcase
looking up at the leaves. I who am so
wondrous, I who always looked for Messiahs,
I who gave opinions, caught up now
in a new strangeness thousands of miles away
from my own cold river, learning quickly to eat
the other foods, learning to love
the way they do, walking after them
with my mouth half open, starting gently to teach,
doing the wind first, doing the dark old days
before there was even wind, saving Picasso
for Monday or Tuesday, saving the two dark strings
for Wednesday night, the night of the dozen tears,
saving New York
for the trip back to the airport, pushing the door
with tapered fingers, racing down the belt
with all that fire around me, sitting by the window
with only three minutes to go. Swinging my briefcase
with all the secrets inside. Keeping my secrets.
Thinking of Poland again. Getting ready for snow.

The Dancing

In all these rotten shops, in all this broken furniture
and wrinkled ties and baseball trophies and coffee pots
I have never seen a post-war Philco
with the automatic eye
nor heard Ravel's "Bolero" the way I did
in 1945 in that tiny living room
on Beechwood Boulevard, nor danced as I did
then, my knives all flashing, my hair all streaming,
my mother red with laughter, my father cupping
his left hand under his armpit, doing the dance
of old Ukraine, the sound of his skin half drum,
half fart, the world at last a meadow,
the three of us whirling and singing, the three of us
screaming and falling, as if we were dying,
as if we could never stop—in 1945—
in Pittsburgh, beautiful filthy Pittsburgh, home
of the evil Mellons, 5,000 miles away
from the other dancing—in Poland and Germany—
oh God of mercy, oh wild God.

Moscow

for Diane Freund

I love to bend down over my love,
my crayon at her breast, my lips just over her neck.
I love her eyes following my left hand,
her fingers rubbing the Greek blanket.
I love the sunlight on the cold windows,
the horns of Scriabin rising through the dreary street,
the carved houses forever on our wild faces.

May 15

Look at our poor rhododendron
blooming its heart out
and our red petunias
trying to come to life in the wet dirt.

Look at the thorn tree
gone wild with seed
and the white lilacs
turning brown and spongy.

Look at my eyes
in the clear glass
and my hairy hand
coming to rest on the greasy sash.

Look at my heart there
underneath the white sweater.
Look at my two red lips
opening and closing again, look at them singing and dancing.

Bee Balm

Today I'm sticking a shovel in the ground
and digging up the little green patch
between the hosta and the fringe bleeding heart.
I am going to plant bee balm there
and a few little pansies till the roots take
and the leaves spread out in both directions.

This is so the hummingbird will rage
outside my fireplace window; this is so
I can watch him standing in the sun
and hold him a little above my straining back,
so I can reach my own face up to his
and let him drink the sugar from my lips.

This is so I can lie down on the couch
beside the sea horse and the glass elephant,
so I can touch the cold wall above me
and let the yellow light go through me,
so I can last the rest of the summer on thought,
so I can live by secrecy and sorrow.

Vivaldi Years

I lay forever, didn't I, behind those old windows,
listening to Bach and resurrecting my life.
I slept sometimes for thirty or forty minutes
while the violins shrieked and the cellos trembled.
It was a crazy youth, wasn't it, letting
my mind soar like that, giving myself
up to poetry the way I did.
It was a little like Goethe's, wasn't it,
a little like Eugene O'Neill's, one joyous
sadness after another. That was the everlasting
life, wasn't it. The true world without end.

Saying the First Words

I could live like that,
putting my chair by the window,
making my tea,
letting the light in,
trapping the spider in my left hand.

I could pull the one book down
and find my place inside the four worlds
and face the wrong way
and live forever by mercy and wisdom.

I could love the pine tree,
and the road going back and forth like a blue thread,
and the fire inside the hills,
and the grass going down to the river—my wildest dream.

Night Again

I'm finally listening to my own radio
after a long and almost heartless day.

I'm folding my wings in front of my chest
and rubbing my beak through the inner feathers.

I'm warbling and warbling,
like some tenor from the 1940's,

matching song for song,
hating the sorrow with all my heart,

loving the pleasures, loving the sullen pockets,
reaching notes beyond my hearing or caring.

Today a Leaf

for William Merwin

Today it was just a dry leaf that told me
I should live for love.
It wasn't the six birds sitting like little angels
in the white birch tree,
or the knife I use to carve my pear with.
It was a leaf, that had read Tolstoi, and Krishnamurti,
that had loved William James,
and put sweet Jesus under him where he could be safe forever.
"The world is so bright," he said. "You should see the light."
"We are born without defenses, both babies and leaves."
"The branch is necessary, but it is in the way."
"I am not afraid. I am never afraid."
Then he stretched his imaginary body
this way and that.
He weighs a half a gram, is brown and green,
with two large mold spots on one side, and a stem
that curls away, as if with a little pride,
and he could be easily swept up and forgotten,
but oh he taught me love for two good hours,
and helped me with starvation, and dread, and dancing.
As far as I'm concerned his grave is here
beside me,
next to the telephone and the cupful of yellow pencils,
under the window, in the rich and lovely presence
of Franz Joseph Haydn and Domenico Scarlatti and Gustav Mahler
forever.

The New Moses

Look at those poor cattails
putting up with the noise of engines.
Look at them using that great wind
in their own lives.
They will be all that's left
when the airport is dismantled
and the city is gone
and the roads are ruined and scattered.
Some new Moses will float by then
and some sad princess will find him
and kiss him a thousand times on his eyes and nose
before she gives him up.
She will stand one minute in the throne room,
or in the hallway staring through the glass,
and almost run, and almost fall,
as she makes her way down through the buried brick and iron
on the almost forgotten fringes of modern Thebes,
not far from the man-made islands and lost skyways,
the hundred heavily guarded tunnels and bridges,
of ancient New York.

Singing

I have been waiting for a month
for this squirrel to dissolve in water.
I couldn't afford the disgrace
of dumping it on to the ground
and watching its body lurch and its teeth chatter.

There is such ghoulishness now
that it might drag its back legs after it,
such desperation
that I might rub its shoulders or brush its lips
to bring it back to life.

You who rushed home to masturbate,
you who touched the same red flower every day,
you know how I must skirt this lawn
to avoid the barrel.
You know how I live in silence.

You who knelt on the frozen leaves,
you know how dark it got under the ice;
you know how hard it was to live
with hatred, how long it took to convert
death and sadness into beautiful singing.

The Seine at Night

You would have to see Virgil Thomson creeping down here,
studying most of all these oily shadows
and see his face in the water
with a doorway behind it
to know that those horns are just the ticket,
and those edgy violins,
and that long slow resonant snare.

The applause too,
the water lapping up the stone steps,
a piece of light wood against the window,
a barrel rolling down the floor;
paper on fire,
cracking and spluttering for five minutes
before it goes out.

This loverboy from Kansas City,
this judge,
this collaborator.
Virgil the Baptist,
the perfect transplant,
the half-mother of us all,
our Vivaldi.

At Jane's

for Gil Orlovitz, 1919–1974

I touch the rose to see what happens there
before I go inside to eat, I pull
the clothesline down and kick the cracked cement,
I howl to myself for mercy. One more time
I walk through the rotten tomatoes. I will end
with little leaves on my shoes, with spoonfuls of mud,
with a beating heart, with a mouth that's open—
I hold my arm out straight like a nervous drunk,
I walk the plank between the rhododendron
and the little pear. For all I know
I could live here happy, I could walk
from here to the river and back without a thought.
I could stop at the Super-America
and read the morning paper. I could sit
at my pancake dreaming of heaven, smiling like a lamb,
listening vaguely to all the garbage, finding
my cave and my twine, my dark place, chewing and listening
while inside I wander—I beg for justice—I crawl
through hell for a little justice. I turn to the wall
and sing a little, and dance a little—
just as the fall is breaking on the Ohio
and leaves are turning yellow, in Marietta,
the backyards stretching out for hundreds of yards
the way they do in America, all that richness,
all that Utopia, wasted, a little dog
howling out there, inside we're barking, inside
I'm finding another heaven, I'm turning around
this way and that, I'm finding my hole in the sun . . .
We're talking now about Spanish music, the difference

in soul between northern Europe and southern Europe;
we're talking now about Crete, we're talking
about Robert Lowell and Delmore Schwartz; I'm lecturing
on Orlovitz, I'm talking about his sonnets,
I'm talking about his death on West End Avenue,
about the poet we lost, about his life,
about the dull politics of poesy,
about the nineteenth century, about Keats,
eighty miles from Wheeling, West Virginia,
a million miles from Rome. Poor Orlovitz,
he wrote 500 poems. I remember the letters:
"Is this a poem, could you send me twenty bucks?"
What do I do with him now? He fell in the street
in front of a doorman; oh his death was superb,
the doorman blew his whistle, Orlovitz climbed
into a yellow cab, he'd never disappoint
a doorman. Now I'm brooding a little, absent,
the way I get, listening to the refrigerator,
the only music we have in North America,
cursing the Reagans a little, saying inside
one of Orlovitz's poems, going back again
into the cave, remembering Shelley's words
about his cave, and Virgil's, and Milton's, knowing
that mine is like theirs, a half mile underground,
where you go on your knees, where you keep the candle outside—
the underground journey—shivers and tremblings. We walk
to the river after breakfast, I'm in heaven,
I saw the meadow, I heard the voices, I felt
the light on my face—in Marietta, Ohio—

with Rachael Stern and Jack Killian and Jane
Somerville, there are alleys between the yards,
it is the oldest city in Ohio,
I wore my black suit for the reading, I roared
and whispered through twenty poems, I sat like a lamb
in the mayor's living room, I sat like a dove
eating cheese and smiling, talking and smiling,
thinking my thoughts, my wise and tender thoughts,
the mayor's palace, Marietta, Ohio.

John's Mysteries

I've been seeing these tombstone beef sticks
and that umbrella tree in so many cities
that I forget where it is I am,
whether it's dirty John's I'm standing in line in
with onions and T-bone steaks in my hands,
or Bishop's, I think it was Bishop's, with hard salami,
safflower mayonnaise and two-percent milk.
My own system of perfect retrieval
tells me it's a big-leaved catalpa,
not an umbrella tree, and what it grows
is not cigars, but intricate seed stalks, terrible
to smoke, cancerless, tasteless, drooping and beautiful.
But I believe only in the islands
so I will insist on emptying the parking lot
of the two beer trucks and putting a table there
under the cigar tree, for me and my friends to eat at.
We will take three hours and end by turning
on the lights and leaning back in exhaustion.
We will be so happy about where we are
that we will cry for sadness, cursing everything
and anything from changed emotional conditions
to polluted leaves to emigration laws
that could threaten to end our mysteries and pleasures.
We will keep the napkins as souvenirs
and write, in ink, what it was like to live here
on Gilbert Street and Market, on Sixth and Pine,
in a town in Crete eight miles from Omalos,
a mile or so from the crone and her great-granddaughter
selling warm Coca-Colas on the flat

along with the baskets and the red vases.
I'll walk across here touching one beer truck
with my left hand and one with my other.
I'll put my old stone arms around his neck
and kiss him on the lip and cheek, I'll sing
again and again
until he remembers me, until he remembers
the green catalpa pushing through the cement
and the little sticks of meat inside, his own
wild voyage behind him, his own long life ahead.

Soap

Here is a green Jew
with thin black lips.
I stole him from the men's room
of the Amelia Earhart and wrapped him in toilet paper.
Up the street in *Parfumes*
are Austrian Jews and Hungarian,
without memories really,
holding their noses in the midst of that
paradise of theirs.
There is a woman outside
who hesitates because it is almost Christmas.
"I think I'll go in and buy a Jew," she says.
"I mean some soap, some nice new lilac or lily
to soothe me over the hard parts,
some Zest, some Fleur de Loo, some Wild Gardenia."

And here is a blue Jew.
It is his color, you know,
and he feels better buried in it, imprisoned
in all that sky, the land of death and plenty.
If he is an old one he dances,
or he sits stiffly,
listening to the meek words and admiring the vile actions
of first the Goths and then the Ostrogoths.
Inside is a lovely young girl,
a Dane, who gave good comfort
and sad support to soap of all kinds and sorts
during the war and during the occupation.
She touches my hand with unguents and salves.

She puts one under my nose all wrapped in tissue,
and squeezes his cheeks.

I buy a black Rumanian for my shelf.
I use him for hair and beard,
and even for teeth when things get bitter and sad.
He had one dream, this piece of soap,
if I'm getting it right,
he wanted to live in Wien
and sit behind a hedge on Sunday afternoon
listening to music and eating a tender schnitzel.
That was delirium. Other than that he'd dream
of America sometimes, but he was a kind of cynic,
and kind of lazy—conservative—even in his dream,
and for this he would pay, he paid for his lack of dream.
The Germans killed him because he didn't dream
enough, because he had no vision.

I buy a brush for my back, a simple plastic
handle with gentle bristles. I buy some dust
to sweeten my body. I buy a yellow cream
for my hairy face. From time to time I meet
a piece of soap on Broadway, a sliver really,
without much on him, sometimes I meet two friends
stuck together the way those slivers get
and bow a little, I bow to hide my horror,
my grief, sometimes the soap is so thin
the light goes through it, these are the thin old men
and thin old women the light goes through, these are

the Jews who were born in 1865
or 1870, for them I cringe, for them
I whimper a little, they are the ones who remember
the eighteenth century, they are the ones who listened
to heavenly voices, they were lied to and cheated.

My counterpart was born in 1925
in a city in Poland—I don't like to see him born
in a little village fifty miles from Kiev
and have to fight so wildly just for access
to books, I don't want to see him struggle
half his life to see a painting or just to
sit in one of the plush chairs listening to music.
He was dragged away in 1940
and turned to some use in 1941,
although he may have fought a little, piled
some bricks up or poured some dirty gasoline
over a German truck. His color was rose
and he floated for me for days and days; I love
the way he smelled the air, I love how he looked,
how his eyes lighted up, how his cheeks were almost pink
when he was happy. I loved how he dreamed, how he almost
disappeared when he was in thought. For him
I write this poem, for my little brother, if I
should call him that—maybe he is the ghost
that lives in the place I have forgotten, that dear one
that died instead of me—oh ghost, forgive me!—
Maybe he stayed so I could leave, the *older* one
who stayed so I could leave—oh live forever!

forever!—Maybe he is a Being from the other
world, his left arm agate, his left eye crystal,
and he has come back again for the twentieth time,
this time to Poland, to Warsaw or Bialystok,
to see what hell is like. I think it's that,
he has come back to live in our hell, if he could
even prick his agate arm or even weep
with those crystal eyes—oh weep with your crystal eyes,
dear helpless Being, dear helpless Being. I'm writing this
in Iowa and Pennsylvania and New York City,
in time for Christmas, 1982,
the odor of Irish Spring, the stench of Ivory.

I Pity the Wind

I am taking off my glasses
so I can stare at the little candles
and the glass of water
in pure darkness.

I am letting a broom stand
for my speech on justice
and an old thin handkerchief
for the veil of melodrama I have worn for thirty years.

I am dragging in Euripides
for his strange prayer
and my own true Hosea
for his poem on love and loyalty.

After a minute I fall down dead
from too much thought
and turn to the freezing wall
for an hour of quiet sadness.

I start my practice later,
twenty minutes for breathing,
twenty minutes for song,
twenty minutes for liberation and ritual.

My poem is about the airshaft
and Zoroaster
and the soul caught in its last struggle
with the two-headed cow, father of everything.

My elation has something to do with light,
my misery with darkness,
my secrecy and fear and distance
with neither.

I end up with a pillow
and a painted floor, as I always do,
my head on the flowers, a little pocket for air,
my right arm drifting and dangling.

I end up just humming,
true to myself at last,
preparing myself for the bridge
and the hand that will lead me over, the hand I adore.

I pity this hero,
so in love with fire,
so warlike,
so bent on teaching.

82/83

Before the winter is over I'll have some sticks
for my dining room table and one or two large blooms
to take the place of the Norfolk pine
shredding and popping in the cold rain.

I'll pick some berries from the thin viburnum
and eat them as a bird does, one at a time,
jerking my head and looking around with terror,
studying the world with softened eyes.

I'll walk between the kitchen and the birch tree
a hundred times, a broom in one hand and either
a shovel or an ax in the other. I'll tie
a piece of frozen string around my finger

and either chew some bark or do a little
Esquimaux shuffling, and moaning, around the broken
circle of slate. I'll look for either a robin
or some other monster, maybe a yellow warbler

to go with my scarf. I'll count the days till Easter,
the thirteen Sundays, the Virgin Days, the Martyr Days,
the days of sleep and waking. Groundhog Day.
Valentine's Day. Ninety days in all.

The one or two cars that come by will be farting
their brains out trying to make it in the cold,
and no one will see me dying there in the twilight,
holding my hands up in the slippery branches.

I'll stay for ten more minutes before I go in,
enjoying the cold and letting the ice come into
my lungs and heart. Whatever my struggle is
I'll let it take place in this yard where the pile of stones

was, and the little hill—I'll keep it
between one tree and another, mostly away
from the flower bed and the wall, as close as I can
to the cement steps and the walk. I'll say goodnight

to one thing or another, maybe a headlight
from Route 611, maybe a brilliant oriole
come here to die in the dark. I'll drink my tea
and my Popov over the heater and with a knife

and screwdriver I'll scrape the snow from my boots.
I'll rest for six good hours and start my watch
again at six in the morning—who's to say
what happens in the night?—I'll look for a jay

to start me right, some pale-crested bluejay
lost and gone wild, some giant from the south
remembering his pine, some frightened animal
screaming for life, sliding on the branches,

wanting his meadow back. I'll pick him up,
though it's too late to put him inside my coat
against my chest, and it's too late to breathe
into his bony mouth. I'll wait for three

minutes, to do him justice, then I'll start
my icy walk—a part of the mystery—
and end up shaking *my* feathers from the cold,
a monster myself, with a piece of the loblolly

in my hip pocket, deciding, certainly before
Washington's Birthday, and certainly before Mother's Day,
whether it was worth it for our birds
to come so far for their wisdom, little simulacra

dying, as I do, from hunger and disease,
maybe two more to go today, the bastard
love and the bastard hope, maybe three,
the bastard pity, before I pull the blind up

and look at the moon, full and weeping tonight,
although it's past its prime and getting ready
for the last sliver again, then darkness again
and the first sliver again, ferocious phases.

Romance

After thirty years
I am still listening to the pipes,
I am still enchanted
with the singing and moaning of the dry boards.

I am lying there night after night
thinking of water.
I am joining palms, or whistling Mozart
and early Yeats.

I am living without savagery,
stretching my body and turning on my left side
for music,
humming to myself and turning on my right side
for words.

Villa-Lobos

I don't know if it's the one great sadness of my life
that I have to return this way every night
to the same small yard and the same small tree
and touch the buds and pick the ancient leaves
or if it's the one great joy. Let there be
one blue space in the sky above to match
the blue between the branches. Let there be
spaces between the chords to match
the spaces between the leaves. It took me
half a life to come here, one small house
on a battered hill, one small tree
to match the house, a man against the tree
with cello strings in his hand, a little dull gleaming
to match his gleaming, a little sobbing
to match his own, a kind of painful sliding
from string to string to match the hill
or the house itself, or even the man himself,
his elbow out in space, his left eye shut,
his heart already bursting from the sounds.

The Nettle Tree

Mine was the nettle tree, the nettle tree.
It grew beside the garage and on the river
and I protected it from all destroyers.

I loved the hanging branches and the trunk
that grew like a pole. I loved the little crown
that waved like a feather. I sat for hours watching

the birds come in to eat the berries. I read
my Homer there—I wanted to stay forever
sleeping and dreaming. I put my head on the trunk

to hear my sounds. It was my connection for years,
half hanging in the wind—half leaning, half standing.
It was my only link. It was my luxury.

Sycamore

It was March third I came outside and saw
for the first time the buttonwood tree with last year's
leaves hanging in the wind like little hearts
and one or two crazy birds going mad with choices
in the hideous leftover snow and the slippery mud.
March the third. The branches were more a silver
than either green or tan, there was no fuzz
yet. Spring was still in Arizona, the Sonora
desert somewhere, somewhere in Ensenada,
and we were still gluing our frozen ears
to our crystal sets in Fairchild and Waterloo.
    The lower branches bend as if they were holding
castanets in their hands—this tree is Greek!—
maybe as if they were limp, the left hand is limp,
it is a tree from Greenwich Avenue,
from Fire Island, but the upper arms
reach out to plead for mercy, reach out to bless
us, she is a twenty-arm goddess, leaning
over a little, dancing her dance, making
little obscene gestures to the lord of lords,
a tiny finger here, a whole fist there.
    I open the windows, I pull the wooden strips
away from the sashes, I tear the dirty plastic,
I let the sun in. Soon my ties will be dancing,
soon my poems will be on the floor, I am
old Shivers, I do a turn to the left, to the right.
Where shall I go this year? What door will I open
and put a little primitive iron against?
Where shall I put the bucket? I want to live here

beside my tree and watch it change, the brown
give way to green, the green give way to brown.
I want, for once, to understand what happens
when the skin falls off. This tree is like a snake.
How many years does it live? What does it do
in its sleep? March thirty-first, this year,
is the little passage; we will get on our knees
and howl with freedom, not one of us can bear
to live without howling, we were given voices
so we could scream. I sing a song from Florida
about the life to come, someone is singing—
she is a flute, I am a silver harp—
about the seven openings, the soul
skittering, sacred things. I want her to go
so I can become a tree, so I can bury
myself as Daphne does, she is the one
who understands what it means to be tormented;
she calls the spring Apollo, Apollo tortured her,
he followed her from one bare tree to another.
I call it Apollo too, I take my place
inside the silver wood, at least for a year.
Next March the third I'll struggle out of my skin
like a sleepy girl, my hair will be too dry,
my nails too long, my mouth will start to work,
at first it will be too hoarse, and then too shrill;
I'll see the streets will be empty, there will be peace,
I'll walk to the graveyard and back, I'll walk to the lake,
no one will see me, no one will follow me
with rage in his eyes, with brutal love in his hands.

It is like death, isn't it, living in the tree,
listening to what were noises, feeling those changes
and knowing they weren't for you—I love the bells
when they come, I love standing in a grove
and guessing which one she's in—I'm in—if I were
Apollo I'd turn myself into this sycamore
and reach my arms through hers, I'd do some flashy
two-step that's made for heavy sycamores,
and when we lie it would be like two great animals,
sweat running down our faces, tears down our legs.
    This year when I sit at the table with bitter bread
in my hands I'll stop for one full minute to give
some lonely praise to the sycamore; I'll say,
let's stop a minute and think of the sycamore,
let's think of the lovely white branches, let's think of the bark,
let's think of the leaves, the three great maple lobes.
What does it know of liberation? I'll say.
What does it know of slavery, bending over
the streams of America? How does it serve as a text
for lives that are pinched, or terrified? Were there sycamores
along the banks of the Rhine or Oder? Tell me
about its bells again, those most of all,
the hard gray balls that dangle from the stems,
tell me about the bark, the large thin flakes,
and the colors, dark at the bottom, light at the top.
And I will go on for an hour storming and raving
before I drink my final cup of wine
and shout to the Egyptians—as I do every year—
you are my Apollo, you are my fleshpot, forgive me

for turning into a tree, forgive me, you lovers
of life for leaving you suddenly, how foolish
and cheated you must have felt, how foolish the body
must feel when it's only a carcass, when the breath
has left it forever, as it always does,
in search of something painless; and I'll end
by sprinkling the tree and sprinkling the ground around it
and holding my hand up for a second of silence,
since I am the one who runs the service—I am
the only one in this house, I do my reclining
all alone, I howl when I want, and I am,
should anyone come in, a crooked tree
leaning far out, I am a hundred feet tall,
I am a flowering figure, I am staggering
across the desert, and here I am now in New York
and here I am now in Pittsburgh, the perfect wilderness.

Baja

These tiny Mexican mosquitoes are like lost souls
looking for blood among the white visitors
in their own land. They come to lead us through
some four or five old trees. They stoop to bite
our hands, they make that wailing sound I live
in terror of, they sing in our ears, they walk
between the seams, they reach for the drink they love,
they bend half over drinking,
they walk along the sand and through the flowers,
they look for work, they are looking for work, they pound
on the windows of our casita shouting *trabajo*,
trabajo, casting mournful eyes on the sea-wrack,
touching the broken sewer line and pointing
at the broken steps.
                                    I catch one in a bottle
of Hellmann's and I let it loose outside
on the little plaza where the Citation is parked.
I tell him, my blood is for you, I tell him, remember
one Pennsylvanian who stopped to talk with the souls
and listened to them even if there was murder
and hatred between us; I ask about my future
as if I were Odysseus in hell
and he were Tiresias, that dear old lady,
or some other dead one, a Hercules or an Ajax.
He tells me, I think, to look out for my own
soul in the years to come, he tells me how long
it will be before I can rest a little, although
what he calls rest it may be some other thing
he talks about. He tells me there is a tree

and a yellow rock and a cloud. I should go left
around the tree, I should walk over the rock,
I should walk under the cloud; it is a Mexican
vision, full of darkness and secrecy.
I thank him for his kindness. Maybe he said
there is a room with terrible noises, tie
yourself to the kitchen table, hold your left hand
over your mouth, concentrate on living
a week at a time, divide your life into threes,
the terror can be digested, take care of yourself
when you are in New York, when you are sleeping,
when you are dying, there is a life to come—
or maybe he said, I love you more than anything,
have pity on me, please help me, take me with you,
I want the chance to live again, I can't
believe how large your limes were, oh I can't
believe how huge and clean your markets were;
take me with you, take me with you, wailing
and howling in front of me, in back of me,
pulling me down, the way they do, a swarm
of spirits, stumbling, pushing; I had to run,
I had to slam the door, I stood there freezing,
blood on the walls where I killed them, blood on my palms,
my forehead foolishly pounding, my two hands shaking,
all alone in the darkness, a man of the heart
making plans to the end, a screen for the terror,
a dish for the blood, a little love for strangers,
a little kindness for insects, a little pity for the dead.

Of Blessed Name

Here in this huge dining room
with its crimson and gold-flocked wallpaper
and its etched glass and nude paintings and brass trimmings
I think of Spinoza sitting at his own table,
practicing what he believed in,
the good days.

And over there in the fish tank
with the pipe of white oxygen
going in and out of the lobster's last redoubt
I think of the red salmon and the pink flounder
as a backdrop to his thought.

Water was his main element.
Only then could God be understood
in all his modes.
The salmon loved him for this;
the lobster in all his fury grudgingly acknowledged his genius.

He dragged God into everything.
It gave him his distance.
It made him dream and figure twenty-four hours a day.

It kept the world at bay,
the carp going over and under
the bamboo bridge,
the mussels in white gravel,
the living grasses.
It kept it wonderful and flowing.

No one was ever more pure
or logical.
Even the crab loved him,
the bow-legged crab,
eternal enemy of the lobster.

I think of him here in Florida
under the boring chandelier,
a thousand little glass tassels going this way and that,
a carpet to keep him warm,
a fish tank to amuse him;
and I save him for the shameful end,
his lungs half filled with glass,
his body weak with fever,
carefully sealing a letter,
wisely adding a word here and there,
saying something terrifying,
something amorous and musical and elegant
as always.

Kissing Stieglitz Goodbye

Every city in America is approached
through a work of art, usually a bridge
but sometimes a road that curves underneath
or drops down from the sky. Pittsburgh has a tunnel—

you don't know it—that takes you through the rivers
and under the burning hills. I went there to cry
in the woods or carry my heavy bicycle
through fire and flood. Some have little parks—

San Francisco has a park. Albuquerque
is beautiful from a distance; it is purple
at five in the evening. New York is Egyptian,
especially from the little rise on the hill

at 14-C; it has twelve entrances
like the body of Jesus, and Easton, where I lived,
has two small floating bridges in front of it
that brought me in and out. I said goodbye

to them both when I was 57. I'm reading
Joseph Wood Krutch again—the second time.
I love how he lived in the desert. I'm looking at the skull
of Georgia O'Keeffe. I'm kissing Stieglitz goodbye.

He was a city, Stieglitz was truly a city
in every sense of the word; he wore a library
across his chest; he had a church on his knees.
I'm kissing him goodbye; he was, for me,

the last true city; after him there were
only overpasses and shopping centers,
little enclaves here and there, a skyscraper
with nothing near it, maybe a meaningless turf

where whores couldn't even walk, where nobody sits,
where nobody either lies or runs; either that
or some pure desert: a lizard under a boojum,
a flower sucking the water out of a rock.

What is the life of sadness worth, the bookstores
lost, the drugstores buried, a man with a stick
turning the bricks up, numbering the shards,
dream twenty-one, dream twenty-two. I left

with a glass of tears, a little artistic vial.
I put it in my leather pocket next
to my flask of Scotch, my golden knife and my keys,
my joyful poems and my T-shirts. Stieglitz is there

beside his famous number; there is smoke
and fire above his head; some bowlegged painter
is whispering in his ear; some lady-in-waiting
is taking down his words. I'm kissing Stieglitz

goodbye, my arms are wrapped around him, his photos
are making me cry; we're walking down Fifth Avenue;
we're looking for a pencil; there is a girl
standing against the wall—I'm shaking now

when I think of her; there are two buildings, one
is in blackness, there is a dying poplar;
there is a light on the meadow; there is a man
on a sagging porch. I would have believed in everything.

Two Trees

This is where I reach for the scarlet bud
and this is where I snap the little chicken claw
twenty feet from the water. Daylight has come
to the Iowa River amidst the blaring of horns
and the frantic splashing across the bridge. I stand
on the northeast corner in the upper branches
of two interlocking maples. I am engaged
in a ritual silence. I am listening to leaves
and flowers come. I look into the river
for backward spills and eddies, I look into the hills
for dreams and losses. There are two silver maples
half buried in water, starting to bud; there is
the shadow of pigeons under me; there is
a path with stones and a golden willow. I live
for this silence now. I stay in the tree. I think
like a bird for five or ten minutes. I see the cloud
on the water, I see the food. There is a Japanese
tulip tree a minute away from the river
half sitting in a sea of petals, there is
a day or two left, the weather is cold, I walk
like a man, like a human being, through the curled flowers,
I almost can't stand the beauty, the insides are white,
the color is in the veins, they are like onions
when you tear them apart, there is an odor; my house
is eighty yards away, I go there to think
and write, I put the blossoms down, I live there
beside them for two or three days, I line them up
on my table, it is my void, a dancing table,

a plastic cover, with other blossoms, some of them
floating as if they were seeds, it is the only
void I know, the only emptiness.

One Bird to Love Forever

If I were to pick one bird to love forever
it would be the desert sparrow, sweetest
thing to ever live in Arizona,
sweetest thing of Mexico. I'd hold it
against my neck where the blood goes through, that soft
little nest underneath the chin, and stare at its eye
to hold it still, to keep it quiet. I'd let it
flutter, or let it fly, if it wanted. I'd rest
beside the acacia, beside the ironwood; I'd sit
for hours listening and loving.
                              When it flies
it rises like a junco, quick and crazy
to get away, and when it sits the softness of
birds is in its throat and chest. It has two
stripes, that is how we know it, one on the eye
and one extending down from the corner of the mouth
to make a pattern, white against the black,
and it has secret habits, it builds its nest
in some demented brush a hundred miles
from water—it never drinks, it seems to live
on nothing—I call it nothing but naturally
it thrives there. Joseph Wood Krutch, when he writes about the desert,
reminds us always that it is a paradise
for whatever lives there, the crazy trees, the lizards,
and nothing is deprived there, and nothing suffers,
it is their world, the funny quails and doves,
the sun shines on the needles, the spiders are huge,
the ground is always dry.
                              It is a madness

to think of loving that bird again. How could I
go back there anyhow? How would I live?
What would I do, go out to touch the thorns
and smell the flowers? Stand beside the boojum
and stare at the sky? Smile again like a lizard?
And Krutch is right—he's mostly right—the loving
of birds is useless, there is no true connection
between their lives and ours, they are only ideas.
It's always been that way, except when I read him—
I read him over and over—I see him using
his own bitterness as I have always used mine
to hide his weak heart behind, although the heart,
he'd say, is something like the liver, only coarser,
and he'd prefer the kidneys again for the seat
of all that soft emotion.
                                        I only spent
five days in the desert but I'm going to drive
from Mexico to Salt Lake City next time.
My sparrow ranges from Texas to California
and north into Nevada and Idaho.
There is a photo in Cruikshank, she is perched
on the edge of her nest and four huge mouths are screaming
for food; the nest is almost buried between
the pads of a heavy cactus and the spines—
two inches, three inches long—surround the nest,
it looks like one or two go through the twisted
grass itself, but somehow they seem indifferent,
the delicate babies, the mother. I want to touch
the thorns and see how sharp the needles are.

I want to live there, I think, wake up with the sun
on my face, wake up with the light making a diamond
or hexagram on my chest and arms and glide
to the sink to drink my water, like a gecko.
My dream of dreams has me staring out the window,
my blue pants are held up by a rope,
and my elbows are leaning on a wooden washboard.
She looks at me for a second. She. A chittering
sparrow. Almost eating her way through the glass.
And then she moves to her tree, a hundred miles
away, for all I know, from my world, this silly
and rotten concrete shack, a poet's ugly
home away from home, a little flowerpot
holding the window up, a vague amazement
to her, a curiosity.
                              I look at the wind,
if you can look at the wind, and then I walk
for twenty or thirty minutes so I can find
my kidney on the road; I want to see it
weeping with pure self-pity, wringing its hands
the way a kidney wrings its hands, much better
than the liver, much better than the heart, more sadness
than either other organ. If I stand still,
if you catch me just right there is a cactus growing
out of my shoulder and my glasses are falling
as always; there is a look of wretched wisdom
on my red face—maybe there'll be a feather
with little bits of white on the outer edge
I'll put in my left pocket, maybe the stone

that goes with the feather, a tiny bit of pearl
to hold it down, you must hold feathers down,
and tiny bits of sand for the other pocket,
something to give me the desert again when I want it,
the blazing sunlight for grief, a little shade for the sorrow.

Fritz

This is too good for words. I lie here naked
listening to Kreisler play. It is the touch
I love, that kindness, that ease. I saw him once
at the end of the 40's, in Pittsburgh, I thought what he did
had something to do with his being old, his moving
to the front of the stage, his talking and smiling. I study
the cracks in the ceiling, the painted floors. I love him
because he strayed from the art, because he finished
his formal training at twelve, because he was whimsical
and full of secret humors. He is another one
I missed—I'm sick about it—there is no table
for us, no chairs to sit on, no words to remember.
He knew both Schönberg and Brahms, he visited
Dvořák, he studied theory with Bruckner,
he was a friend of Caruso's, he was a friend
of Pablo Casals.
                    Something like terror moves me,
walking on 611. What have we lost?
Does Kreisler belong to the dead? Was that a world
of rapture that he lived in? In what year
did he fix his imagination? Will there be strings
two hundred years from now? Will there be winds?
—There is a bank that leads down from the towpath
and I have walked there a thousand times, each time
half tripping over a certain root—I think
it is the root of a locust, maybe a lilac.
Tonight I am partly moody, partly in dread,
there is some pain in my neck, but I am still
possessed a little. I rush into the living room

to listen to either the Elgar or the Mendelssohn.
Something left us forever in 1912,
or 1914. Now we live off the rot.
I wonder if it's true. Kreisler was fifty
when he came back to Paris, over seventy
when I saw him in 1948. The root
was in the nineteenth century. I'm lost,
I'm lost without that century. There is
one movement left. *Con amore.* I began
my journey in 1947. I wrote
four hours a day, I read five books a week.
I had to read five books. I never knew
the right hand was raised like that. I never knew
how trapped the body was. I didn't believe
you gave yourself to the fire like that, that after
awhile—if the brain was in the fingers—the heart
was all that made the sound, whatever I mean
by "sound," and that we have to start with feeling—
we poor machines—which stood me in good stead
for ten or twenty years, that and Marlowe's
tears, and Coleridge's soft flight, and Dostoevski's
rack—it was the fire that moved me.

Three Skies

I always remember the crone. I always think of her
at that card table selling us Cokes. I sit in Dante's
drinking my coffee, my left hand is walking through Crete,
my right hand is lying exhausted on the roof
looking up at the stars. It was the stars
that helped me then. I stood on the cracked cement
on the same hill I know where Minos stood
looking for heavenly bulls and for the first time
in Greece I had my lightness. I saw the link
between that life and mine, I saw the one
outside me stand for my own, like Dante himself
in Paradise. I felt I was standing inside
the sky, that there were other lights below me
and other worlds and this one could be restored.
And there were other feelings I have forgotten
or can't quite put in words. I saw myself
moving from body to body. I saw my own
existence taken from me. I lost the center.
—It lasted for fifteen minutes, then I slept,
with three or four others, scattered on that roof
as if we each had little rooms, the brilliance
of the night keeping us quiet, all our efforts—
at least my own—going into lying still,
going into some secret humming and adoring,
I was so changed, I was so small and silent.

In Crete the heart gets filled up, there is a joy
there, it is the mountains and sea combined,
it is the knowledge you have that there was a life

there for centuries, half unknown to Europe, half
unknown to Asia, Crete is a kind of moon
to me, a kind of tiny planet,
going through the same revolutions, over and over.
That was the first time I had been in the stars
for maybe twenty years, and it was odd
that I was not in the woods or on the water
in upper Michigan or Maine or Canada,
thousands of miles from civilization, now
it was thousands of years, although it was almost the same.
I dreamed of my bus ride back, some perfect village
in the mountains, and I dreamed of staring through the window
at some small child in blue or smiling at a man
with huge boots on. I wanted to sit in the square,
what little square there was, and talk again
about the ancient cities and the forest
that once filled Crete before I returned again
to my little room on the roof and my crazy pillow
and my sky of bitter lovers and animals,
three hundred miles from Africa, from Egypt.

It wasn't lost on me that it was Dante's
Café that I was sitting in—a coffee house
in Greenwich Village with an overblown photo
of Florence on the wall, squeezed in among
my loved ones, reading books, or talking, or waiting
for someone to come, for someone new to walk in
and catch our interest, the irony—even the comedy—
wasn't lost on me. I think I had been there

over an hour frowning and writing. It was
a disgrace! Thank God for New York! Thank God for tolerance!
Thank God for envy! Except that in New York City
I think there are no heavens, I think you live
without a sky there. I remember one Sunday
a little girl came out to my house in Raubsville,
Pennsylvania. I don't remember her mother.
The girl was black, the mother was white, after
supper we went outside to look at the sky
and smell the river; the girl was terrified
when she saw the stars; we had to take her inside
and hold her, and love her; she had never seen the sky
except in New York, it was half sad, half horrible.
I remember one night on a hill in Pittsburgh
we tried to look at the stars; we had the charts
in front of us—no one would ever laugh
at either my rages or my fantasies
if he had spent *his* twenty years in Pittsburgh
looking for kindness in that rotten sky.
—My left hand is tying my folder, my right hand is helping.
I am getting ready to leave, I look for
a tip, I touch my hat, I am still living
a little in the age of politeness. I walk
through the cement playground at Sixth and Houston and down
to Vandam Street. My poem is over. My life
is on an even keel, though who's to say
when I will waver again. I start to call
my friends up one at a time to talk about the stars,
my friends on the Upper West Side and my friends in the Village,

my friends in New Jersey and Brooklyn. I listen to them rave,
those poor stargazers, everyone with a story,
everyone either a mystic or a poet,
one a musician, one an astrologer,
all of them illuminated, all of them ecstatic,
every one changed, for a minute, by his own memory.

Red Bird

for Greg Pape and Marnie Prange

Now I feel safe,
I've gotten my cardinal back again.
I'm standing in Tuscaloosa,
watching her hop through the puddles.
I'm watching her eat and drink, a brown-chested
queen, living outdoors in clarity and light
with a loose and rotten sparrow as her playmate,
some common thing not fit to touch her hem,
not fit to live with her in the same puddle.

I have to walk over a sick dog to see them,
and through some bicycles and cardboard boxes.
One has a heavy beak and a scarlet headpiece
and one has ruffled feathers and a black throat.
As long as there is a cardinal in my life
I can go anywhere; she was the bird
that, as it turned out, freed me fifteen years
ago in a town in western Pennsylvania
in some unbearable secret rite involving
a withered pear tree and a patented furnace.
There is a pear tree here too, just to add
a little mistiness, and a truck, and a car,
waiting beside the puddle like two kind horses.
But the cardinal now is sweeter and more whimsical
than the last time, maybe a little smaller, and gentler.
I talk and the sparrow flies away, for God knows
what kind of seed or God knows from what kind of shadow.
Someone will say, as he always does, this sparrow
is English, you know, you have to make a distinction

between him and our own, he is the sloppiest
sparrow of all, he is aggressive and promiscuous,
just as he lands on the pear tree, just as he lands
on the roof of the truck, and someone will say, it is
a female cardinal, the male is redder, his chest
is bigger and brighter, just as she lands on the car
and just as she disappears, a little speck
somewhere, a kind of messenger, her throat
abounding with information, little farewells
to the English sparrow, little bows to the scholars
with bird-stuff on their brains and beautiful cries—
something between a metallic chirp and a whistle—
to the one from Pennsylvania, the one who loves her.

Adler

The Jewish King Lear is getting ready
for some kind of horror—he is whispering
in the ears of Regan and Goneril: I know
the past, I know the future, my little hovel

will be in Pennsylvania, I will be
an old man eating from a newspaper,
I will stop to read the news, my fish
will soak the petty world up, it will stretch

from Sears on the left to Gimbels on the right,
my table will be a crate and I will cover
the little spaces with tape, it is enough
for my thin elbows. They will look at him

with hatred reminiscent of the Plains
of Auschwitz—Buchenwald—and drive him mad
an inch at a time. Nothing either in England
or Germany could equal his ferocity,

could equal his rage, even if the Yiddish
could make you laugh. There is a famous picture
of a German soldier plucking a beard; I think
of gentle Gloucester every time I see

that picture. There is a point where even Yiddish
becomes a tragic tongue and even Adler
can make you weep. They sit in their chairs for hours
to hear him curse his God; he looks at the dust

and asks, What have I done, what have I done,
for Him to turn on me; that audience murmurs,
Daughters, daughters, it cries for the sadness that came
to all of them in America. King Lear,

may the Lord keep him, hums in agony,
he is a monster of suffering, so many holes
that he is more like a whistle than like a king,
and yet when sometimes he comes across the stage

crowned with burdocks and nettles and cuckoo flowers
we forget it is Adler, we are so terrified,
we are so touched by pity. It is said
that Isadora Duncan came to worship him,

that John Barrymore came to study his acting,
that when he died they carried his coffin around
from theater to theater, that people mourned in the streets,
that he lay in a Windsor tie and a black silk coat.

One time he carried Cordelia around in his arms
he almost forgot his words, he was so moved
by his own grief, there were tears and groans
for him when they remembered his misfortune.

I thank God they were able to weep
and wring their hands for Lear, and sweet Cordelia,
that it happened almost forty years
before our hell, that there was still time then

to walk out of the theater in the sunlight
and discuss tragedy on the bright sidewalk
and live a while by mercy and innocence
with a king like Adler keeping the tremors alive

in their voices and the tears brimming in their eyes.
Thank God they died so early, that they were buried
one at a time, each with his own service,
that they were not lined up beside the trucks

or the cattle cars. I think when they saw him put
a feather over her lips they were relieved
to see her dead. I think they knew her life
was the last claim against him—the last delusion,

one or two would say. Now he was free,
now he was fully changed, he was *created*,
which is something they could have to talk about
going back to their stairways and their crowded tables

with real streaks of remorse on their faces—
more than forty years, almost fifty,
before the dead were dragged from their places
and dumped on the ground or put in orderly piles—

I think they used a broom on the charred faces
to see if there was breath—and a match or two
was dropped on the naked bodies. For the sake of art
there always was a German or Ukrainian

walking around like a dignified Albany,
or one made sad repentant noises like Kent
and one was philosophical like Edgar,
giving lectures to the burning corpses,

those with gold in their mouths, and those with skin
the color of yellow roses, and those with an arm
or a hand that dropped affectionately on another,
and those whose heads were buried, and those whose black tongues—

as if there were mountains, as if there were cold water
flowing through the ravines, as if there were wine cups
sitting on top of the barrels, as if there were flowers—
still sang in bitterness, still wept and warbled in sorrow.

The Expulsion

I'm working like a dog here, testing my memory,
my mouth is slightly open, my eyes are closed,
my hand is lying under the satin pillow.
My subject is loss, the painter is Masaccio,
the church is the Church of the Carmine, the narrow panel
is on the southwest wall, I make a mouth
like Adam, I make a mouth like Eve, I make
a sword like the angel's. Or Schubert; I hear him howling
too, there is a touch of the Orient
throughout the great C Major. I'm thinking again
of poor Jim Wright and the sheet of tissue paper
he sent me. Lament, lament, for the underlayer
of wallpaper, circa 1935.
Lament for the Cretans, how did they disappear?
Lament for Hannibal. I'm standing again
behind some wires, there are some guns, my hand
is drawing in the eyes, I'm making the stripes,
I'm lying alone with water falling down
the left side of my face. That was our painting.
We stood in line to see it, we loved the cry
that came from Eve's black mouth, we loved the grief
of her slanted eyes, we loved poor Adam's face
half buried in his hands, we loved the light
on the shoulder and thighs, we loved the shadows, we loved
the perfect sense of distance. Lament, lament,
for my sister. It took ten years for the flesh to go,
she would be twenty then, she would be sixty
in 1984. Lament for my father,
he died in Florida, he died from fear, apologizing

to everyone around him. I walked through three feet
of snow to buy a suit; it took a day
to get to the airport. Lament, lament. He had
fifty-eight suits, and a bronze coffin; he lay
with his upper body showing, a foot of carpet.
He came to America in 1905, huge wolves
snapped at the horse's legs, the snow was on the ground
until the end of April. The angel is red,
her finger is pointing, she floats above the gate,
her face is cruel, she isn't like the angels
of Blake, or Plato, she is an angry mother,
her wings are firm. Lament, lament, my father
and I are leaving Paradise, an angel
is shouting, my hand is on my mouth, my father
is on the edge of his bed, he uses a knife
for a shoe horn, he is in Pittsburgh, the sky is black,
the air is filthy, he bends half over to squeeze
his foot into his shoe, his eyes are closed,
he's moaning. I miss our paradise, the pool
of water, the flowers. Our lives are merging, our shoes
are not that different. The angel is rushing by,
her lips are curled, there is a coldness, even
a madness to her, Adam and Eve are roaring,
the whole thing takes a minute, a few seconds,
and we are left on somebody's doorstep, one of
my favorites, three or four marble steps and a simple
crumbling brick—it could be Baltimore,
it could be Pittsburgh, the North Side or the Hill.
Inside I know there is a hall to the left

and a living room to the right; no one has modernized
it yet, there are two plum trees in the back
and a narrow garden, cucumbers and tomatoes.
We talk about Russia, we talk about the garden,
we talk about Truman, and Reagan. Our hands are rubbing
the dusty marble, we sit for an hour. "It is
a crazy life," I say, "after all the model
homes we looked at, I come back to the old
row house, I do it over and over." "My house"—
he means his father's—"had a giant garden
and we had peppers and radishes; my sister
Jenny made the pickles." We start to drift
at 5 o'clock in the evening, the cars from downtown
are starting to poison us. It is a paradise
of two, maybe, two at the most, the name
on the mailbox I can't remember, the garden
is full of glass, there is a jazzy door
on the next house over, and louvered windows. It is
a paradise, I'm sure of it. I kiss
him goodbye, I hold him, almost like the kiss
in 1969, in Philadelphia,
the last time I saw him, in the Russian manner,
his mouth against my mouth, his arms around me—
we could do that once before he died—
the huge planes barely lifting off the ground,
the families weeping beside us, the way they do,
the children waving goodbye, the lovers smiling,
the way they do, all our loss, everything
we know of loneliness there, their minds already

fixed on the pain, their hands already hanging,
under the shining windows, near the yellow tiles,
the secret rooms, the long and brutal corridor
down which we sometimes shuffle, and sometimes run.

Groundhog Lock

This is a common plantain, the simple weed
of my solemn childhood, and this is a staghorn sumac,
the weed of my adolescence. I rushed down
to get here before the state got busy pulling
and sawing and cutting. The plantain was our wheat
and it waved in the wind for us; we loved the heads
of tiny green and white flowers, we loved to snap
them loose from the stem and leave them dying there,
for birds, or rabbits, for all we knew. The sumac
was somehow reeking with sex, the branches were covered
with tender velvet and the heavy fruit
was thick with bright red hairs. As I recall
the twigs, when we broke them, had a creamy sap—
we called it milk, or juice—and though the poor shrub
was innocent enough, and no more monstrous
than either the violet or the bitter daisy,
our minds were already ruined.
                              I'm torn between
two stages of my life; the next will be
the stage of silence, of course, and centered around
the sunflower or the hollyhock although
I'm thinking of smoking punk again and sitting
half stoned on nothing under a pussy willow
or a drooping lilac. Maybe I'll live for space
the next time, and practice denial, and sit
on the wooden seesaw and blow the white dandelion
into the river; maybe I'll practice reunion
and pluck the petals: "she loves me, she loves me not,"
a kind of gnosticism; I have ten chances,

sometimes twelve; maybe I'll wait for the milkweed
to come my way, that way I can sit forever
on either the sand or the gravel.
                                    There are some steps
going down to the water. I will end my search
on those steps, my own Benares, sixteen risers,
and Budweiser all around me. My last plant
is a morning glory. It comes as if to hide
the chain-link fence, the vine is wrapped around
the heavy wires, a bird is singing, the smell
is more like cotton candy than urine, more
like White Shoulders, there is a dead fish, the flowers
are five to a stem, the leaf is heart-shaped, my arms
can hang between the stone wall and the wire,
my legs can wrap themselves around the roots,
and my back, underneath the neck, the point of exhaustion,
can rest on the worm-like and succulent laterals,
although it could have been a wild carrot
and I could have concentrated on the ivory,
or it could have been the chicory
and I could have concentrated on the blue,
or it could have been crown vetch, there is some
growing on the towpath, I sleep beside it,
three more kinds of existence on the river,
among the picnic tables and the spruce and the pump,
one of the two corners of the universe.

July 2, 1983

This is what it's come to on my primrose path,
a delphinium growing out of a cabbage,
a hosta
or August lily.

This is what a July day looks like
in the 1980's,
a white butterfly,
a shimmer of heat, a shadow.

O ugliest of flowers,
be with me forever,
now that I've lifted my left hand against the tubers,
now that I've lifted my right hand against the motor boats.

O mugho pine,
bless my swallows,
flying madly in and out of their woven duplex,
living for two great weeks with heartbreak and wrangling and terror
and a minute and a half of sleep, and a minute and a half of silence.

The Dogs

Sometimes the dogs don't hear me. Sometimes I walk
a mile each way—to the locks and back—singing
a Japanese song, humming a little, remembering
the dry roses. Sometimes I walk through the geese
and they don't move, the guards look up in boredom
and hardly notice, sometimes I see each leaf
is burning from lack of rain, sometimes I reach
the first bridge out of breath, sometimes I rest
in front of the spillway and wait for a breeze. I stand

on the great catwalk, I feel the spray in my face,
I look at the bubbles, I look at the wavering sun,
I look at the winches and wheels, I look at the water
roaring around the bend. There are maples
growing out of the wall, there is giant
purple loosestrife, there are logs and tables,
there are seesaws, there is a well, the lip
is capped, the river is on my left, the sky
is dark and heavy, the island is rich and empty.

Lovesick

Nobody Else Living

Nobody else living knows that song as well as I do.
On bad days I fill the tub with hot water
and rest my head on the freezing porcelain.
I fill the courtyard with sounds.
They come through the frosted glass,
they come through the transom. All that wonderful pity,
all that broken bliss, for twenty or thirty minutes
now rich and reminiscent and warm,
now cloudy and haunted.

Lovesick

The dead straw in those trees, the
dead leaves in those trees
have turned to birds, they have turned
to crows, they are watching a deer
or a piece of tire, my foot
is on the deer's black head,
my face is in the clouds,
I kick the tire over
to see the guts. I want
the whole thing for myself.
They want the eyes, they want
the stinking shoulder, they wait
for me to leave, I kick
the legs, I drag them across
the highway, all those beaks
are snapping, all those tails
are waving in the wind,
their bellies are moaning and howling,
their souls are cooing and cawing.

All I Have Are the Tracks

All I have are the tracks. There were a dog's
going down the powdered steps, there was a woman
going one way, a man going the other, a squirrel
on top of the man; sometimes his paws were firm,
the claws were showing—in fear, in caution—sometimes
they sort of scurried, then sort of leaped. The prints
go east and west; there is a boot; there is
a checkerboard style, a hexagram style; my own
I study now, my Georgia Loggers, the heel
a kind of target, the sole a kind of sponge;
the tiny feet are hopping, four little paws,
the distance between them is fifteen inches, they end
in the grass, in the leaves, there are four toes and a palm,
the nose isn't there, the tail isn't there, the teeth
that held the acorn, the eyes that thought; and the hands
that held the books, and the face that froze, and the shoulders
that fought the wind, and the mouth that struggled for air,
and love and hate, and all their shameless rages.

I Do a Piece from Greece

I do a piece from Greece. I haven't done that
for three or four years. I turn the radio up.
I stare at my ties. I pick a California
and wrap it around my robe. There is a shark
on the ceiling above my shoes. Her nose is pointed
toward the door. She is the streamlined body
we dreamed about in the thirties. Her tail is monstrous,
her brain is a pea. I pluck the strings
in a kind of serenade. I raise the bow
above my head and bend a little, my hair
is hanging down. I am at last the musician
my mother wanted. My aunts and uncles are sitting
on wooden boxes, they are sobbing and sighing,
I take my time, I have a Schubert to go.
I have a light beside me. I am lying
under the Sea of Azov, it is a joy
to be here, they are howling. I raise my elbow
to make a sound. I wait for the moon to shine
on the Allegheny. I look at their faces, they turn
the pages, eleven uncles and aunts, a leather
coffin. I start to play, it is the only
way I have of weeping, it is my way
of joining them, my tears were taken away
when I was eight, this way we end up singing
together. I am a note above them, it is
the thirteenth century, singing in fifths, in parts
of the south they sing like that; the violin rises
above the alto, a shrieking sound, we humans

shriek at the end, we want so much to be heard.
My way was with the soaring and the singing.
Once I heard it I could never stop.

I Hate My Moaning

I hate my staring. I hate my moaning. Sometimes
I lie there in the morning arguing
against myself. I hold a mirror up
above the telephone so I can snip
a long hair from my eye. I balance a cup
of coffee on my stomach. Sometimes I sing,
sometimes I hold a feather against my nose,
sometimes I prop the clock against my ear,
sometimes I drag the speakers across the floor
and turn the volume up. There is a hole
above my head, the plaster is dropping, the lath
is exposed; there is a blanket over the window;
I hold it up with nails, it tears in the center
and lets a stream of light in; I can tell
when it's six o'clock, and seven o'clock, it is
my hour, the blanket is full of holes, the light
comes through the threads, it is a greyish light,
perfect for either love or bitterness,
no exaggeration or deceit.

This Was a Wonderful Night

This was a wonderful night. I heard the Brahms
piano quintet, I read a poem by Schiller,
I read a story, I listened to *Gloomy Sunday*.
No one called me, I studied the birthday poem
of Alvaro de Campos. I thought, if there was time,
I'd think of my garden—all that lettuce, wasted,
all those huge tomatoes lying on the ground
rotting, and I'd think of the sticks I put there,
waving goodbye, those bearded sticks. De Campos,
he was the one who suffered most, his birthday
was like a knife to him; he sat in a chair
remembering his aunts; he thought of the flowers
and cakes, he thought of the sideboard crowded with gifts.
I look at the photo of Billie Holiday;
I turn the light bulb on and off. I envy
those poets who loved their childhood, those who remember
the extra places laid out, the china and glasses.
They want to devour the past, they revel in pity,
they live like burnt-out matches, memory ruins them;
again and again they go back to the first place.

De Campos and I are sitting on a bench
in some American city. He hardly knows
how much I love his country. I have two things
to tell him about my childhood, one is the ice
on top of the milk, one is the sign in the window—
three things—the smell of coal. There is some snow
left on the street, the wind is blowing. He trembles
and touches the buttons on his vest. His house

is gone, his aunts are dead, the tears run down
our cheeks and chins, we are like babies, crying.
"Leave thinking to the head," he says. I sob,
"I don't have birthdays any more," I say,
"I just go on," although I hardly feel
the sadness, there is such joy in being there
on that small bench, watching the sycamores,
looking for birds in the snow, listening for boots,
staring at the begonias, getting up
and down to rub the leaves and touch the buds—
endless pleasure, talking about New York,
comparing pain, writing the names down
of all the cities south of Lisbon, singing
one or two songs—a hundred years for him,
a little less for me, going east and west
in the new country, my heart forever pounding.

I Sometimes Think of the Lamb

I sometimes think of the lamb when I crawl down
my flight of stairs, my back is twisted sideways
in a great arc of pain from the shoulder down
and the buttocks up. I think of the lamb through my tears
as I go down a step at a time, my left hand
squeezing the rail, my right hand holding my thigh
and lifting it up. As long as there is a lamb
I can get on my hands and knees if I have to
and walk across the floor like a limp wolf,
and I can get my body to the sink
and lift myself up to the white porcelain.
As long as there is a lamb, as long as he lives
in his brown pen or his green meadow,
as long as he kneels on the platform staring at the light,
surrounded by men and women with raised fingers,
as long as he has that little hump on his rear
and that little curve to his tail, as long as his foot
steps over the edge in terror and ignorance,
as long as he holds a cup to his own side,
as long as he is stabbed and venerated,
as long as there are hooves—and clattering—
as long as there is screaming and butchering.

Stopping Schubert

Stopping Schubert, ejecting him, changing the power,
I make it from Newark to the shores of Oberlin
in less than nine hours, Schubert roaring and groaning
halfway there, the violins in the mountains,
the cellos in the old state forests.
When I reach Clarion I know I am near Pittsburgh.
I turn the tape down; I can live off the music
of childhood for a while—I still know the words
in both languages—I am not that different
even today. My mouth makes a humming sound
just as it did back then. I take my comb out
and my piece of paper. I bang the swollen dashboard
thinking of my golden trombone; I ruined
the lives of twenty-four families in those days
sliding from note to note, it was my fate
not to make a sound on the French Horn,
to rage on my trombone. I still love Schubert
most of all, *Death and the Maiden, Frozen Tears,*
Der Lindenbaum.
I have kept it a secret for forty years,
the tortured composer from central Pennsylvania,
Franz Schubert.

I Am in a Window

I move from chair to chair. Thinking of Liszt.
I am in a certain century again
going from city to city. I am in a window
with Berlioz on my left and Czerny on my right;
Liszt is looking into the clouds, his wrists
seem to be waiting. I am in an oil painting.
Victor Hugo is there, and Paganini,
and Sand and Dumas side by side. A bust
of Beethoven is half sitting on the piano,
half sitting in the sky. We live by the light
of Saint-Simon—it is our socialism,
freedom from rage, freedom from marriage,
freedom from money; or it is Weimar
forty years later, Liszt is at the window,
Wagner has come and gone, the world is whistling
Brahms and Debussy; in a few years
Gandhi will be born, then Frank Lloyd Wright.
The continent has shifted half an inch,
a little joy has come to Zuyder Zee,
a little horror has come to the Crimea.
I move from table to table, from room to room,
I try to think of Gurdjieff, what was the work
he had in store for me? Where were the shovels?
I think of Rudolf Steiner, all the reading
he did on Hegel and Goethe; I think of the gatherings
in Switzerland, and France, I see his hand
in a book, his eyes are radiant. I pack
my bag, a leather strap, a leather pocket—
how well the goods were made in 1910,

fifteen years before my birth—my soul
was probably born too late, it had a certain
zest, I think, for the wrong century
and fluttered along for decade after decade
with the wrong digits—that is the way it is
with souls—I have a rug upstairs to roll in,
something to keep me warm, it came from Crete
and has three green and yellow flowers on it,
on a field of crimson; I bought it in Chania.
I'll lie there for hours thinking of my mountains,
reading Keats.

Béla

This version of the starving artist
has him composing his last concerto
while dying of leukemia. Serge Koussevitsky
visits him in his hospital room
with flowers in his hand, the two of them
talk in tones of reverence, the last
long piece could be the best, the rain somewhere
makes daring noises, somewhere clouds are bursting.
I have the record in front of me. I drop
the needle again on the famous ending, five
long notes, then all is still, I have to imagine
two great seconds of silence and then applause
and shouting, he is in tears, Koussevitsky
leads him onto the stage. Or he is distant,
remembering the mountains, there in Boston
facing the wild Americans, he closes
his eyes so he can hear another note,
something from Turkey, or Romania, his mother
holding his left hand, straightening out the fingers,
he bows from the waist, he holds his right hand up.
I love the picture with Benny Goodman, Szigetti
is on the left, Goodman's cheeks are puffed
and his legs are crossed. Bartók is at the piano.
They are rehearsing Bartók's *Contrasts*. I lift
my own right hand, naturally I do that;
I listen to my blood, I touch my wrist.
If he could have only lived for three more years
he could have heard about our Mussolini
and seen the violent turn to the right and the end

of one America and the beginning of another.
That would have given him time enough to brood
on Hungary; that would have given him time
also to go among the Indians
and learn their music, and listen to their chants,
those tribes from Michigan and Minnesota,
just like the tribes of the Finns and the Urgo-Slavics,
moaning and shuffling in front of their wooden tents.

There is a note at the end of the second movement
I love to think about; it parodies
Shostakovitch; it is a kind of flutter
of the lips. And there is a note—I hear it—
of odd regret for a life not lived enough,
everyone knows that sound, for me it's remorse,
and there is a note of crazy satisfaction,
this I love, of the life he would not change
no matter what—no other animal
could have such pleasure. I think of this as I turn
the music off, and I think of his poor eyes
as they turned to ice—his son was in the room
and saw the change—I call it a change. Bartók
himself lectured his friends on death, it was
his woods and mountain lecture, fresh green shoots
pushing up through the old, the common home
that waits us all, the cycles, the laws of nature,
wonderfully European, all life and death
at war—peacefully—one thing replacing another,
although he grieved over cows and pitied dogs

and listened to pine cones as if they came from the sea
and fretted over the smallest of life.
He died

September 28, 1945,
just a month after the war was over.
It took him sixty days to finish the piece
from the time he lay there talking to Koussevitsky
to the time he put a final dot on the paper,
a little pool of ink to mark the ending.
There are the five loud notes, I walk upstairs
to hear them, I put a silk shawl over my head
and rock on the wooden floor, the shawl is from France
and you can see between the threads; I feel
the darkness, I was born with a veil over
my eyes, it took me forty years to rub
the gum away, it was a blessing, I sit
for twenty minutes in silence, daylight is coming,
the moon is probably near, probably lifting
its satin nightgown, one hand over the knee
to hold the cloth up so the feet can walk
through the wet clouds; I love that bent-over motion,
that grace at the end of a long and furious night.
I go to sleep on the floor, there is a pillow
somewhere for my heavy head, my hand
is resting on the jacket, Maazel is leading
the Munich orchestra, a nurse is pulling
the sheet up, Bartók is dead, his wife is walking
past the sun room, her face is white, her mind
is on the apartment they lost, where she would put

the rugs, how she would carry in his breakfast,
where they would read, her mind is on Budapest,
she plays the piano for him, she is eighteen
and he is thirty-seven, he is gone
to break the news, she waits in agony,
she goes to the telephone; I turn to the window,
I stare at my palm, I draw a heart in the dust,
I put the arrow through it, I place the letters
one inside the other. I sleep, I sleep.

A Song for the Romeos*

for my brothers
Jim Wright and Dick Hugo

I'm singing a song for the romeos
I wore for ten years on my front stoop in the North Side,
and for the fat belly I carried
and the magic ticket sticking out of my greasy hatband
or my vest pocket,
the green velvet one with the checkered borders
and the great stretched back with the tan ribs
going west and east like fishes of the deep looking for their covers.

I'm wearing my romeos
with the papery thin leather
and the elastic side bands.
They are made for sitting,
or a little walking into the kitchen and out,
a little tea in the hands,
a little Old Forester or a little Schenley in the tea.

I'm singing a song for the corner store
and the empty shelves;
for the two blocks of flattened buildings
and broken glass;
for the streetcar that still rounds the bend
with sparks flying through the air.

* Romeos were a kind of indoor/outdoor slipper or sandal.

And the woman with a shopping bag,
and the girl with a book
walking home one behind the other,
their steps half dragging, half ringing,
the romeos keeping time,
tapping and knocking and clapping on the wooden steps
and the cement sidewalk.

A Slow and Painful Recovery

Richard Strauss, my hero, here you are
finally letting go of both sword and breast,
and there you are escaping from our bleeding world
onto a mountain or into a cloud. I stare
at the pink fixture, it is a flattened breast
with a longish nipple, breasts half over the world
are covering light bulbs, there is a light bulb out
and a darkened breast in the other room; I stay here
with my lilacs and daisies, I am in my bed
of needles. Now it's Schumann again, the second,
his deep depression gone by the final movement
and soon it will be Mozart, Europe again,
the true Europe, lilacs everywhere,
the cellos of the plant world. This is the last
good day for the first bouquet. I know there are some
daisies left among the lilies. The second
bouquet is better, it refuses to bow,
it brings the outside in, I think it's the bluebell,
I think it's the red bud crawling and twisting, a kind of
Japanese dancing, maybe more formal than twisting.

I'm writing the fourteenth now. I'm doing it
in a room with all my boxes and boots and paintings.
I'm getting ready to move. My bed of needles—
crooked, antique—is in the midst of it all.
Each day I walk a mile, I crawl and twist
like a broken branch, I pass the scented tree,
I pass the poppies, I pass the lilacs, I climb
two giant hills, my face is twisted, I hold

the rusted rail—this house is historical—
and pull myself up the steps. My crisis was the spine,
one or two flattened discs, I had the pain,
I had the depression, I had the boredom. There are
paths I know that no one knows. I know
the color of tulips in every yard. I know
the sheets of green with yellow discs. I watch them
turn white. I know a house so small the owners
are either midgets with squeaky voices or giants
with little chairs and tables, little beds
they and their children play in. There is a mailbox
nailed onto the shingles. There is a railing
falling over—the giants' heavy touch,
the midgets' swinging. There is a small backyard
with white and purple lilacs. I am listening
to Haydn's sixty-sixth, the ever loyal
Haydn, Haydn the good, Ben Franklin Haydn.
I take my pills—daily at bedtime—I look at
my Cretan rug. I fought for days to save
five or ten dollars, every day the dealer
sent out for coffee, every day he told me
about his life in Chicago and every day
we struggled in silence. I turn the lights out, my mind
is all alone, it begs for valium, it cries
for milk and scotch. At four in the morning the birds
and I are screaming. I start my long walk at five;
the shadows let me alone, the perfume tree
is silent, my hands are shaking—a little residual
weakness—my leg is dragging, I turn the corner

to a kind of dawn, there is a weak light over
the sycamores—the perfume tree is apple—
the red bud is split in two, the poppies are opening.
It was a slow and painful recovery.

My First Kinglet

I saw my first kinglet in Iowa City
on Sunday, April twenty-second, 1984,
flying from tree to tree, and bush to bush.
She had a small yellow patch on her stomach,
a little white around her eyes. I reached
for a kiss, still dumb and silent as always. I put
a finger out for a branch and opened my hand
for a kind of clearing in the woods, a wrinkled
nest you'd call it, half inviting, half
disgusting maybe, or terrifying, a pink
and living nest. The kinglet stood there singing
"A Mighty Fortress Is Our God." She was
a pure Protestant, warbling in the woods,
confessing everything. I said goodbye,
a friend of all the Anabaptists, a friend
of all the Lutherans. I cleared my throat
and off she went for some other pink finger
and some other wrinkled palm. I started to whistle,
but only to the trees; my kinglet was gone
and her pipe was gone and her yellow crown was gone,
and I was left with only a spiral notebook
and the end of a pencil. I was good and careful,
for all I had left of the soul was in that stub,
a wobbling hunk of lead embedded in wood,
pine probably—pencils are strange—I sang
another Protestant hymn; the lead was loose
and after a minute I knew I'd just be holding
the blunt and slippery end. That was enough
for one Sunday. I thanked the trees, I thanked

the tulips with their six red tongues. I lay
another hour, another hour; I either
slept a little or thought a little. Life—
it could have been a horror, it could have been
gory and full of pain. I ate my sandwich
and waited for a signal, then I began
my own confession; I walked on the stones, I sighed
under a hemlock, I whistled under a pine,
and reached my own house almost out of breath
from walking too fast—from talking too loud—
from waving my arms and beating my palms; I was,
for five or ten minutes, one of those madmen you see
forcing their way down Broadway, reasoning with themselves
the way a squirrel does, the way a woodpecker does,
half dressed in leaf, half dressed in light, my dear face
appearing and disappearing, my heavy legs
with their shortened hamstrings tripping a little, a yard
away from my wooden steps and my rusty rail,
the thicket I lived in for two years, more or less,
Dutch on one side, American Sioux on the other,
Puerto Rican and Bronx Hasidic inside,
a thicket fit for a king or a wandering kinglet.

I Slept Like That

It was always a soothing position,
holding my arm up with the elbow locked
and the fingers bent.
I was always a birch tree,
with a long curved bough and a limb hanging down
half touching the grass.
I slept like that
and dreamed of the light coming through and my five dry fingers
returning to life.
That was in Pittsburgh and New York and Trenton and Camden.
And Philadelphia. Philadelphia, P.A.
I slept by the river—always—and followed the devious way.
In five old cities, each with an ancient and brutal government,
I lived with my arm in the sky and my fingers bent.

Lillian Harvey

This is lovesick for you—Charles Koechlin
covering his paper with tears, he shushes his wife
and his children, he is crying for Lillian Harvey—
or this is lovesick—sending his wife to meet her,
he is too shy to go, and he is married;
when she comes back he asks a thousand questions:
What was she wearing? Does she like his music?
How old did she look? Was she like her photograph?
But he never met her, she whose face haunted him,
although he wrote a hundred and thirteen compositions
for her, including two *Albums for Lillian*,
and he wrote a film scenario and score,
which he imagined, fantastically,
would star the two of them. He was himself
twice in America, both times in California,
but they couldn't meet—it would be a violation.
I know that agony myself, I stood
on one foot or another four or five times
and burned with shame and shook with terror. You never
go yourself. I know he must have waited
outside her house, a crazy man, he must have
dialed her number a hundred times, even risked
his life for her. But you never go, you never
stand there smiling—he never stood there smiling,
he never reached his hand inside her dress,
he never touched her nipple, he never pressed
his mouth against her knee or lifted her thighs.
For she was the muse. You never fuck the muse.

There I Was One Day

There I was one day
in the parking lot of the First Brothers' Church
on one foot, a giant whooping crane
with my left ibex finger against my temple
trying to remember what my theory of corruption was
and why I got so angry years ago
at my poor mother and father, immigrant cranes
from Polish Russia and German and Jewish Ukraine—
the good days then, hopping both ways like a frog,
and croaking, and trying to remember why it was
I soothed myself with words
at that flimsy secretary, not meant for knees,
not meant for a soul, not least a human one,
and trying to remember how I pieced together
the great puzzle, and how delighted I was
I would never again be bitten twice,
on either hand, the left one or the other.
I stopped between the telephone pole and the ivy
and sang to myself. I do it now for pleasure.
I thought I'd trace the line of pure decadence
to either Frank Sinatra or Jackie Gleason,
and thence to either the desert or the swamp,
Greater Nevada or Miami Beach;
or I would smile with Stalin or frown with Frick,
Stalin and Frick, both from Pittsburgh; Mellon,
Ehrlichman, Paul the Fortieth, Paul the Fiftieth.
I learned my bitterness at the dining room table
and used it everywhere. One time I yanked
the tablecloth off with everything on top of it.

It was the kind of strength that lets you lift
the back end of a car, it was the rush
of anger and righteousness you shake from later.
My Polish mother and my Ukrainian father
sat there white-faced. They had to be under fifty,
maybe closer to forty. I had hit them
between the eyes, I had screamed in their ears
and spit in their faces. Forty years later I stutter
when I think about it; it is the stuttering
of violent justice. I turned left on Third—
it was called Pomfret in 1776—
and made my way to the square—I think I did that—
past the Plaza II and the old Huntington,
and did an Egyptian turn. There were some other birds
sitting there on the benches, eating egg salad
and smoking autumn leaves. They didn't seem to care
or even notice. We sat there for the humming
and later we left, one at a time, and limped
away at different speeds, in different directions.
I ended up doing a circle, east on one street,
north on another, past the round oak table
in the glass window, past the swimming pool
at the YW. Just a walk for me
is full of exhaustion; nobody does it my way,
shaking the left foot, holding the right foot up,
a stork from Broadway, a heron from Mexico,
a pink flamingo from Greece.

One Animal's Life

for Rosalind Pace

This is how I saved one animal's life,
I raised the lid of the stove and lifted the hook
that delicately held the cheese—I think it was bacon—
so there could be goodness and justice under there.
It was a thirty-inch range with the pilot lit
in the center of two small crosses. It was a Wincroft
with a huge oven and two flat splash pans above it.
The four burners were close together, it was
a piece of white joy, from 1940 I'd judge
from the two curved handles, yet not as simple as
my old Slattery, not as sleek. I owe
a lot to the woman who gave me this house, she is
a lover of everything big and small, she moans
for certain flowers and insects, I hear her snuffle
all night sometimes, I hear her groan. She gave me
a bed and a kitchen, she gave me music, I couldn't be
disloyal to her, yet I had to lift
the murderous hook. I'll hear her lectures later
on *my* inconsistencies and hypocrisies;
I'll struggle in the meantime, like everyone else, to make
my way between the stove and refrigerator
without sighing or weeping too much. Mice
are small and ferocious. If I killed one it wouldn't be
with poison or traps. I couldn't just use our weapons
without some compensation. I'd have to be present—
if it was a trap—and hear it crash and lift
the steel myself and look at the small flat nose
or the small crushed head, I'd have to hold the pallet
and drop the body into a bag. I ask

forgiveness of butchers and hunters; I'm starting to talk
to vegetarians now, I'm reading books,
I'm washing my icebox down with soda and lye,
I'm buying chicory, I'm storing beans.
I should have started this thirty years ago,
holding my breath, eating ozone, starving,
sitting there humming, feeling pure and indignant
beside the chewed-up bags and the black droppings.

Silver Hand

There is that little silver hand. I wrap
my fingers around the wrist. I press my thumb
on the shiny knuckles. There is a little slot
in the empty palm—the lines are crude and lifeless,
more like an ape's hand, more like a child's, no hope
for the future of any kind, a life line dragging
its way through civilization, the line of destiny
faint and broken, a small abandoned road,
the heart line short, no sweetness, no ecstasy,
and no dear journeys, and no great windfalls. I shake
the wrist, there are some dimes and nickels inside,
but it is mostly empty, an empty hand
reaching out. It is the hand that acts
for the spirit, there is a connection, the hand has mercy,
the hand is supple and begs, the hand is delicate,
even if it is brutal sometimes, even if it is evil—
and it is penniless and lost, a true
spirit, that sings a little and dances a little,
green or shiny on the outside, black on the inside.
Give to the hand!

Washington Square

Now after all these years I am just that one pigeon
limping over towards that one sycamore tree
with my left leg swollen and my left claw bent and my neck
just pulling me along. It is the annual
day of autumn glory, but I am limping
into the shade of that one sycamore tree.
Forget about Holley crumbling out there in the square,
forget about Garibaldi in his little hollow;
remember one pigeon, white and grey, with a touch
of the old blue, his red leg swollen, his claw
dragging him on and on, the sickness racking
his skinny neck; remember the one pigeon
fighting his way through the filthy marijuana,
sighing.

Arranging a Thorn

I am wandering through Newark, New Jersey,
among the gymnasts, the accountants and the kings
and my arms are breaking from all the weight I carry.
I am wearing the same blue pants and jacket
I have worn for the last twenty years
and mumbling to myself as always
as I go out of one long corridor and into another
or up an escalator
and into a jazzy bar
or through the beeper, over and over again,
discarding my metal, dropping my keys and watches.
I am ranked below the businessmen
with their two-suiters and their glasses of ice
and I get a slightly bored or slightly disdainful look
from the flight attendants and the drunken crew
and the food gatherers.
This is the trip I'm going to think about Rexroth
and what it was like in 1959
reading his poem on murdered poets,
and Shelley's *Adonais*
and Dunbar's *Lament*,
half a dirge for Dunbar,
half a dirge for the reader, sick and dying.
—Ah brother Levine and brother Stanley Plumly,
what hell we live in; we travel from Tuscaloosa
to Houston; we go to Chicago; we meet the monster
and spend our night at the Richmont or the Hyatt,
there is a table by the bed, the rug
on the wall is there to ruin us, coffee and toast

is seven dollars. Murphy meets us in leather
at the South Street station and drives us over a curb;
I pay for my own meal; twenty people show up
for the reading; it is the night that Carter loses;
my back is out of place. It was in the *Ion*
that Plato doomed the poets. There is no peace
in any land, we stand in the dust and kick
our shoes, some with holes in the toes and some
with holes in the soles. That's all there is. The prizes
are there for delusion. Oh brother Ignatow, oh br'er
Bly, there is such joy in sitting here knowing
one thing from another; I feel like singing;
that darkness is gone, that angry blackness. I sort
the leaves, my life is full of leaves again,
I make a garland for my head, it is
a garland of pity—I won't say glory—poets
are full of pity, I talk to them, they hate to
think about glory, it is the terror, everything
lost, their poems shredded and burned, their music
boring, or insignificant, or derivative,
a critic somewhere keeping time, but *pity*,
pity is for this life, pity is the worm
inside the meat, pity is the meat, pity
is the shaking pencil, pity is the shaking voice—
not enough money, not enough love—pity
for all of us—it is our grace, walking
down the ramp or on the moving sidewalk,
sitting in a chair, reading the paper, pity,
turning a leaf to the light, arranging a thorn.

The Dog

What I was doing with my white teeth exposed
like that on the side of the road I don't know,
and I don't know why I lay beside the sewer
so that lover of dead things could come back
with his pencil sharpened and his piece of white paper.
I was there for a good two hours whistling
dirges, shrieking a little, terrifying
hearts with my whimpering cries before I died
by pulling the one leg up and stiffening.
There is a look we have with the hair of the chin
curled in mid-air, there is a look with the belly
stopped in the midst of its greed. The lover of dead things
stoops to feel me, his hand is shaking. I know
his mouth is open and his glasses are slipping.
I think his pencil must be jerking and the terror
of smell—and sight—is overtaking him;
I know he has that terrified faraway look
that death brings—he is contemplating. I want him
to touch my forehead once and rub my muzzle
before he lifts me up and throws me into
that little valley. I hope he doesn't use
his shoe for fear of touching me; I know,
or used to know, the grasses down there; I think
I knew a hundred smells. I hope the dog's way
doesn't overtake him, one quick push,
barely that, and the mind freed, something else,
some other thing, to take its place. Great heart,
great human heart, keep loving me as you lift me,
give me your tears, great loving stranger, remember

the death of dogs, forgive the yapping, forgive
the shitting, let there be pity, give me your pity.
How could there be enough? I have given
my life for this, emotion has ruined me, oh lover,
I have exchanged my wildness—little tricks
with the mouth and feet, with the tail, my tongue is a parrot's,
I am a rampant horse, I am a lion,
I wait for the cookie, I snap my teeth—
as you have taught me, oh distant and brilliant and lonely.

Shaking Myself and Sighing

What a sweet urinal it was in Narbonne,
the smoke coming up in the form of thin wisps,
the tough little roots sticking out above our eyes.
You could hear music there, something that
wailed and something that snorted, it was a
perfect place for sound. I touched the stone
above my head with the flat of my hand, it was
the right hand, elbow bent and forehead almost
touching the roots. I hummed a little and listened
to cars on the wall. Pleasure would drag me down
to the wide canal and fate would drag me through
the five hundred years of silt. My eyes would water
thinking of the Saracens or thinking
of the Jews arriving from Spain and Africa
with books and shawls. I thought of Moses Khimki,
the Blue Book mentions him; I thought of the Jewry
leaving their city forever, going down to Poitiers,
going back to Barcelona, I stood there sighing,
shaking myself and sighing. If I had stayed
I would have come back in 1960, half
a scholar, half a poet. I would have spent
two years teaching in Perpignan, I would have
lived in Carcassonne, I would have walked
the road from Montpellier to Sête again
and spent another Thanksgiving there, still dreaming
of renting a boat—with two or three others—still singing
American songs, among the Phoenicians,
visiting Valery's grave, bicycling back
to Montpellier at two, or three, in the morning,

singing in French, or being silent. I would have
done that three or four times. God forgive me
for coming back, there I am standing and talking
to two or three Arabs—we kiss—there I am sitting
at six A.M. across from the park; I have
a roll in my right hand, I have lifted the white
coffee to my lips, God forgive me
for my desertion—I am a heavy moaner,
can that be forgiven?—I owe a song to Basnight,
he lived in Turkey for twenty years; I owe
a song to Brett, he lived in Greece for almost
twenty-five. I would have packed my silver
in straw, I would have packed my books in paper
and dropped the key inside the lion's mouth
and left when the chairs and cushions were still burning.

A Pair of Hands

That is a pair of white hands I see
floating in the mirror, the fingers on the left
are blunt and rounded, the ones on the right are raised
as if in thought. They are almost like gloves,
the lines are gone, they are abstracted, the suffering
is in the creases, somewhere in the folds
underneath the knuckles, or somewhere in the spaces
over the fingertips. I choose them this time
over the mouth, the mouth with two great trenches
and two great cheeks beyond the trenches, the mouth
with a curled smile, and I choose them over the eyes,
surrounded by wrinkles, wounded and bloodshot. The hands
are permanent and heavy, they are the means
both to pain and pleasure, thus the ancient
Peruvians buried them inside their clothes,
thus the Arabs cut them off and fed
them to their dogs. Our age is weak—and vague—
in what it does with hands, there is a history
both of terror and loathing. My first forty years
were an agony. I lived by touching and holding.
It was my ruin.

Bob Summers' Body

I never told this—I saw Bob Summers' body
one last time when they dropped him down the chute
at the crematorium. He turned over twice
and seemed to hang with one hand to the railing
as if he had to sit up once and scream
before he reached the flames. I was half terrified
and half ashamed to see him collapse like that
just two minutes after we had sung for him
and said our pieces. It was impossible
for me to see him starting another destiny
piled up like that, or see him in that furnace
as one who was being consoled or purified.
If only we had wrapped him in his sheet
so he could be prepared; there is such horror
standing before Persephone with a suit on,
the name of the manufacturer in the lining,
the pants too short, or too long. How hard it was
for poor Bob Summers in this life, how he struggled
to be another person. I hope his voice,
which he lost through a stroke in 1971,
was given back to him, wherever he strayed,
the smell of smoke still on him, the fire lighting up
his wonderful eyes again, his hands explaining,
anyone, god or man, moved by his logic,
spirits in particular, saved by the fire and clasping
their hands around their knees, some still worm-bound,
their noses eaten away, their mouths only dust,
nodding and smiling in the plush darkness.

It Was in Houston

It was in Houston I saw the heavy sideboard
with dogs and foxes and lobsters carved into
the wood, a giant stag was hanging down
from a polished rope, there was an eagle on top
and bowls of fruit and plates of fish—all carved.
I opened the drawer and put my message inside.
The drawer was smooth and faultless, one of the hidden
ones without knobs, curved and rounded, with nice
round insides that soothe the soul. It might
take a year for someone to open the drawer.
It would be either a mother or her son;
the mother would be mad with cleaning, her fingers
would itch to get at the inside of that furniture
and rub some oil into the corners, the son
would long to take the piece apart, to loosen
the stag, to free the eagle, to find a dime
inside the hidden drawer. This would be before
she turned to books and he turned to motorcycles;
or it would be a musician, someone who loves
to touch old wood. It never would be a poet—
they are all blind—who pulls the drawer and finds
my secret words. For any of these three,
here is the white pen I am writing with,
here is my yellow tablet, there are no
magic thumb prints, nothing that is not there,
only the hum, and I have buried that
on the piece of paper. It is a small envelope;
I always have one in my jacket; the words
are simple, half music, half thought, half tongue, half tear,

and made for the pocket book or the hip pocket,
or the inside of a wallet—I like that best—
folded up, and there are broken words,
or torn, hanging onto the threads, the deep ones
underneath the flap, the dark ones forever creased,
the song half hovering in that cloth lining
as if a moth were struggling out of the leather,
half caught between the money and the poetry,
little white one in the ravaged world.

Neither English nor Spanish

for Heidi Kalafski

It was when I went out to get an angry soul
a little cool and a little windy. Some bird
was clacking his beak or maybe rubbing his gums
together either for singing or for crushing
a watery insect. I was driving with one sister
to find another and the car we drove in
was huge and fast and dangerous. I thought
the darkness we drove in was something like daylight although
the lights on the body seemed more like lamps, just lighting
the ten or twelve feet in front of us. It is
the madness of northern New Jersey I'm describing,
a sulphur day and night, a cloud of gas
always hanging above us. We drifted down
to Newark, there were clusters of people in front of
every bar and drug store, they were mostly
very young, as if the population over twenty
had disappeared and the care of life and the care of
the culture were in the hands of babies, all our
wisdom, our history, were in their hands. I stopped
over and over to ask directions, the language
they spoke was neither English nor Spanish, they either
pointed in some odd direction or stood there staring.
I bounced up over the curb into a radiant
gasoline island; there was a psycho-pomp
in a clean white suit who calmed me down and told me
where the phone booth and the park was I wanted.
His English was perfect. I was shocked to see him
in a job like that, reaching over and wiping
the mist away, holding his hand on the pump,

staring at nothing. He should have been a lawyer
or engineer, but he was black, although
he could have been a student. I gave him a tip
and turned around. This time I found the park
in half a minute but there was nothing in sight,
not even a police car with its fat dog yowling
or some stray bleak berserker on the burnt grass.
I locked the car, the other sister sat there
trembling. I tried to smile. I found a dime,
and then a quarter, for my phone call. I stood there
on the sidewalk holding the black receiver
and listening to noisy insects. The sweet life
outside is different from the life of the car.
I suddenly wanted to walk. I wanted to touch
the trees, or sit on the ground. There was a ringing
but no one answered, as I recall. I shouldn't
have made a mystique of that but I was shouting
"bad connection" to myself and "vile connection"
and "fake connection," all that we hold dear
in twentieth-century evil communication.
That was where I could have lifted my fist
and played for the dirty trees, but I was tired
and struggling with the stupid lock, a Ford
Galaxy Superba. Anyhow, I got bored
with the park and its shadows, I did a fainthearted dance,
a mild frenzy on the sidewalk, and sang me
a primitive note, a long moaning note,
as I put my car into "drive," the lever hanging
somewhere in oblivion, the meshes

ruined, no right connection between the orange
letters and the mushy gears.
                                     This was
my futile descent into Newark. We returned
empty-handed, empty-hearted. I smoked
a single cigarette in the blackness and ranted
against New Jersey, as if there was a difference
between one land and another. That dear girl
we looked for would be sitting in the kitchen,
surrounded by her family, thin and exhausted,
full of terror, her mind erasing one horror
after another; and I would hold her and kiss her
along with the others. We would be some tragic
group somewhere, someone would boil water,
and we would talk all night, even end up laughing
a little before the streaks of light and the morning
noises brought us to our senses. I turned
right where I had to turn right and found the buried
driveway as always. I was right, the kitchen
lights were burning and there were cars and trucks
parked wildly in the yard. I looked at the dawn
behind the A&P and the pizzeria—
that takes two seconds in New Jersey—and climbed
over a sled, a tire and an ironing board—
I who saw the dead and knew the music—
and opened the door to that embattled kitchen
and shook hands all around, I and the sister.

I Am in Love

Everyone who dances understands what I am doing,
standing for hours in front of the card catalogue
and walking up and down the black riverbank.
He understands it how I stop and gesture,
that talking to the dead, and how I make
a face for every age, a vile one for ours,
a sweet one for one I half forgot, a wrinkled one
for the one that is Peruvian and a smooth one
for the one that is Egyptian. I have been working
among the O's; I started with Orpheus
and have been there for months; there are some libraries
where you can live in the stacks, you bring your lunch
and sleep on the heated floor. My scholarship
is hectic, I can start with an O and stray
to everything in sight, Pound and paideuma,
Palladio—I steal that from my son—
his trips through Italy, his view of the sky.
There is a dance in which I sit for one hour
with warm milk in my hands, the furnace is roaring
and just outside the window one or two cars
are driving by in the darkness. In it I either
find a book, or I find a piece of paper
and a yellow pencil. I sway a little and moan
all to myself. When I am done, when the milk
is done, I stand and bow to the shopping bag,
to the Sears rug—I have an audience—
and climb the fifteen steps with my head down
and my legs dragging—another dance. I have
a helpless fascination with myself,

I love to watch myself when I climb stairs,
or when I drink that milk. I stay alive
that way, I am amazed at myself. I have
no power over it, whether I'm lying and sleeping
or lying awake and staring. Sometimes I sit
like a stone, I do the lines of wind and rain,
sometimes I do the birch tree searching for the sun,
sometimes I do Route 30. I am in love.

My Favorite Demon

My favorite demon holds me by the hair
and gnaws behind my ear. Though one hand digs
into my neck, the other holds my head
almost lovingly and her deep frown
is only the frown of concentration. My lips
are full and red and my face is gaunt. My eyes
are closed as if to receive the pain. A tear,
always the tiny symbol, rests on the bridge
before descending, as it must, to the valley
between the cheek and the lip, or sometimes even
down to the tip of the nose. There is a tail
somewhere out in front and a pair of horns
protruding from the lobes, although her face
is human, and aside from the gnawing and sucking
she is almost kind. My own joy was
walking and thinking. I had a fascination
with secret knowledge. Also I sighed and moaned.
Also I hated controversy. Mostly
I was slow in learning and slow in changing,
but that had nothing to do with chewing and gnawing—
at least I think not. If anything it was
the closeness I loved, as ludicrous as that sounds,
and if we chose each other, if I chose her,
if she chose me, it was for the closeness. Imagine
calling that love, the skin ripped off and the red
bones exposed, such wild distortion, my head
half rolling, half bouncing, imagine my eyes, imagine
them pleading, imagine my screaming, I, the soul
of sanity, caught up in violence and sorrow.

Another Insane Devotion

This was gruesome—fighting over a ham sandwich
with one of the tiny cats of Rome, he leaped
on my arm and half hung on to the food and half
hung on to my shirt and coat. I tore it apart
and let him have his portion, I think I lifted him
down, sandwich and all, on the sidewalk and sat
with my own sandwich beside him, maybe I petted
his bony head and felt him shiver. I have
told this story over and over; some things
root in the mind; his boldness, of course, was frightening
and unexpected—his stubbornness—though hunger
drove him mad. It was the breaking of boundaries,
the sudden invasion, but not only that, it was
the sharing of food and the sharing of space; he didn't
run into an alley or into a cellar,
he sat beside me, eating, and I didn't run
into a trattoria, say, shaking,
with food on my lips and blood on my cheek, sobbing;
but not only that, I had gone there to eat
and wait for someone. I had maybe an hour
before she would come and I was full of hope
and excitement. I have resisted for years
interpreting this, but now I think I was given
a clue, or I was giving myself a clue,
across the street from the glass sandwich shop.
That was my last night with her, the next day
I would leave on the train for Paris and she would
meet her husband. Thirty-five years ago
I ate my sandwich and moaned in her arms, we were

dying together; we never met again
although she was pregnant when I left her—I have
a daughter or son somewhere, darling grandchildren
in Norwich, Connecticut, or Canton, Ohio.
Every five years I think about her again
and plan on looking her up. The last time
I was sitting in New Brunswick, New Jersey,
and heard that her husband was teaching at Princeton,
if she was still married, or still alive, and tried
calling. I went that far. We lived
in Florence and Rome. We rowed in the bay of Naples
and floated, naked, on the boards. I started
to think of her again today. I still
am horrified by the cat's hunger. I still
am puzzled by the connection. This is another
insane devotion, there must be hundreds, although
it isn't just that, there is no pain, and the thought
is fleeting and sweet. I think it's my own dumb boyhood,
walking around with Slavic cheeks and burning
stupid eyes. I think I gave the cat
half of my sandwich to buy my life, I think
I broke it in half as a decent sacrifice.
It was this I bought, the red coleus,
the split rocking chair, the silk lampshade.
Happiness. I watched him with pleasure.
I bought memory. I could have lost it.
How crazy it sounds. His face twisted with cunning.
The wind blowing through his hair. His jaws working.

The Blink of an Eye

Twilight is like the blink of an eye;
this one comes in and this one goes out
and it is impossible to grasp.
I stand with day behind me and night ahead.
There is the sun and there is the moon, both moving
across the sky. I stretch my hand for silence
before I put my fingers up to straddle
the two orbs. If I can bend down I'll touch
my forehead to some stone. If I can remember
the music I will sing although the words
may be a little shaky. What is the thought
between two states? Which way should I turn? Deliver me,
I say to the sun, deliver me, to the moon.
It is the hour of love, I walk on the white
highway north of the city; I have abandoned
my Datsun, there is a field of wagons, there is
a valley of trees, an ice pond, a windmill. I walk
behind two calves, they are in a pickup, they slide
in terror, one is a dirty white, one is
a dirty black and white, their eyes are wild,
darkness will save them, sleep will save them. This way
is best, walking behind the calves. I have
my story. I have been walking here for an hour,
I am thinking of twilight. I am studying
the mountains of dust and the clouds. I am living
on the edge of total blackness. It is the time
it takes to walk two miles, at this time of year
at such and such a height in such a place.
I can see the yellow bands with borders

of red and purple, there is ice in the ditches
and wind inside the trees. I have my story
in case I'm stopped by a farmer or a state trooper,
in case a calf should splinter the wood, in case
Rabbi Akiba should stop me or Rabbi Judah,
asking about night and the first three stars,
testing me on purification and prayer,
in late February, outside Iowa City,
between one long-faced birthday and another.

Making the Light Come

My pen was always brown or blue, with stripes
of gold or silver at the shaft for streaks
of thought and feeling. I always wore the nib
on the left side. I was a mirror right-hander,
not a crazy twisted left-handed cripple,
trying to live in this world, his wrist half broken,
his shoulder shot through with pain. I lived by smiling,
I turned my face to the light—a frog does that,
not only a bird—and changed my metal table
three or four times. I struggled for rights to the sun
not only because of the heat. I wanted to see
the shadows on the wall, the trees and vines,
and I wanted to see the white wisteria
hanging from the roof. To sit half under it.
Light was my information. I was an immigrant
Jew in Boston, I was a Vietnamese
in San Jose, taking a quick lunch hour,
reading Browning—how joyous—I was worshiping
light three dozen years ago, it led me
astray, I never saw it was a flower
and darkness was the seed; I never potted
the dirt and poured the nutriments, I never
waited week after week for the smallest gleam.
I sit in the sun forgiving myself; I know
exactly when to dig. What other poet
is on his knees in the frozen clay with a spade
and a silver fork, fighting the old maples,
scattering handfuls of gypsum and moss, still worshiping?

It Was a Rising

It was a rising that brought the worms. They came
when the bodies came, the air was muddy, it was
a small mistake, the fingers were gone, the lips
were eaten away—though I love worms, they have
bags on their backs and pointed sticks, they come
by the thousands, they can clean a beach in an hour,
they can clean the ground of fruit and bottles,
paper and plastic. I was a worm once, I wore
an olive uniform, my specialty was Luckies,
I speared them by threes, I hooked a bone to a cup,
I caught the silver foil. The rain when it comes
forces the worms to the surface; that is another
rising but not as cataclysmic. Love
of one thing for another brought them up,
and love will bring them back. This is the flesh
that dies and this is the flesh that lives. The bone
at the base of the spine is called the almond, it is
the nucleus of our birth. I had my chance
when the worms were in the air. I went out swimming,
I started to float, I held my arms up sideways
and let myself be eaten. I lie on the beach
planning my future. I am a mile away
from the motors out there and I am a yard away
from the wet footprints. There is a bird half crying
and there are the waves half moaning, these are the sounds.
My nose alone is showing, most of my head
is buried, I should have a straw in my mouth
to breathe with and a periscope for my eye
to see the flags and see the derrick. I lie

in coldness, only my lips are burning; I crack
my blanket, I am free again, I rise
with sand on my shoulder, stomach, thighs. The calcium
ruins my arm; I try to wipe my back
and scream in pain; I crash into the water;
it is my justice there, in the blue, in the brown,
and I am happy. I find my stone with one breath
and rub the hatchings. It is a rolled-up scroll.
It is a book. I swim a few short lengths,
to Ireland and back, and end up walking the planks.
It is either the dream of Asbury Park
where it is built on clouds and there are cherubs
holding it end on end, or it is the city
itself, a state senator at one end,
a Confederate Legionnaire at the other,
in front of Perkins, with an unlined notebook,
ready for my own visionary window,
ready for a whole morning of sunlight and silence.

Hobbes

I am here again
walking through the long-term parking,
fighting the cold.
My mind is on Hobbes,
how he would fare on the small bus,
what luggage he would carry,
what he would do with his meanness.
I climb the two steps
and with my two red eyes
I make peace with the driver.
He will drop me at Piedmont
and I will drag myself to another counter
and another nasty and brutish computer.
All is poor and selfish
sayeth the monster;
only pride and fear of death
move us.
I hold my little contract in my hand
and walk down the ramp all bloody and sovereign.
I give my number up
and lie down in my padded seat
and tie myself in.
After a while I will be warm and happy,
maybe when breakfast is carried in,
maybe lunch;
and though Hobbes be with me
I will sing in my seat
and fall asleep over Kansas and southern Utah.
I will wake in the dark

and put my left shoe on over one mountain
and my right shoe on over another.
When the time comes
I will put my ugly suitcase in the narrow aisle
and wait for the bodies in front of me.
He who meets me, or she,
will know me by my flower
or the lines around my eyes
or my wolf walk,
and I will be his or hers forever,
three full days or more.
I will live in the sunshine
and breathe the air
and walk up and down the brown grass
and the white cement.
I will keep the beast
in my breast pocket
or the inside of my briefcase
next to the wine stain and the torn satin.
Going back
I will reconsider all my odd connections
and prepare for that long slow descent
through Altoona and Harrisburg and Whitehouse, New Jersey,
by whispering and sighing as always.
If Hobbes is there
we will get on the Long Term bus together
and I will be his—or hers—forever,
two or three minutes or more,

at least until we reach the shelters.
I have my number in one of my twelve pockets
and he has his.
He sings, you know, in bed,
and still plays tennis,
not so bad for an Englischer.
We drift apart on Route 22
and Route 24, going west and east.
This was a lifetime friend,
although we'd be apart sometimes for years.
I know no one
who loved his own head more.
I'll tell this story:
when Charles II turned against him
he stayed in bed for seven days and nights
murdering bishops.
He wrote a complete version of the *Iliad* and the *Odyssey*
when he was ninety.
He never gave up his wild attempt
to square the circle.
I make the turn on Route 78
singing Villa-Lobos.
I am a second soprano.
Life has been good the past eight years,
the past two months.
I write a letter to myself
on force and fraud in the twentieth century.
I write a long and bitter poem

against the sovereign,
a bastard, whoremonger and true asshole,
as always, my darling.

Grapefruit

I'm eating breakfast even if it means standing
in front of the sink and tearing at the grapefruit,
even if I'm leaning over to keep the juices
away from my chest and stomach and even if a spider
is hanging from my ear and a wild flea
is crawling down my leg. My window is wavy
and dirty. There is a wavy tree outside
with pitiful leaves in front of the rusty fence
and there is a patch of useless rhubarb, the leaves
bent over, the stalks too large and bitter for eating,
and there is some lettuce and spinach too old for picking
beside the rhubarb. This is the way the saints
ate, only they dug for thistles, the feel
of thorns in the throat it was a blessing, my pity
it knows no bounds. There is a thin tomato plant
inside a rolled-up piece of wire, the worms
are already there, the birds are bored. In time
I'll stand beside the rolled-up fence with tears
of gratitude in my eyes. I'll hold a puny
pinched tomato in my open hand,
I'll hold it to my lips. Blessed art Thou,
King of tomatoes, King of grapefruit. The thistle
must have juices, there must be a trick. I hate
to say it but I'm thinking if there is a saint
in our time what will he be, and what will he eat?
I hated rhubarb, all that stringy sweetness—
a fake applesauce—I hated spinach,
always with egg and vinegar, I hated
oranges when they were quartered, that was the signal

for castor oil—aside from the peeled navel
I love the Florida cut in two. I bend
my head forward, my chin is in the air,
I hold my right hand off to the side, the pinkie
is waving; I am back again at the sink;
oh loneliness, I stand at the sink, my garden
is dry and blooming, I love my lettuce, I love
my cornflowers, the sun is doing it all,
the sun and a little dirt and a little water.
I lie on the ground out there, there is one yard
between the house and the tree; I am more calm there
looking back at this window, looking up
a little at the sky, a blue passageway
with smears of white—and grey—a bird crossing
from berm to berm, from ditch to ditch, another one,
a wild highway, a wild skyway, a flock
of little ones to make me feel gay, they fly
down the thruway, I move my eyes back and forth
to see them appear and disappear, I stretch
my neck, a kind of exercise. Ah sky,
my breakfast is over, my lunch is over, the wind
has stopped, it is the hour of deepest thought.
Now I brood, I grimace, how quickly the day goes,
how full it is of sunshine, and wind, how many
smells there are, how gorgeous is the distant
sound of dogs, and engines—Blessed art Thou,
Lord of the falling leaf, Lord of the rhubarb,
Lord of the roving cat, Lord of the cloud.
Blessed art Thou oh grapefruit King of the universe,

Blessed art Thou my sink, oh Blessed art Thou
Thou milkweed Queen of the sky, burster of seeds,
Who bringeth forth juice from the earth.

A Garden

for Gretchen Caracas
and Howard Rogovin

This was my garden in 1985,
a piece of jade in a plastic cup, a bell jar
full of monarchs, a bottle of weeds, a Jew
hanging out of a glass, and one live flower,
a thin geranium in a jar of water,
the roots in slime, the brown leaves on the surface,
half reaching up for light and down for shadows.

I lived in the kitchen—all day—moving between
the stove and the sink, between the clock and the door.
I sat at the table reading, one foot over
a painted chair, an eye on the window, a pencil
pulling and pushing, helping me think, a bent
and withered daisy, dead for days, sticking out
of a brass vase, a postcard hanging over me.

I watered a few things, sometimes I moved the weeds
to the left, the jade to the right, sometimes I cleaned
the two sea shells and wiped a bottle, but mostly
I studied the Jew or lifted the jar of monarchs
and shook a little dust down. They were my tulips,
if anything was, my gory roses, just as
the twisted geranium was my hollyhock

and the bottle of weeds my phlox or my rhododendron.
I had no milkweed—there was a weakness. Next year
I'll plant a seed in a plastic glass. And I had
no parsley. Other than that I lived all summer
with a crowded windowsill and a dirty window;
as if I could find a little intelligence there
and a little comfort, as if I could find some refuge

between the shells and the coffee can, some pleasure
among the red petals, and even some in the leaves
that hang down over the sink; and as if I could find
five seconds of richness, say, as I bent my head
to taste the water, five seconds of pity, say,
as I wiped away the bugs, as I loosened a root,
or cleaned a leaf or found another bottle.

No Longer Terror

In the sunset glow and early twilight and first star-sprinkling
I start to wander again. That way when the gloom
comes I can be in the hills, when darkness
is in the trees I can be in the open
with all that light going up and down, the pink
and yellow streaks, the variations, I can
come back to the lilacs and the wooden fence
before it's dark. I sit for three straight evenings
in a basket chair above the vines, my eyes
go over the roofs, I only look at shadows.
I spend my whole day waiting for this. There is
a bat and a dove. I have my choice; there are
the insects, it is May—the end of April—
there are no flowers but the tiny leaves
are curled and shining, as if there were; the grapes
will be here soon, they will be green at first
and then they will be black; the leaves will hide them,
the leaves will be like a roof. I will reach under
and pull at the stalks. I sit two feet away,
there is a ledge for my coffee, there is an urn
with dead leaves in the dirt. I put my book
on top of the leaves; on June twenty-first the light
will last another hour, it could be two
except for the clocks, there will be birds and bird song,
a little more wind than now, the train will roar
as it does now, only it will be daytime,
an hour from now—or two. I walk inside
when it gets dark. On my small porch there is
no lamp. I live by daylight, and dusk; Eurydice

is weeping on the radio, she has just
tramped on the snake and she is waiting to die;
Orpheus is singing in contrapunto.
Tomorrow I will look at the top three wires
and count the birds; the curtains in the living room,
I could watch that for hours. I put my head
on a heavy grey pillow—there are three others—I listen
to one thing and another, tomorrow morning
I will go back to my chair, life will be different,
it will be early, I will sit there reading
for hours, eating, answering the phone. At night
I'll wait for a certain light, I'll wait for the moon
to come between those houses, I'll wait for the sun
to leave, to have those two great hours, three,
if you count the shadows. What I will do depends
on the clouds and the dust. If there is a purple light
I will walk out again to see it, maybe
touch some bush or look at an insect still eating
and crawling at that hour, if it is a dull light
with a little yellow coming through—and green—
I will just sit there. I think the last thing I'd see
would be the clouds, a little yellow and pink
and a little whitish blue beyond the garages—
an hour earlier there. It is the darkness
I'm waiting for. Sometimes there is a glow
as if it were acid, sometimes it's black, that moonless
black, I feel my way, I stumble over
a plant and a table, I bang my knee on a trunk,
I trip on a rug. It is that last five minutes

I love, that last five seconds. I feel the wall
as I leave my chair—there I was sitting in darkness,
there I was starting to moan, I didn't even know,
I thought there still was daylight. I stood beside
the lamp, I rubbed the brass, I had to decide
whether or not to pull the chain. I stood
in front of the windows, there were thirteen plants
either hanging or on the window seats,
or on a table in front of the window seats,
a little forest; maybe there were eleven,
I watered them once a week; I saw their shapes,
even a little detail. There was some light
coming from the south, there were some stars,
some houses—somewhere—I looked out the side window,
I thought I saw some grapes, the leaves were brushing
against the screen, they were huge, there was a stick
holding the window up, there was a carpet
on top of the trunk—there may be just a board
from window to window, and not a window seat;
these plants will flower; outside the wind is blowing;
the last thing I see will be a green VW;
the last thing I see will be a cut-glass bottle,
blue I think; the Volkswagen is black,
the license plate is green; the last thing I'll do
is touch the plant above me; the last thing I'll do
is take my shoes off. Ah I still wear shoes,
though I am alone, I still wear socks and a shirt
with every button buttoned, I eat my meals
course by course, as if I were in a restaurant,

though I am alone, either thinking about the Greeks
or thinking about the bees gorging themselves
or—like tonight—thinking about the light,
how long it stayed, how long I will be in darkness,
how I couldn't lose a second, how sometimes I knelt
with my elbows on a chair to see the sky,
what joy it gave me, walking into the bedroom,
closing both doors, propping up the window.

Nobody Else Alive

Nobody else alive knows the four heart sounds
and nobody touches the four soft places
and raises his wing to look for lice; and nobody
else sees himself as one of the skeletons
with another old white one in his arms
or looks for his keys in the long-term parking
and ends up with his pockets inside out
and his head pounding from the iron telephone pole.

Nobody is as clumsy.
Nobody breaks his darling's six new wineglasses
with a yellow sponge
or spills a pitcher of ice over his warm hand
or rubs his puzzled fingers over the butter
looking for paper.
Nobody carries his small notebook with such sorrow
and crosses his bloody femurs with such joy.

Knowledge Forwards and Backwards

This was city living in the 1930s,
making machine guns out of old inner tubes,
fighting above the garages. It was peaceful
killing and spying and maiming; sometimes we smoked
cigars, or roasted potatoes—we used gloves
to reach into the coals; sometimes I put
a cinder to my lips, a charred and filthy
piece of wood, then stirred through the fire hunting
my lost potato. We were not yet assimilated,
nothing fit us, our shoes were rotten; it takes
time to adjust to our lives, ten and twelve years
was not enough for us to be comfortable—
after a while we learn how to talk, how to cry,
what causes pain, what causes terror. Ah, we had
stars, in spite of the sulphur, and there was dreaming
as we came into the forties. I remember
the movies we went to—I am spending my life
accounting now, I am a lawyer, the one
with blood on his lips and cash in his pockets. I reach
across for the piece of paper, it is cardboard
from one blue shirt or another, there are columns,
I whistle as I study them. There is
a seal on the boardwalk, just about the size
of a tiny burro, the one I rode was blind
and circled left, the miniature golf is the same,
the daisies are there on the seventh hole, the palms
are crooked as always, the fences are rusted, the windmills
are painted blue and white, as always, the ocean
is cold, I hated the ocean, Poseidon bounced me

over and over, I was gasping then,
trying to get a breath, and I am gasping
now, my rib is broken, or bruised, the muscle
inside the bone, or over the bone. I have
a hundred things to think about, my mind
goes back, it is a kind of purse, nothing
is ever lost. I wait for the pain to change
to pleasure, after a while my lips will stop moving,
I will stop moaning, I will start sleeping, one day
there is an end, even if at this end
there is lucidity and gruesome recollection
and I am paying for every red mark and blue mark.
I have the calendar in front of me;
I have the pencil at my lips, but no one
can live in place of us, there is no beast
on the seventh hole to save us; the grass is false,
it is a kind of cellophane, it is
produced in shops, above garages, maybe
in spare bedrooms or out of car trunks; there is
no spirit with her finger on her forehead
and her mouth open; there is no voice for sobbing
so we can sob with it a little, although—
and I am only beginning to feel this—I am
accumulating—what could I call it, a shadow?—
I am becoming a kind of demon, you turn
into a demon, with knowledge forwards and backwards,
backwards, forwards, you develop a power,
you develop a look, you go for months
with sight, with cunning, I see it in older men,

older women, a few of them, you stand
at some great place, in front of the Port Authority
or facing the ocean, you see the decade in front of you,
you see yourself out there, you are a swimmer
in an old wool suit, you are an angry cabbie,
you are a jeweler, you are a whore, the smell
of burned pretzels is everywhere, you walk
backwards and forwards, there is a point where the knot
is tied, you touch your fingers, you make a cage,
you make a roof, a steeple, at last you walk
forwards and backwards, your shirt is thin, your elbows
are getting longer, you are a type of demon,
you can go forth and forth, now it's the ocean
now it's the Port Authority, now you are sixty,
standing behind the pretzel man, amazed
at the noise around you, amazed at the clothes, amazed
at the faces; now you are twelve, you stand in a little
valley of water, you study the sand, you study
the sky, it was a violent journey, you end up
forgetting yourself, you stand at some place, there are
thousands of places, you stand in the Chrysler Building
beside the elevators, you stand in a lookout
on Route 78, you stand in the wooden post office
in Ocean Grove, in front of the metal boxes;
it is a disgrace to dance there, it is shameful
snapping your fingers, if we could just be singers
we'd walk down Main Street singing, no one as yet
has done this, three and four abreast, the language
could be Armenian, it could be Mohawk—

that is a dream too, something different from Whitman
and something different from Pound. What a paradise,
in front of the Quaker Inn, the women are watching,
I'm singing tenor, someone is taking a picture.
For me, when there is no hierarchy, for me,
when there is no degradation, when the dream
when lying is the same as the dream when walking,
when nothing is lost, when I can go forth and forth,
when the chain does not break off, that is paradise.

Two Moons

I'm looking at the moon, I'm half resting
on my right knee until the water settles.
There is a tree in the upper left-hand corner,
there is a house beside it. No one is watching,
I'm dying out here in the cold, I move my leg,
my knee is muddy, I shift to the other knee,
there are some waves between the cracks, there is
some grass inside the windows, it is marsh grass,
the blades are thick and sharp; I lean half over
to see my face, it is that Jewish face,
or Slavic face, that Spanish, I am grieved
by the lines around the eyes and by the fat
around the neck, around the chin; I stir
the water a little, near the mouth, a light
is coming on somewhere, someone is watching
me having my heart attack or dropping my key;
the moon is in its final phase, it drips
thick milk, there is a branch that looks like a calf,
it suckles the moon, it digs its feet in the ground,
its eyes are wild, the slaver is on its chin;
I have been still enough, I stand on my feet,
I stamp a little, the light goes out, I howl
silently, silently, I have learned that from dogs,
though I have learned when not to howl, I learned that
from parents and teachers, clerks and principals,
dentists and rabbis, doctors and lawyers—I hear
baying in Chile and baying in Africa,
men look up and see the moon, they scream
from pain, their backs are smashed, their faces are swollen,

their eardrums are broken, their genitals are purple,
there are welts from their shoulders to their buttocks,
they have been drinking gasoline—it is
too brilliant to bear, it should be dark, such beauty
is agonizing. There is a telephone wire
above the house, and a cigarette butt on the chimney
beside the grass, wet and useless. I drop
a stone in for a hurricane, there was
too much of crystal, I will leave when the sirens
go off, there will be a truck or an ambulance,
I will play footsie with the girl beside me,
she is nine, ah those are the girls that know me,
and love me and understand me, their poor mothers
are nervous, helpless. I am thinking of Yeats,
and Keats and Pound, on beauty. Somewhere a general,
somewhere a tall policeman is looking at the moon,
he wipes away some blood from his boot, there is
a tooth, and a piece of tongue, caught in the laces,
he waits for his daughter, she is nine, he gives her
a gentle touch, how gentle he is. Somewhere
up there the dust is falling, I have read it,
somewhere valleys and mountains, somewhere lake beds—
Darling Li Po, I bend my lips to the moon,
I wait for the tide, I touch myself with mud,
the forehead first, the armpits, behind the knees,
clothes or no clothes; now I walk on my face,
I had to do that, now I walk on the wires,
now I am on the moon, I am standing
between two moons, always there are two moons,

one for us and one for them, we know it,
visiting famous hills, following shadows,
believing in water, bowing to sparrows, bowing
to white deer, refusing to shame the spirit.

Lyric

I wonder who has pissed here
and stared—like me—at those wild petunias
or touched a purple leaf from that small pear tree.

Has anyone lain down here
beside those red peppers
or under those weak elm withers
standing in shame there?

Dear God of that grape,
has anyone snapped off a little curlicue
to see if it's wood or wire
or stripped the bark off those thick vines
and leaned against that broken fence?

Has anyone put some old parsley in his mouth
to see what the taste is
or lifted a rose mum to his face
to see if he'll live forever?

My Favorite Farewell

There is a kind of mop hanging down from the tree.
It is a willow. It has its own sad branches
somewhere. There is a huge Greek crypt
in front of the tree and there are stairs going down
to some kind of darkness. In the other corner
there are three cypresses—they stand alone
against a light blue sky—and there are flowers
around the crypt and bushes on the hillside.

Sadness is everywhere. Hector is holding
his wife's thin wrist and staring into her eyes.
Her hand is hanging loosely on his neck
and she is holding back her tears. A plume
is sitting on his helmet and a beard
is hanging from his neck; his skirt is made
of gorgeous pelts and there are purple thongs
around his leg tied in a little ribbon.

What else? The nurse is holding the baby. He is
enormous. Andromache's robes are flowing.
There are pompoms on her shoes and disks
holding her sleeves up, and her girdle. Her hair
is wavy and hanging to her waist but the nurse's
is just below her fluted ear. Hector
is resting his right hand on a shield—it's more
like a lopsided wheel. He doesn't have a spear.

What else? There is a pond underneath the cypresses
and they are on a hill. There is an effort
at vegetation beside the pond. Hector's
sleeves are rolled up. Andromache is in motion.
The crypt is out of proportion; the background is missing
on the left side; the steps seem to go up
instead of down; there is a violet filagree
behind the steps; the pillars are covered with disks.

It is my favorite farewell. As I watch it
I know Achilles will tear the helmet off
and drag the body through the dust, and I know
his enemies will spit on him and stab
him and the dogs will feed on his blood. I pay
attention to these things. It is the only
life we have. I am happy to be here
in front of the silk work and embroidery

watching them say goodbye. They will have to
make do with their sentiments and banalities.
That is all they have. Their hands are clumsy.
Their hills are unconvincing. Their clouds are muddy.
They are lucky to have the cypresses
and they are lucky that there's a streak of blue
behind the willow. I press against the glass.
There is a nail stuck inside the silk

that adds another oddness to the painting,
that makes it flat and distant and ruins illusion—
if there was any illusion—although it may
have fallen from the backing and slid down
the sky and down the shield and through the ribbons
into the dirt. I kiss the baby goodbye.
I kiss the nurse goodbye. The snow is falling
and I will be walking in the street half buried

inside my overcoat. I remember
the ending now. They put his white bones
in a golden box and wrapped it in soft purple
before they covered it up with dirt and stones.
That was a nice farewell—Andromache sobbing,
Hecuba howling, Helen tearing her hair out.
I think it is the cypresses that moved me
the most although it is the mop-faced willow

that is the center of the grief. The cypresses
are like a chorus standing on top of the sky
and moaning—they are moaning about the wind
and moaning about the narrow steps; they sit
on the edge of a hill, they hardly are planted, they whisper
about Achilles: "Think of Achilles," they whisper.
"Think of his tapered spear, think of his shield
with three kinds of metal, thicker than a wrist,

heavier than a door, think of lifting it
and holding it up with one huge hand while the other
searches the air and dances"—I find it moving
in spite of the stiffness and pallor of the figures,
in spite of the missing leg and floating branches.
It is my fondness for those souls. It is
my love of childish trees and light blue skies
and flowing robes. I have to be forgiven.

For Once

It was in southern Florida I reached
my foot across to trap a soul. He strayed
from one orange tile to another; he would live
for twenty seconds under my shoe, then run
to his door and pant an hour or two. I watched him
climb his wall. He turned his head and stared.
He lifted one gluey leg, then another.

He was from Enoch, one of the little false ones
full of mathematics and wizardry,
a slave to the moon. We yodeled and sang together—
it was like scraping chalk—I touched his throat.
It was translucent. I could see the spiders
going down his gullet. "Just one more song," I sang,
and there, two blocks from the ocean, six thousand years
into our era, we stood on the street and shouted.

There was a sunset somewhere. Someone cranked
a window open, as if to listen. Beyond that
there were our noises, an airplane droning, a car
beginning a trip, a baby screaming, a woman
yelling in Spanish. We stood beside each other—
if you could call that standing, and speculated.
We were mediators. I rubbed his head
and his yellow eyes began to close. The two of us
were getting ready for something—I could tell that—
before we lost each other.
                              I was left
with the bougainvillaeas and the narrow sidewalk

and the chain-link fences and the creeping vines.
I kept the music secret, walking south
on the left side of the road, beside the mosses.
Our sound was southern, mixed a little with Spanish,
mixed a little with French, and Creole. For once
there was no Polish, or German. I was adjusting
to the dunes and swamps, although there was some forties,
and thirties too; the last thing I did was whistle
and ring the fences. I was alone now and wandered
up and down those streets. I thought of the tail;
I thought of the heart. I don't know about the heart,
how many chambers there are, how cold it gets,
where it shunts the blood to, what the pulse is,
if it's a *clumsy* heart, if it can love
like ours can, if it can be grown again, if food
destroys it and exercise renews it, if memory
can make it flutter, if passion can make it flow.

This I thought about going south on one street
and east on another, picking up coconuts
and holding them to my ear, tearing the fronds up
and wearing them like a shawl. It was a kind
of happiness, shrieking and hollering in the tropics,
watching my skin grow dry and my blood grow thin,
wandering through a forest of cypress roots,
finding someone that old and wise. I loved it.

Stolen Face

Piazza St. Andreas, Lucca, Italy

There is a face stolen from the twelfth century
I come back to over and over. I wait for
the train for hours and hours, sometimes it's raining,
sometimes the sun is beating down—although I
like to wait for evening, there's that golden
light you get in some of the painters, cities
are in the distance, trees are small but clear,
there are tiny churches and walled-in saints
and miniature rivers and miniature clouds and mountains.
The eyes are a little crossed and the head is thrust
forward, in either stupidity or terror—
I'll say that now—although it could be curiosity
that made him stretch his neck like that. There is no
neck, of course, there is a moon face, a disk,
that is the last link in a frieze, the bottom
of an arch—I think it was taken from something else
and put there—and it matches another disk
at the other side of the arch, although the other
face for me is insignificant
compared to the first. For one thing the stone lion
underneath it *hides* the face and even
casts a little shadow over it
in almost every light. There are *two* lions,
one on the left and one on the right, each of them
is standing over a man, their looks are vague
and even aloof; it is the look of a cat
straddling a rat, he knows every move but seems
almost bored. The man on the right is terrified,
his eyes are bulging, his hands are holding on,

one to the lion's leg, one to his paw;
the one on the left is twisted sideways, his right hand
is holding the lion's mouth, his left the paw—
the very same place. The hair on the left is wavy,
the man's hair and the lion's; the hair on the right
is curled, all of it, mane and beard and forehead;
and there are other lions—with rats—in sets,
just like this one; one has a fat stone snake
under his belly, one has another lion,
a mirror lion, biting and snarling. The face
on the right, above the lion, has a pipe
coming out of the mouth, and he is cross-eyed.
I don't know if it's part of a drainage system,
a kind of fountain, or a huge cigar,
either way the face is ugly. The eyes,
as I say, are crossed, and the cheeks are puffed a little
from blowing out water—or smoke—and the soul is drowned.

I know there are other faces like these faces
all over Lucca. In St. Martin's alone I counted
fourteen faces though most of them were covered
by scaffolding and netting. There are faces
like it on St. Michael facing the mountain
and there is a face on the front of St. Christopher
that stares at the sky as if it were drunk on sleeping
though none of them has the spirit of the one face.
They look as if they were being punished. One
has his mouth open, his teeth are showing, the lines
are carved in his jowls and forehead; one is screaming

because of some hidden terror, one is straining
with all his might to hold a pillar up.
They are like masks, these faces, carrying life
and death like masks do, they are like drawings, one line
crossing another line, just that, and the flesh
is suddenly there. There is a book I love,
a face with two lines on it showed it to me,
a face fat from sitting. It is a book
showing the faces of Jesus for five hundred years,
including the Botticelli at Bergamo,
including the Veronese at the Louvre,
including the Juan Juares at Madrid,
sometimes tender, sometimes thin and careworn,
sometimes broken with pain. Sodoma's Christ
is silent, the lips are open, horror and sadness
are in his eyes; Guercino's Christ is foolish,
huge drops of blood are trickling down his face,
his eyes are looking up, he is insipid
and full of self-pity. The Christ of Jan Van Eyck
is matter-of-fact and unemotional,
it is a portrait, someone stood in front of him
and stared at the window. Giorgione's Christ is thoughtful,
his eyes are full of light, his look is gentle,
the crown doesn't pierce his brow, there is no anguish,
nothing is sickly. It is the opposite.

Now I have eighty-nine steps to climb. Each landing
is another burden—you should forgive me—I gasp
at number four, at number five. How crazy

it is to climb someone else's steps. I'm tired
of always living this way. At every window
I touch my throat. What was it like to have
your own city? What is that round face doing
above its Renault? What is the rat doing staring
down at the shoemaker, down at the street cleaner?
This is my evening: I light the stove and boil
a little tea. I stare at St. Michael's—I live
behind the façade. I can see the steps
above the roof. It is as if the ceiling
were meant to be raised. St. Michael has his arm up,
he is letting the sun down. He has a wand,
his two assistants are playing horns. The snow
is always on the hills. I start to break
the sticks, we need some kindling, we need some paper,
the wood is hard and green, the chimney is crude,
it is the sky we heat, a little smoke
among the stars. I fool myself by blowing
air on the coals. I make a wobbly face
of smoke and fire. I put the nose in. It is
a Spanish face, ascetic and melancholic
and overcome with grief; it is a Dutch face,
almost coarse, wholesome and unimaginative,
not one nimbus, every line exact.
I stare at myself, the trick is finally to do it
without a mirror. The teeth have separated
a little, the hair is whiter, the neck is thicker,
but who would know that in this light? I put
the lines in the cheek—I think I like them wavy—

I am the one from Asbury Park, I am
the one from New Orleans, the one from France,
the one from Philadelphia. I believe
the Jews of Russia came from Asia, but the Jews
of Poland came from Spain and Africa.

Tomorrow I will wake up freezing. I'll get there
before the market is open, it is two blocks
east and two blocks south; the moon at six
in the morning is tired, his eyes are closed, the bulging
one follows my eyes, there is a cast in *his* eyes—
were they not crossed? He stares all night. The crudeness
must get to him. I listen. I learned that idleness
from Moses. I listen for a sound but nothing
comes—it is too hard to speak. I show him
my sack of old clothes, he likes that, I show him my permits
to trade with the East, I show him my medicines—
I am allowed to practice—I show him my bills
of lading—they are just old receipts but he is
impressed. I sit on the hood to hear his sermon—
ah, I will convert, believe me. This is the last
time we will see each other, or maybe I'll pass
him again with pears in one hand, wine in the other,
and only remember when I am walking past
the furniture store and stop to look in the window
or when I am sitting at one of the metal tables
under a striped umbrella, my pen half balanced
as if it were a spear, my paper white
from the morning sun. If he is a Lombard I

am happy, if he is something Byzantine I
am happy too. If we are allowed one face
it must be this one, hard and coarse as the eyes are,
thick as the nose is, round as the head is. I make
my way to the station walking like a lobster,
with ninety pounds on my back; the last thing I did
was visit that square again. I keep coming back
as if I would learn something, as if the next time
there would be a surprise. It took one second
and everything there was to know I knew.
Now I'm leaving. I walk down some steps. I'm dragging
my body through a tunnel. I'm counting to fifty
to make the load lighter. Now I'm counting to thirty.
I check my two main pockets. I shift the burden.
I practice a verb. I check my shoes for water.
I check my brain for air. I follow the arrows.

Steps

There are two hundred steps between my house
and the first café. It is like climbing a ladder.
I gasp and pant as if I were pulling a mule,
as if I were carrying a load of dirt. I do
the journey twice—I left the key in the car
the first time down. There is another hill
above the first—the road to the car—another
one hundred steps. But I was born in Pittsburgh
and I know hills; I know that second rise
after a leveling off; I know the gentleness
between the two pair of steps, I know the wear
at the center, if it is stone, the soft splinters,
if it is wood, and I know the broken spaces,
the rhythm stoppers—railroad ties—but even
worse, I know the broken heights, four inches
and then a foot, and then another foot,
or fourteen inches, and the curves that carry you
around and around. There is a street on the South Side—
Pittsburgh again—that goes up hundreds of feet.
It is a stairs. I walked until my thighs
had turned to stone; and there were walkways like that
on the side of streets and cars that only made it
partway up, some turned around, some facing
the houses, abandoned cars. I am in Samos,
a village called Stavrinidhes, halfway up
the mountain of Ampelos. The town of Ampelos
is two miles away, a forty-minute walk.
I sit all day and watch. The sea is on my left.
The hills are all around me. Today is the walk

to Manolates, an hour and a half by foot,
a little less by car; it is a mulepath
up and down the ridges. I like the streets
in Ampelos. You climb for fifteen minutes,
your legs go slower and slower; this time there is
the long slope, the slant between the steps,
no relief at all, and there are two steps
twenty-five inches apiece, and there is a stairs
with a tree at the top, it is a kind of pyramid,
a kind of throne, the tree is a king, it sits there
painted white, and there is a waterfall
of steps, it almost pours. I touch a window
on my left, I touch a curtain, there is a trumpet vine
in front of the house, there is wisteria—
a limb that stretches half a block—I touch
a cactus, I touch a telephone pole, I reach
the hill above the town. The thing about climbing
is how you give up. I sit on a rock. I am
in front of a mountain. There's a white horse behind me,
there's a two-foot cypress beside me, it's already
burdened with balls. I am waiting for Hera,
she was born on this island. Zeus must have roared
on every mountain, he must have lifted a pine tree
to make a bed for them, or scooped out a valley.
Ah, Lord, she was too full of anger. The clock
says something on one side, something else on the other.
It rises above the houses. There are some towns
in Pennsylvania like this, and West Virginia;
I have sat on mountains. Imagine Zeus

in West Virginia, imagine the temple to Hera
in Vandergrift, P.A. My heart is resting,
my back feels good, my breathing is easy. I think
of all my apartments, all that climbing; I reach
for a goldenrod, I reach for a poppy, the cross
is German more than Greek, our poppies are pale
compared to these. I gave up on twenty landings,
I gave up in Paris once, it was impossible,
you reach a certain point, it is precise,
you can't go further; sometimes it's shameful, you're in
the middle of a pair of stairs, you bow
your head, your hand is on the rail; your breath
is hardly coming; sometimes you run to the top
so you can stop at the turning, then your legs burn,
sometimes they shake, while you are leaning over
and staring down the well or holding your arm
against the wall. Sometimes the stairs are curved,
that makes a difference, sometimes the risers are high,
sometimes there are too many turns, your knees
cannot adjust in time. Sometimes it's straight up,
landing after landing. Like a pyramid.
You have to lean into the steps, you have to
kneel a little to stop from falling backwards.
I turn around to look at the mountain. There is
a little path going up, some dirt and stones;
it would take two more hours. The wind is almost
roaring here—a gentle roar—the ocean
is green at first, then purple. I can see Turkey.
Who knows that I have given up? I hear

two women talking, I hear a rooster, there is
the back of a chimney, seventy bricks, there is
a cherry tree in blossom, there is a privy,
three hundred bricks to a side, there is a cat
moaning in Greek. You would look at the cherry tree,
you would rest your feet on a piece of marble,
you would be in semi-darkness; there are
dark pink cherries on the roof, the bowl
is sitting on a massive base, the floor
is dirt, there is no door. I wave to a donkey,
I read his lips, his teeth are like mine, I walk
to the left to see the oven, I count the bricks,
I look at the clock again, I chew my flower.

Bread Without Sugar

1

Sylvia

What is Eros doing
standing naked among these gravestones almost
6,000 miles from Paphos?
What does he want *now*, another handful
of yellow hair, two blue eyes
and a spine in pain? How is it that he is standing
without a skullcap on? Does he
think it is he who will bring her in? Does he pine
for his mama, does he want to
simper, or stamp his foot, or scratch his back
with his tiny arrow? When was he last
in Pittsburgh, what does he think of these Jews reclining
off route 51? What is love now
doing with death and what is love now planning
in such a garden? What is desire
to him—and longing—what, when he lifts her, is in
his mind?—Where is my plot?—
And where will he take her? Does he think that love
destroys the world, does he think
that love is death, does he think that love
should drop his lyre and throw away
his torch, why does he have to be death too
and carry a vial of mint and a vial
of myrtle? Where does he stash his coins? Where is
Sylvia's meadow? How is this light the
light par excellence? Why is she buried so close
to Pete and Jenny Kaplan, was it
a truncated poplar or a truncated cyprus
that stood above her—was it limestone?

Was there a leaf on her tree? Was it too crowded
        in upper K? Eros should trip
over the graves of Libbie and Barrel Barach
        once he starts climbing. Eros should
tell me something; Eros should turn his worms
        around so they face north; he should
decide on one song, then he should sing, or he could
        let the plectrum decide. Eros
should cry when he lifts her, he should have wet cheeks
        this time—how does he get there, does he
land like a fly? What does he think of defilement?
        Eros should have her picture, he should
kiss her curls, he should brush her lips
        with medicine. Who was *his* sister?
How did *his* mama grieve? Is he more heartless
        as love or death? I think Sylvia's own granddaughter
would have touched her cheek and stroked her hair
        as she did her darling Libbie. As I did too.

Three Hearts

A chicken with three hearts, that is a vanished
breed, a day of glory in the corn,
romance against a fence. It was the sunset
just above New Egypt that made me wince,
it was the hay blown up from Lakewood. God
of chance, how much I loved you in those days,
how free I felt and what a joy it was
sitting there with my book, my two knees braced
against the dashboard. How empty it was then,
and how my mind went back. How many hearts
did the chickadee have? How much whistling and singing
was in those fields? How far did I have to go
to disappear in those grasses, to pick those trillium?

The Bull-Roarer

I

I only saw my father's face in butchery
once—it was a horror—there were ten men
surrounding a calf, their faces were red, my father's
eyes were shining; there might have been fewer than ten,
some were farmers, some were my father's friends
down from the city. I was nine, maybe eight;
I remember we slept a few hours and left
at four in the morning, there were two cars, or three,
I think it was West Virginia. I remember
the pasture, the calf was screaming, his two eyes
where white with terror, there was blood and slaver
mixed, he was spread-eagled, there was a rope
still hanging from his neck, they all had knives
or ice picks—is that possible?—they were beery,
drunk, the blood was pouring from the throat
but they were stabbing him, one of them bellowed
as if he were a bull, he was the god
of the hunters, dressed in overalls and boots,
the king of animals; they seemed to know—
some of them seemed to know—the tendons and bones,
they were already cutting and slicing, pulling
the skin off, or maybe that was later, I stood there
staring at them, my father with a knife;
we didn't even have a dog—my mother froze
whenever she saw one—we were living in Beechview,
we had the newest car on the street, it was
an ugly suburb, everything was decent,

there was a little woods, but it was locust,
it would be covered with houses, we didn't even have
a parrot, my father left at eight in the morning
and drove his car downtown, he always wore
a suit and tie, his shoes were polished, he spent
the day with customers, he ate his lunch
at a little booth, I often sat with him,
with him and his friends, I had to show off, I drew
their likenesses, I drew the tables and chairs,
it was the Depression, none of them had brass rings
hanging from their ears, they all wore socks,
and long-sleeved shirts, they ate and drank with passion.

II

My mother is eighty-seven, she remembers
the visit to the farm, there was her brother,
my uncle Simon, and there was his friend, MacBride,
Lou MacBride, he was the connection, he was
a friend of the farmer's, maybe a cousin. I asked her
about the killing—"that is the way those farmers
got their meat, they lived like that, they butchered
whatever they needed." I asked if she could remember
anything strange, was she nervous or frightened?
"There was the tail, they cut the tail off
and chased each other; it was like pinning the tail
to the donkey." Both of us laughed. I didn't have the heart
to mention my father's face, or mention the knife—

and, most of all, my pain. What did I want?
That he should stay forever locked inside
his gold-flecked suits? That he should get up in the dark
and put his shoes on with a silver knife?
That he should unbutton his shirts and stuff the cardboard
into a chute? That he should always tie
his tie with three full loops, his own true version
of the Windsor knot? And what did I want for myself?
Some childish thing, that no one would ever leave me?
That there would always be logic—and loyalty?
—I think that tail goes back to the Paleolithic.
I think our game has gory roots—some cave,
or field, they chased each other—or they were grimmer,
pinning that tail, some power was amassed,
as well as something ludicrous, always that,
the tail was different from the horns, or paws,
it was the seat of shame—and there was envy,
not just contempt, but envy—horns a man has,
and he has furry hands and he has a mane,
but never a tail. I remember dimly
a toy we had, a kind of flattened stone,
curved at the sides, with a long rope at one end
we whirled around to make a thundering noise.
This was a "bull-roarer"; we made thunder
and felt the power in our shoulders and legs.
I saw this toy in southern Italy;
I saw children throwing it over their heads
as if they were in central Australia

or ancient Europe somewhere, in a meadow,
forcing the gods to roar. They call it Uranic,
a heavenly force, sometimes almost a voice,
locked up in that whirling stone, dear father.

My Death for Now

I have settled down to watch the branches
growing vertically from two dead limbs.
It's what I do all day. I raise my left arm
and hunch my shoulder over. My leg is asleep,
which is my death for now, although sometimes
I raise both arms and let the fingers turn on
the vertical branches; then my hands are dead,
not just my leg. It is the middle of January
and there is a sheet of ice and there are berries
and leftover leaves and even a few old weed stalks.
I wave my fingers—there is a little wind—
I arch my neck—there is a twisted trunk
against a wire fence. It is a window
I sit in. I am marking a day for wisdom.
I give that to myself. I give myself
a day for mercy. I turn my hand around;
it is an amaryllis. The wrist is bent,
the fingers are spread. I give myself a basket;
I brought it from Pennsylvania; I put the flower
inside the basket. The wire is gorgeous. The handle
was rubbed by German farmers. It was filled
by yellow peaches. There is a certain dryness
that makes them small and juicy. Too much rain
will make them mealy, or stringy. I touch my lips
to the little leaves; it is the flower of fruits,
delicate, aromatic, yet they are heavy,
they weigh the basket down. I stretch my palms;
I look at them in awe. I straighten my fingers.
I bend for water. I drink the snow. I lie

on my stomach drinking snow. Two of the peaches
are bruised. I turn them around. I try to keep them
free of each other. I do it by concentration.
I blink one eye; and frown. That is the dream,
just sitting and thinking—frowning; that is the joke,
the juices running down. I bend like a bee,
I lean to the left, one hand is at my neck,
the other is on my cheek. I wipe my chin.
I may as well count the leaves—buried in the snow;
I might as well listen to the diesels or bring the
squirrels back and watch them dig. That was September,
the end of summer, my window was open, a dwarf
was singing in my bedroom, there were books
spread all over the porch, with pencils inside,
there were mosquitoes still, my birch was turning,
the noise was insane, birds were screaming, walnuts
were dropping on the roof. I might as well die
from the past; I might as well die from longing.

One Day an Arbor Vitae

I always went for natural shapes, I slid
on the mud to get away from my street, I ripped
my leather jacket on the hill hanging on
to a broken branch; I swung there, one foot turned,
one foot almost lost. It took me an hour
to find a certain willow; I say an hour
but it was more like twenty minutes. I went
to the roundhouse and back in fifteen or twenty minutes,
I went to the station itself in half an hour.
Six in the morning was my time, I picked up
three kinds of grass, I wrapped them in my notebook.
Once there was a truck, it was called
a stakesider, I think the bed lifted up;
the wheels were scattered, the cab was gone, a kind of
Eastern tumbleweed hung from the axle.
Once there was an opossum broken in two,
the head was wet from the rain, the tongue was rolling,
there was a pool of water in the thorax.

I always went to the bridge and back, there was a
white angora on the tracks, her bell
was jingling; I tried to keep her away from the carcass,
I tried to help the crows. There was a tire
buried in the mud, someone had thrown it
down, the leaves were planted inside it; I knelt there
hating the cat. I read the Sunday paper
standing on the rubbish. I broke a stick
before I climbed the hill, it helped me think,
one day it was a sword, one day a crutch,

one day it was a broom. I held it up
with two of my fingers, I smashed some branches, I cut
some ugly roots, it helped me sleep at night,
having it there beside my bed, leaving it
behind the door, either inside or outside.
One day it was an insect, one day a flutist
leaning with one arm out and one leg splattered;
one day an arbor vitae, one day a maple.

Brain of My Heart

Thank God for the walnut in 1986.
Thank God for the hard green shell and the greasy center.
All you, you thirty white worms and forty green grubs,
I know what you are, burrowing like pigs,
running like moles inside your bulging rooms.

I pick up a rubber ball, it may be a walnut
gone black on the sidewalk, it may have a hundred worms
drinking the juices and drying up the husks.
I do a Pittsburgh twist, a double-handed
reverse action, I learned it in three short hours.
I put my foot on the mound, the rubber juices
fall like blood on the street; I'm doing the fiend's work;
I kick the tennis balls. I drive my car
over the hard green stones, it is the bounce
I learned in Philadelphia, pebbles piled up
in every alley, a terrible screaming and wailing.

Deep in the recesses two yellow brains
are facing each other. They are like human brains,
the hills and valleys make an expanded surface,
the neurons are popping, the chemicals are charging,
the eyes are already staring, the mouth is running.

Deep in the recesses there is a Twelfth Crusade.
A murderous knight is already on his knees.
His right eye is gone, his left arm is lopped at the wrist,
the skin is sewn together. He is back
in Europe. He has given up. His murders

will take five years to repay, his shoulder is raw
from the leather. There are two heads at his belt,
he has combed their hairs. Their little tongues
are whispering, one has the grating voice
of Billie Holiday, one has the voice
of Jimmy Durante, one is tormented, one
is full of sappy wisdom. It is freezing,
winter has come in one day, the few brown leaves
will turn to pieces of ice. I start to huddle
inside my blanket. I start to store my blood,
my brain is moving south, my mind is wandering.

The Founder

There was a kind of drooping bronze head
I stole in the Catskills and put in my living room
in Philadelphia. I put a sledge hammer
beside it so my friends and I could smash him
and change his shape from thoughtful oppressor
to tortured victim. This was just to show
the close connection between the two, the liquid
life of Capitalism; we got to kick him,
we got to gouge his eyes out, we were elated
breaking his nose and flattening his ear; it was
a kind of funeral rite, sometimes the hammer
hummed in our hands, there was a jolt, his pain
was in our wrists; sometimes we were exhausted
from so much pounding; after a while his face
was old and twisted, it was a little shameful.
I finally sold him—by the pound, I think;
he was too ugly for us, too demented;
we were starting to turn to pity—we pitied
that bronze bastard, he who must have presided
over the burning of mountains, he who managed
the killing of souls, the death of every dream.

I reached inside once to get the brain
but it was only rough casting in there,
nothing to suck on, even though the cavity
was widened at the base of the skull. He was
a brainless founder, his eyes stared at the wall,
or if we turned him around his eyes stared
with a kind of wonder at the dining-room table

catching the pools of beer. I remember
it wasn't all raw Socialism and hatred
of the rich; there was a little terror in it.
I think sometimes I got out of bed early
and put a towel or a T-shirt over his face
to cover his eyes and his ugly deformities.
He was for a while a mutilated ancestor,
someone we had buried twice, a monster,
something that could ruin us. It took an effort
to put him on the back of a station wagon
and free ourselves from fright. I had to struggle.
Although I'm sorry I sold him, he deserved
to be buried somewhere. I should have driven
to one of the dumps and thrown him into a valley
between a sofa and a refrigerator,
or just gone into the woods and made a grave
between two birches and shoved him in. I'm glad
there wasn't a river; I would have dropped him
down in the muck with the black Budweiser,
and one cold spring the current would have carried him
through a park or into a muddy backyard
on top of the poison and the wild strawberries,
or carried him into the open, his crushed head
going faster and faster, turning around in the garbage,
his face forever swollen, his eyes squinting,
the sorrow coming from his metal lips,
the sun shining down, the melodies never ending.

The First Lewd Offering

I am one of the squirrels—I have a dogwood
in my breast pocket, I am *smitten*, I squeeze
the four red corners back together, I make
a purse to hold the seeds again. I tried
to *pluck* the flower, to snap it off, but there was
rage in the branches, there was glue, I had to
pull the wood loose, there is such brute strength
in a blossom. I had no idea the mouth
was in those leaves or there was a yellow brain
half buried under ground. I walk with greed
up every mountain, there is always a mark
of courtesy between us, I could turn it
to love if I wanted, the ground is so soft, the branches
are all so careful. There were thorns getting here,
there was water—at first—up to my ankles,
there was a wire fence. I lean my head
against a hemlock. There is no loyalty.
The honeysuckle will come, then the catalpa.
I will drink the nectar, I will study
the magic prints, one out of four is crimson—
it is the blood, I guess. If there was a tree
that kept me sane I know it was that one; if there
was a life it was that life. I first got the blossoms
in a brown envelope, the *blossoms* were brown—
and dry—I put them on my dashboard; that was
the first lewd offering; I was forgiven.

Nice Mountain

Great little berries in the dogwood,
great little *buds*, like purple lights
scattered through the branches, perfect wood
for burning, three great candelabra
with dozens of candles, great open space
for sun and wind, great view, the mountain
making a shadow, the river racing
behind the weeds, great willow, great shoots,
great burning heart of the fields, nice leaves
from last year's crop, nice veins and threads,
nice twigs, mostly red, some green and silky,
nice sky, nice clouds, nice bluish void.

I light my candles, I travel quickly
from twig to twig, I touch the buttons
before I light them—it is my birthday,
two hundred years—I count the buds,
they come in clusters of four and seven,
some are above me, I gather a bunch
and hold it against my neck; that is
the burning bush to my left, I pick
some flaming berries, I hang them over
my tree, nice God, nice God, the silence
is broken by the flames, the voice
is a kind of tenor—there is a note
of hysteria—I came there first,
I lit the tree myself, I made
a roaring sound, for two or three minutes
I had a hidden voice—I try

to blow the candles out, nice breath,
nice wagon wheel, great maple, great chimes,
great woodpile, great ladder, great mound of tires,
nice crimson berries, nice desert, nice mountain.

Love Is the Opposite

I carry the white head with me
and stare at it eye to eye. I'd say it's a
bobcat, not an opossum, I'd say it
trembled for half an hour once in a sweet gum
before it jumped; I'd say an opossum
had softer teeth, a flatter jaw, I'd say
that anger drifted through the species, that we were
lucky we learned it from the cats. For my part
I sit on a silken couch, there is a bolt
of extra cloth in the cellar once the stain
covers these cushions. If I had a tree
it would be a cottonwood, one long trunk,
to claw my way up, to hump and then pull, a narrow
limb, covered with leaves, for my two eyes
to hide behind, my eyes and my shoulders. Love
is the opposite, some kind of love, maybe tenderness,
maybe regret. I dig my claws in, the pads
would be enough but I have nails; I scream—
that is my way—I watch the curtains blow.
It takes a year for the flesh to go, for rage
to be reduced to fluff; some time next summer
I will be bleached—ah Yorick, I know you well,
you carried me in your pocket, ah opossum,
I carried *you*; your skull is the size of an apple,
my pockets are full, they are like cheeks; oh bobcat,
bobcat, you were betrayed, you are unloved,
you rage at yourself, you are an accomplice; oh bobcat,
you are in grief—and frightened—it is your death
you lick, you are humiliated, the stars

discarded you, the clouds withdrew. For a year
you shook, the leaves of the cottonwood curled up
as if the ground had lost its water. I know it
so well, for a year I shivered, and sighed, oh rabbit.

The Age of Strolling

I loved a certain period; I wore
an overcoat that came down to my ankles.
I carried a stick—a cane—I had that stiffness.
Now, to this day, whenever I take a picture,
I pose as if I were living then. I take
the world in with a glance, although you'd think
my eyes were riveted on a pin of light
or to a streak of dirt. There was a way
we ate then, there was a way we walked, we trundled,
we rolled, the hips in a line with the shoulders; it was
an age of strolling—who knows that word?—you lift
one leg at a time, your toes are pointed out,
your shoes have crease after crease. There were our cities,
there were our railroad stations, there were our newspapers,
Switzerland was our country. We used to sit there
behind our panes of glass; those were our mountains
we stared at, those were our crude and dirty cities.
Always there was one drama. I am spending
my life on that. I have the magazines,
I have the photographs. I think it was fear.
I used to call it happiness—nervousness—
that's what it was. My book was always Job.
Where can wisdom be found? Could we go out
and scrub some building down, a Gothic high school
with garbage on the staircase, one old light bulb
hanging from a wire? There in the branches
is Absalom the beautiful. A mule
was his undoing, he rode it into the woods
and he was taken up between heaven and earth.

It was a mule of great stupidity;
it was a prince of loveliness. They stuck
spears in his body; they were tipped with metal
to make him hemorrhage more; he was murdered
and buried in the woods. How could his head
be lifted up like that? Was it his hair
that ruined him? How could he hang without a word?
David was sitting in the gate; he saw
a messenger crawling across the field, he thought
it's like a beetle; he thought, it's like an ant;
there should be something white, there should be black,
there should be a bird. He climbed into the room
above the gate. He thought of Absalom's mother.
His body began to shake—the king of music—
he thought of the Philistine giants. What is a giant?
He thought of Saul. How just he had been. He thought
of Bathsheba—and poor Uriah. What was his God
doing to him? Where would the messenger stand?
Should he not kneel? Should he not prostrate himself?
—I think myself there was a trap; Absalom
was snapped up into the sky. I saw a zebra
hanging like that—a photograph. Life
in 1887 was different. I heard
the *Symphony Pathétique* last night. Forgive me
for saying this, I loved the gloom itself.
What joy there was to settle into that sadness,
to sit in the first row of the balcony
and hold my hand on my breast, to stand on the steps
and talk for a minute about Tchaikovsky's death,

to solve the secret suicide, to smile
over the scandal and the vicious code,
to say goodbye—in the street—to hold my glove
so the fingers fell against the palm, to walk
across the river, to stop in the middle, to lean
facing east where all the bridges were—that pleasure.
It started when I was twenty. As I recall
I walked across the Sixth Street bridge, there were
the row houses first and then the mansions; I walked
on the wooden porches and looked into the windows.
I studied the gas lamps and the wallpaper.
I loved it when there was no *conversion*. I was
already sacrificing. I was a slave
or I was a ghost. This has been
a long distracted life. I have carried
my secrets with me. That is my explanation.
When I stood there cupping my right hand
and when I looked at the barges struggling up
my river I was already changed. I spent
a lifetime doing this, grieving and arguing.

Sending Back the Gloom

for Kerry Keys

One time I rose from my bed, I had to walk
to the bridge and back, I had to listen to water
move under me. There was a tree to look at,
it was a dead tree, really a giant stump,
with a bird hole in the back and a dangling wing.
—It is three miles to the bridge and back, a little
under maybe, but "three" is convenient; I walk
as if I were running, I slow down only once
to wait for the cows or study the shredded sky.
I dream of my drink—boiled sumac—the juices
are drained through cheese cloth, the long hairs and the pulp
are left behind; I drink it as I walk.
It is the hawthorn I wanted—I have a thorn
in one of my pockets, it is a toothpick—the hawthorn
leans to one side—I have seen it—the branches
are close together, sometimes touching, dense
is what the Field Guide calls it, almost a shrub,
perfect for nesting, sometimes hundreds of birds
fly out of a single tree, sometimes they huddle
and shriek all day in the midst of their fruit and flowers.
—I lean on my elbows when I reach the bridge;
I dangle my wrists, I spread my fingers, I stare at
the water, the river curves through an open field,
there are no banks, there are no obstacles.
I love that kind of river, the water and the land
are level with each other; I don't know
if a river like that can have a name, or if
it's a river at all; if there's a flood the water
will spread over half an acre, maybe the curving

is what I like, the endless curving; the walk
back is different, the sky is purple and the sun
is lighting the fields, the sumac is on my left,
the hawthorn is on my right; I reach for a straw,
I reach for a stick of grass, I pass the Texas
pipeline, I stop in a valley, the sky is over me,
the trees are close, every ten yards the view
is different; I count up to seven colors, the day
is over at 3 o'clock, the last half mile
I walk through the woods, the dead tree is on a hillside
on top of me—it is a hummock—a rusted
wire fence runs through one side, the bark,
what there is of it, is dry and gray, the wood
is rotten, you can pull it off in pieces,
or you can pull the bark off separately.
Dirt is piled up inside, it keeps the tree
together, dirt and leaves and grass—it must be
twenty feet tall from top to bottom; from the front
it is a piece of sculpture, Garibaldi
with one arm in the air, Demosthenes
cursing the Blue Mountains; from the rear
it is a one-eyed monster, the bird hole
is thick and protruding, there the graceful and pleading
arm is almost invisible; I carry
a thorn in one hand, a scarred branch in the other,
the flowers are gone, this isn't one of the limbs
that bloom all winter, white and brown memories
of dreams gone by; half of my life is pleasure
and half of it is dread, I turn my corner

shouting to myself, the smoke is pouring
from eleven chimneys, we are sending back
the gloom, I hold my branch up, it is unlucky
to sing in this tree, or underneath it, I hang
my hat from the thorn, I look like a florist crossing
the highway, I am branched and perfumed.

One Gift

If I have one gift it is rising in the dark
and falling to my death down a vertical stairway.

It is walking with my feet spread out in both directions
and pressing the white plaster with my red fingers.

One time I was paralyzed, my leg disappeared,
and there was mist between my right knee and the floor.

One time I rose to the ceiling. I closed like a knife
after banging my head against the gritty stucco.

Sometimes there is fleece, the sheets are in shreds
and a white face is floating over the window;

sometimes there is blood, my hand is sticky,
the back of my head is wet, my mouth is salty.

Blood is my terror, blood just under the skin,
blood in the toilet, blood on the pillow. I hear

of every disgrace. I shake from fear. I hate
the heart being where it is, a piece of leather

covered with jelly, pressed against the backbone;
I hate the rotten lungs; I feel like a chicken

lying open, there is a speck of liver
above the gall—what pain if I were alive!—

what sadness there is for the spirit! There is the rope
that carries thought, there is love behind

the bladder. Down I go on one knee.
Sometimes I snore; I do that while I am lying,

it is my other gift. I crawl outside
to get at the moon. There is a balcony

over my head. I should be up there moaning.
Sometimes I end up wandering, sometimes sleeping.

First Day of Spring

for Bruce and Fox McGrew

I have been such a follower,
first Porphyry, then Alexander,
I have gone so long without shaving,
that now I have nothing
except this mustache and this forked stick.
Behold one T-shirt
I have traveled with from one wrinkled continent to the other;
behold one leg
that lifted me up over 40,000 thresholds.
My heart—such as it was—
always surprised me,
and my curved back,
it never gave out on the stairway,
it never paused once in spite of
the lifeless ankle
and the unlubricated lung.

There was a red carpet once
in the north of France
that wandered like a river
from the staircase to the first turn
and lapped against the plastered walls.
I stood outside a door
listening to two cries,
one gutteral and despairing,
one frantic and birdlike.
I shifted my trunk to my left shoulder
and began another climb,
three steps to the landing,

sixteen or eighteen steps to the next river.
As far as I can remember,
even with the closing of the door
and the admiration of my own face
in the unsilvered mirror,
stuck as it was wrongly
between two loose pillars
on a mahogany wardrobe,
I listened to their cries
half with shame, half with desire,
and half with terror and half with unabashed regret.

That was the beginning of grief,
the start of a second life,
although it wasn't that
the love cries themselves did this,
it wasn't the moaning—
or the creaking floor
or the exploding pipes—
it was, for the first time in *my* life,
I was abandoned.
I had to grab some rail
or vestigial fixture
sticking out of the wall
and do a shaky dance
under the heavy trunk.
I was suspended.

I guess I lay on the bed
staring at the ceiling
and the painted wire going into the light bulb,
or I guess I lay there remembering—
although I know I cut short the first years
and I know I concentrated on the early tribes,
crying out with rage and disappointment
in their slide from shelf to shelf;
though what I should have done,
and what I was able to do later,
was smile at what they *did* do
in the 200,000 years,
the first half aeon.
It took me one decade
till I could lie peacefully,
and two or more—
I think it was three or more—
to forgive myself,
or just to ignore myself,
for singing at the wrong time,
for interrupting the way I do,
for moaning, for talking out loud,
for being a dwarf.

In the great and lasting argument
that overwhelmed the Mediterranean
for more than a thousand years

I took the losing side.
I would do that in Spain
in the time of the two Sulimans
and I would do that in America
in the time of the two Stevensons.
I wanted to mourn for kings,
I wanted a bonnie prince,
and I wanted to feel the stinging
salt on my face too—
the silent ship, the sym-
pathetic sailors, the letters
wrapped in leather, a bottle
waiting to be opened,
a ribbon around the neck.
I solved problem after problem
in 1985
in the *campo dei fiore*
not only at the fish stand
but in the freezing movie house
where we sat in leather coats
and rocked in our chairs
watching the Blues Brothers
in English and Italian.
This is where Bruno died,
this is where my foot dragged
on the way to the river,
this is where Brutus—may
the Lord keep him insane—
swam before eating.

My favorite church
both then and now
was Il Gesù
where the Jews were herded together on Holy Thursday
to listen to a sermon
on the joys of conversion,
only a few blocks away
from the Vesuvio Palace, my
own crowded bakery.

It was astounding
to walk up that red carpet
in the fifth decade,
and it was astounding
to rock by the river
in the middle of the eighth.
Something was in my mind
both then and then
and something later brought it back again.
Sometimes you wait for forty years, it was
a little less for me
when I first thought of Alexander and Porphyry.
I have forgotten now, but I remember
it was a sweet elation, I was happy
and I was half-suspended.
                              I am sitting
in Arizona, the moon is full, so check
the twenty-first of March 1989.
I was reading Horace tonight, who never

wrote by porchlight, maybe a dish of oil
outside Brindisi. Ah, the stricken soul,
he sat till midnight waiting for a girl
who never came. I love his *sense*, he knew
where the ludicrous lay, he hated
quackery. I wonder
if maybe in the palace he had seen
a bromeliad once and touched the drooping flower—
the rubbery claws; I wonder if he talked
to a passing fox about the frogs that lived
in those leaves, if he had exchanged some wisdom, how
it only eats air, how it clings to palm trees; I wonder
if March twenty-first was when the plum tree bloomed
in Tivoli, if he had also seen
hundreds of butterflies in those branches, if he
lay down and wept—in spite of his careful mind—
if that is the third suspension, the third abandonment.

R for Rosemary

I heard a fluttering—just inside the door
of my *casita*; it was inside a bush,
a kind of pine, a kind of blue rosemary,
and since I saw two doves wandering under
my window yesterday and over my stones
I thought there had to be a mourning dove—
or two of them—puffed up and asleep,
living inside that bush, one of them frightened
by my loud steps. But I will know them later
by their sweet smell, whether they stretch their necks
or stick their chests out, getting ready to soar,
for they have made the mistake of living in rosemary
and they are spies for now and carry the stench
of betrayal on them. I could have reached inside
and heard them scream and watch the bushes shudder
with terror, but I let them go. More
and more I do that. Why did I wait so long
to let them have their darkness? I rub the leaves
under my chin and over my wrists. I know
the smell will last. I crawl up under my window
and try my keys. I'll have to pull the blinds
and close the curtains, those doves are so rotten; they are
such eavesdroppers. We listen to each other
through the glass, we preen in our mirrors; their cooing
is absurd, it is the noisy sound
of codex international; I know
the tapping, I know the turning of the head;
and it is odd to watch them stretch a wire
between their beaks and under my windowsill,

then walk off unaffected. I put powder
over my shoes. I know that trick. I called it
blue rosemary because of the flowers, I should have
called it lavender; it was my color
when I was a boy; there were *two* doves; we wandered
from bush to bush, it was a disease of the spine
that took the other one; she was a dove. If I
spend year after year explaining it is because
I was left without her. I have a sprig
of the dried-up plant, the leaves and the flowers have mixed,
the color is greenish-blue, almost an olive;
it has some weight, the woody part is heavy,
it is itself a kind of flattened tree;
it is a bookmark; it is a perfumed wing.

How Would It Be?

How would it be at my age to burn some land
between a Chinese willow and a white mulberry?

What would I do with the smoke
that blows first toward the television wires

and then reverses itself to curl some flowers
still hanging from the dwarf apple?

Couldn't my love be in that fire, wouldn't she
just adore those ashes, wouldn't she just love to stir

a stick in that dust, and wouldn't she love to dream
of another birth and another conversion?

Couldn't she get on her knees? Couldn't she also
smear her face with dirt? Couldn't she explode?

Saving My Skin from Burning

There was a hole in the ground once; there was a manhole
I used to get inside. I lowered a rope
and kicked my way down. The walls were two feet thick
and there was at most a foot of leaves where somehow
the wind had crept in, but there was no water. I felt for
the pipe, there was a little ledge—with matches.
I tried to get out. The truth was I fell. My mind
was on vipers, I called my enemies vipers, it was
an old honorific word but now I shook,
they were not just snakes—they were adders—their bodies
were flat, their fangs were huge, my enemies
strike like they do—their heads are triangles,
their eyes are in their skulls. I screamed for rope,
I needed rags, I had to save my skin
from burning—my chest and upper arms.
                                        The hole
is our greatest fear; I grab the air behind me
and stiffen my legs. The greatest joy is rising,
the greatest joy is resting your arms on the ground
and getting ready to swing your body up—
and seeing the clouds again and feeling the wind
on your white legs, and rubbing your eyes. I ran
to touch a tree, I stroked the bark, there was
one stone, it was half-pitted, the sun had turned it
into a pillow; I lay on my back recovering.

Shouting

Now I am reading a psalm,
the lack of mercy here and there,
doves freezing in the doorway.

I sink into something,
water covers me up to my neck,
my throat is burning.

It is a joy like this,
more fat than blind, more blind
than deaf, though that is coming. Either I fly

or I walk, but either way there is no sweetness.
Give me back, it says,
the brilliance of early October. I turn blue

when I think of it. The sun made a shadow on the wall,
the moon had a nimbus. I think of it and I moan.
My breath falters. I keep going back and back.

First there was fear, though I never called it
that, then there was silence. First there was sadness,
then there was anger. There is snow on my roof;

it makes me think of justice. I go back
over and over again. The white footprints
have nothing exactly to do with it. They lie

between the trees, the powder fills them up.
I make one turn—it doesn't matter—I could have
made another. There is a rock, it is

a teacher, it is a shield. I start to sing
a song with my hands; there is a pool of hot water;
I sit there with the rest; this is going back

with a vengeance; life was boiling; what we lacked
was a nucleus; we ate sulphur; there was light
twelve miles away; there was a great disorder.

What good is pity? I shake the needles; snow
slides down my neck. What I sing is buried.
I walk on the left side three or four miles a day,
shouting.

The Eyes Are Always Brown

I spend an hour watching the yellow parrots
swooping in and out of the jacaranda;
I touch each building with an oar; I count
the cars going by—I have a system—I watch
through a window, I see them go into the chairs
and over the vase of flowers; the brass coupling
helps me line them up and steer them through.
There is a bird of paradise here, his cheeks
are like a duck's, although the web is too long;
his crest is like a cockatoo's; a flower
grows out of his skull; his neck is buried. And there is
a fish nearby, her nose is purple, spots
of gold run up and down her body, her tail
is red, her teeth are absurdly small, her fins
are almost demented.
                    I am starting a trip
on the east side of Vandam; I travel south,
although the traffic flows north. I have no qualms—
in fact there is a certain delight. The sun,
what there is of it, is shining on the library
of the blind; the subway shakes my bench, I sit
holding the gunnels; one of my hands is dragging
through the orchids. I am making the sound
of the magpie; there are silken feces floating
in front of me, there is a wave, I smash
a pale scorpion with my palm, I touch
two windowsills. It is the same woman
staring at me, the flowers are always yellow,
the eyes are always brown—or was it chocolate?—

that made me bend over and gasp. I tip my helmet,
it is a *casque*, I offer her sink water,
I offer her bread and cheese, my table is set,
here is a napkin for her. I pass by
and lift my hand a little; I have a foolish
smile. I will have to make a decision
in one or two minutes, either I'll stop on an island
or drift down to the wall. I'll never see her
again, or the jacaranda; we call it death,
we call it worse than death; there was a hook
inside the heart against both walls; the brain
is the best organ for love; more than drifting
I love this jouncing. I give a piece of cheese
to the drowned fish; I'll never see the accountant
with the white cuffs, I'll never see the bus driver.
My back is red from bending over; the sun
is pouring down; I sprinkle a little water
over my head, over the fish's head.
I'll never crash into Kleinsleep. Should I have brought
a harp? What do they have here? What if they planted
harps, what if they knelt in the sand and prayed
to the strings? What is the moon doing now,
drifting through the water towers? Why
did I stop to listen to that music, poor love?

2

A Song for Kenneth Burke

May 7–15, Iowa City, Iowa

I have in mind some dust; a sprite
called Burke shook down some apples once.
It was in Shadyside. I stood
on the same corner, the same tree
blossomed that spring. I loved the bees
going wild. I carved around the rotten
flesh and lifted them up; it was
a miniature world: the teacher was sleeping,
the wife was in her chair, the child
was squirming, there was a soldier screaming,
he was hunched over. What is it called
when the world is sliced apart? I lift
the Victorian Age, I hold it by a stem,
I lift my childhood: there is the frog
in a mason jar, the glass is driven
into his body, it was an accident—
I think it was only three landings—there is
a woman named Liz, her mouth is full
of semen; I hold a tiny cat
in my arms—a diorama! A section!
A slice of life! Ah shades of some school
or other, the girls are walking back
to their sewing machines, the miners are digging
by purple light.
                    I stand by a tree
in the rear of my garden, it is surrounded
by lilacs, yet the blossoms are large
and lovely; I feel like a mother in awe
of her baby—how could those limbs be perfect

like that? How could those blossoms come
again and again? The whole tree is covered
with flowers. Poor Burke! When he finally gets here
there will be just a white rug, but that
is something too. I see him bend down—
the last time I saw him his legs were crooked—
and pick up a blossom. He holds it to his eye,
he blows on the edges. I heard he lived
in a cottage in west New Jersey, it is
ramshackle, no electricity,
a bottle of vodka on the sink,
the papers piled up, a stand of trees
outside the window, little hills
to soothe his spirit, a hand-dug pond—
with pickerel—a tiny sand beach,
with rushes, for Moses, so Moses can lie there
planning the future. My apples are yellow,
and hard and sweet; I eat them all day;
some are rotten, all are rotten
a little; I love a wrinkled skin,
I love the seeds. I pick some flowers—
it's early still—I'll put them in a vase—
with lilacs—I'll arrange them. This is
my month: tulips, lilacs, cherries—
and violets—under the apple—green
and purple and white; this is the month—
under our lake and near our river—
for plans, for visions; not September,
not December.

Burke had a plan
to call things by their other name;
it was an exotic plan. He lived
near hills and water; that was in the blood,
that was in the mind; he lived
by moonlight—there is another race
among us; he was almost Li-Po
for a minute; he pursued that face
for years, he stalked a soul, he cried
in Greek, he spoke to a shadow, he dropped
a stone in the pond, a part of him shivered,
it almost exploded; he spoke to the moon
with caution. Who is to say the moon
loved one of them less? How could you not
turn into a shadow? What would that fish
now eat? What if it nibbled on his hair?
What if it swam through his eye? Sustenance
is in the brain. How could Burke not
derive his knowledge from the talk
in drugstores—was the fish not brainfood?
Didn't the pickerel swim in the mind?
Was there not a reversal? Didn't
the pickerel eat that meal? Was gray food
not what he ate? Did he not gobble
blood and nerves? Did he not dip
his nose into the skull, was he
not a fish of fury?
                    Burke bends down
to pick up a porous stick, he sensed

the lightness, it shone in the moonlight, the holes
were there for the light to come through though water
took over sometimes and mud caked up
his exits—for him they were exits. He floats
his stick, it is another face;
a third; a fourth if you count the moon;
he should have put some feathers on
the forehead and scarred the cheeks. He runs
to the other side, the grasses scratch
his ankles, his slippers are soaked, he picks up
his stick; the water is black, the roots run
into his fingers. For just a minute
he thought of Thales—he could be Thales
explaining the world. Was he not Thales?
Did he not have one explanation—
and then another? If he had a glass
he'd lift it to the moon. Ah, vodka,
with ice. Vermouth. What if love
could be reduced? What are the words
in German and Hebrew? How did the Greeks
help lead him astray? How long did his Lucy
wait? What is the word for sorrow?
What is the word for live fish, for shadow?

Aspiring to Music

My favorite piece of dreck
on the grasses of Houston Street
is a bottle of Bohemia,
green and shiny on the outside,
brown and watery on the inside.

Or the grille of a Mercedes
sitting on the curb,
slightly bent on the left,
slightly haughty, its steel nose
finally up in the air.

I count two hundred pieces
between Thompson and Sullivan,
some of them monstrous and baffling,
some of them dropped from the moon,
all of it oily and dirty.

Today, kind Lord, the mayor
was voted out. In a week
his brilliant ventures in the world
of Thought will be forgotten
and we will have our lives back.

Down there in Tompkins Square
a little cheer will go up
in front of the makeshift hospital
and in the open tents
lining the circular walks.

If I stay too long I'll either
faint from the fumes or I'll die
from the noise—this island is narrow;
I feel the wind from the trucks,
I feel the weight of the tires.

I work up a dance—I always
do that—paper napkins
and broken glass. Dance
and poetry are the close ones,
and all that shameful talk

about poetry and music
is just a high-pitched raving
from one philosopher
to another, one vile German,
one berserk mayor.

Music and poetry
are enemies; the sounds
I make come from my twenty-
stringed tongue. The vile ones hate
not only words but the crude

sources; they hate the tongue,
they hate the blood on those strings,
they hate the sorrow; dancing
they never did, poetry
they never wrote, but they

played piano, and violin.
Poor Coleridge—even Coleridge
submitted. What did *he* play,
the flute? Did Wordsworth play
a little harp? Why is music

the measure? I have met
a ravishing dancer—how
do you say that with notes? It takes
twenty-seven minutes to walk
from Thompson and Houston to Saint

Mark's Place and Avenue A,
the left side of Tompkins, the center
of Bombay, the absolute horror
of the known world. One time I was stuck there
with the other pieces of paper.

I didn't know how to get out,
I couldn't find the gate,
I finally walked through the playground
and ended up going west
instead of east. You have to

be locked in to under-
stand—they didn't even hate me,
they didn't even hate the mayor,
they didn't even hate the mosquitoes,
they were aspiring to music;

not only art—all things
aspire to music. Just ask
a piece of paper. They sat there
in a quiet mode; it was
the hour of reason, some

were smoking tea, some
were sleeping. For how many years
have I been walking like this?
For how many years have I
been dancing and singing? I cross

in front of two trucks; I feel
the heat; I could have sat
in the grass, I could have put up
a tent. How long would they let me
stay? What is the ordinance

forbidding housekeeping? Would I
have gotten support? What prophet
would be my model? What psalm
would I sing? There were four grasses
on that plot—I take

some heart in that. Here is
the toothpick I plucked; it's almost
like wheat. I could have grown
tomatoes—that is for me
the mark of a habitation;

I would have searched for worms
for an hour each morning; I would have
planted my marigolds
in a perfect circle. I have
almost enough money now

to stop my wandering.
I certainly have enough
to live on a grass plot
in the middle of Houston Street
and more than enough to print

some words for the sorrowful
or give away three dollars
a day—that makes a thousand
a year—will you give a thousand
a year to the sorrowful?

I dedicate this poem
to the woman in blue who preached
neighborhood mercy last Sunday
on Sixth near Twenty-first.
I also dedicate it

to the carp on Bleecker Street
who lived in the bleached grasses
underneath the lilies
and fed on the floating pods,
the bloated sunflecked carp.

Grinnell, Iowa

Guy Daniels would have loved May
if he could see those teachers coming toward him
with baked chicken and white wine in their arms.
He would have bent down a little
and closed his eyes the way he did
to smell a lilac or a wet spirea.
When I drive through those empty streets or past
the giant feed stores and storage sheds
I think of how he lived in New York, the shame
of all those steps, the uncontrolled steam, the terrible
darkness of his rooms. I have heard him
rage against five administrations. I have
listened to his jokes—in French and Russian—
and I have heard him shout at three wives and anger
his few friends with his endless self-pity
but I have never heard him talk about this state
with anything but affection. When I drive
four times over the Iowa River, because
it twists underneath our highways, I half-see
Guy Daniels in 1941 just starting
a life in the East, some precious books, a few
shirts and ties, a smile on his face, a young
man's gloom and purity surrounding him
like a white cloud, the cloud of steam that goes by
his unwashed window. I half-see him changing
trains in Chicago, his suitcase is on his shoulder,
his coat is open. The war is what ruined him, Nixon
ruined him, living three years in Washington, living
by his wits in New York City, the best translator

of Russian in America; leaving Iowa,
forgetting the River Road outside Ottumwa,
forgetting the streaks of lightning over the Capitol.

Walking toward those teachers my eyes water
as if I were Guy Daniels. I half-bow
to show respect. I keep thinking it is
the second decade of the twentieth century,
or maybe as late as 1940. I bend
to pick a few spring beauties, they are scattered
like what? like snow? snow in May? They last
one hour I think; I give them to the tall
wife in the linen dress; she would have adored
me once; I can hear a cardinal; there is
nest after nest in the woods; I think of the steamliner
racing toward Cedar Falls, but I am
once removed—I am not Daniels—I think of
the stone hills in the north, the black trucks
pointed into the curb, the bitter farm
holidays, the empty corn palace.

I pick a poppy—made of paper—it is
the color of the one I buy each year
May thirtieth, or the Monday before.
I pull a caterpillar from my shirt;
I give him another home, a green leaf
surpassing all green leaves; I watch him with a straw,
a kind of supple vein I took from a leaf
the next one over to his. I keep away ants

and birds. He is half bursting with desire,
he almost is ready for his molt, he almost
is ready for his week of rage and sorrow.

Ukrainian

for Robin Beeman

Before I go outside I daub my face
with vinegar. That is Ukrainian. I put
one drop behind my knee and one on my earlobe.
I choose a bush. If there is a flower I scatter
a grain of sugar on the twig to help
the flying worms; I pick a weed; I prop
a rain-drenched tulip. There is a part of me
that lives forever. Spring after spring I sit
at my redwood table; at this point the grain is white
with age, the boards are splintered, the hole that held
a grand umbrella is bent, or twisted, nothing
could fit there. Yet I'm enchanted. I sit on the bench—
one of two—half-curved—the table itself
is round, it measures more than a yard, the end boards
are split and shattered. I have one favorite tree
and one favorite bird. I lift my cocoa. Water
is all around me. I make a pact; if the tree
lasts one more year, if it blooms next spring, if the flowers
that cover the twigs and fill the sky come back again
I'll stay here another winter, I'll plant a garden,
I'll trim my branches, I'll rake my leaves. The cardinal
who lives beside the redbud, he whose crimson
is richer than that pink, he who almost
shames the tulips, he whose carnal cry
is always loud and florid, he is my witness.

Coleman Valley Road

This is where I had my sheep vision,
in the brown grass, under the stars.
I sat there shivering, fumbling with my paper,
losing tobacco. I was a spark at the most,
hanging on to my glasses, trying to hide
from the wind. This is how I bent

my head between my knees, the channels and veins
pumping wildly, one leg freezing, one leg
on fire. That is the saxophone
and those are the cymbals; when it gets up here
the roar of the waves is only a humming, a movement
back and forth, some sloshing we get used to.

That is my cello music and those are my headlights
making tunnels in the grass; those are
the clouds going down and those are the cliffs going out.
I am reaching up. I think I have
a carp's face, I have a round nose
and a large red eye and a ragged white mustache.

The strings are stretched across the sky; one note
is almost endless—pitiless I'd say—
except for the slight sagging; one note is
like a voice, it almost has words, it sings
and sighs, it cracks with desire, it sobs with fatigue.
It is the loudest sound of all. A shrieking.

What It Is Like

I will have to tell you what it is like
since I was the one lying on my back
with my arms in the air and a blanket up to my
chin, since I was the one on a mattress
and the one trying to make up my mind
whether it was an early heaven just being there
or whether it was another bitter vertigo.

There were great parties where I went out
on a back porch and stared through the sycamores,
and there were parties, mostly lawless gatherings,
where we stood on the beach apart from each other
studying the sky. For me it's always
the earth; I'm one of the addicts; I can hardly
stand the dreaminess; I get burnt, I blister

at night as others do in the day. Last summer
I lay there crying. It was California
and the sheep vision. I was on a mattress
looking up. I started to talk. Aside
from the stars, aside from the beating heart, I only
remember two things: both hands were in the air
and I was, for the first time in twenty years,

lying down without fear. My friend Robin
was there beside me; she was sobbing; I have
such gratitude toward her. It was her house,
it was her stars. She took me down to see
the sheep first, then she showed me the ocean.

It was an outside room; one wall was a maple,
one wall was made of planter boxes. There were

tomatoes and eggplants in one, there was lavender
and basil in another. I remember
the trees on every side; I know there was oak
and redwood; there was a twisted madrona with leaves
in leathery piles, almost like rhododendron.
Robin knew the shadows, she knew the edges,
she knew the clouds, she knew the sky. It was

the summer of 1989. The charts
have already registered my odd affliction
and the stars absorbed my happiness. Standing—
or lying—you could see a horse to the right,
if you were facing north, and a white dragon,
if you were facing south. I think I never
slept that night. I only dozed. And ranted.

Two Daws

for Stanley Kunitz

The false dawn in Wheeling, West Virginia
is five o'clock—given the season—given
the inclination of two or three daws to sing
outside my frozen room; there is some fog,
there is some light; the birds go back to sleep
then, something like I do, waking themselves I'm sure
just as I do with something of a snort
when finicky memory combines with green sulphur—
in their case maybe it's vile hunger combining
with cold, slightly different. I call it "false" dawn
as if it were a fixture; I will talk
to two or three others, a sweet librarian,
a morose poet; I always check to see
if there is a cosmos to match my own. I learned
thirty years ago how odd my thoughts were,
how I could not be trusted. If *I* described
the morning I would say there are two dawns,
one, if it's late April, if it's in the East,
it's night still, there is a kind of thin blue
over the hills; and, two, the true dawn, then
the trees are almost shaking with noise, the sun
is spread out, light is everywhere. There are
two deaths as well—though I will have to check it—
false death, there is a bird then, still a daw,
or sometimes a jay, depending on the season,
and the location; I think in West Virginia
it could be any of twenty birds, the cardinal
is good, the dove is good, they sing with such a
note—such notes—of pity my nose is red

from weeping, my eyes are swollen, there are creases
of woe in my forehead, I am dragging my feet
like never before, it is a sacrifice
and I am holding the knife; I want it to be
a stone knife—I can pick my weapon. The other
the birds are silent; I would have them screaming
and scolding, but I have no authority there.
Kunitz, may he live forever, says
there's only one dawn. It's like an orchestra,
first, say, a lark, or first a robin, and then
it's the finch's turn; maybe the flutes are first
and then the cellos and the flutes are silent.
That is the lull. We in the trombones slide
slowly, don't we—what a din we made.
But there are *two* deaths, he's wrong—only once—that gorgeous
poet, there are *two* deaths, though now I remember
he only spoke of "dawn," he didn't speak
of "death"—he never said there weren't two deaths—
I was the one who brought up those birds and had them
singing and scratching twice, he kept his counsel
on death, and everyone I talked to we reasoned
together about two "dawns," and almost everyone
said there were two, or they agreed with me
to show how smart they were or they just found
the thought intriguing. No one said there were,
or said there weren't, two deaths; I'm all alone
with my two deaths, I have to make my own birds
and my own cat, for that matter, sitting and watching
or walking slowly by with a flea collar

choking him, or dragging a bell from his throat.
—False dawn maybe is only a light birds are
fooled by, though the light could be from within,
triggered by fear—or hunger; I almost think it's
curiosity—which kills all birds. False death
is almost like it; light from something drags us
out, breathing our last, fresh blood pumping
through our necks and wrists, terror forcing us
down, last-minute cunning, last-minute hope
saving us—counting to ten, humming, laughing,
at what I called light—instead of darkness—knowing
more than I say—more than I can say—but true dawn—
ah sapsuckers singing from my birch, the branches
of my giant arbor vitae shaking, the needles
of my great yews dancing, not to mention the copper
beach, or the weeping willow, not to mention
the crab apple, not to mention the dying
redbud, not to mention the oak. The word
"dawn" it comes from "daw," there has to be
some connection with the bird; "daw"
is middle English: "there are two daws"; "death"
is from old Frisian, that from old Saxon, that from
old High German. When it comes to true death
Kunitz is just like me, I guess, polite
and a little terrified, certainly amazed. I
have nothing to say about which birds; I think
of crows, naturally, although that should be false
death, shouldn't it? I say that with respect
for one soul and another. I think it's geese

I think about, walking with their webbed feet
down some greasy path, honking with caution,
almost with rudeness, yet lifting their huge bodies
and disappearing, in ten or twelve seconds, life
and death are in their rising and falling; swallows
are birds of death, in and out, trees
I won't get started on, either here, wherever
here is, or in the next place, or in the last place,
not one locust, not one cyprus. I
am full of spring these days, I listen to a hundred
sounds of shrieking every morning. Kunitz
is right about the orchestra—and yet,
isn't it reversed? Isn't true dawn
the one that is operatic? Shouldn't I sing then,
breathing my last, fretting over my own death
among the other birds? And shouldn't I sleep
like a wise man through the false dawn even if the first
thin blue is out there, even if there is a call
from one or two creatures, even if the cardinal
is making me moan, and even if the chickadee
is hanging upside down and banging his head
against the shiny glass—even if the worm
is fighting for his life and the lily of the valley
is bowing her head in shame, shouldn't I live on?

3

Her Right Eye Catches the Lavender

for Judy Rock

What is the eastern gull called? Is it the same one
that floats in the Iowa River? I read in *Birds*
it has pink legs—yellow eyelids in summer.
Why did I never see that? Can I drive
a thousand miles to live among them, watch
them hop and lift their wings a little, see them
fold their legs back as they soar? Someone

named Rock was walking by the water; she threw
salami at them. Knowing her as I do
I know she chose one of them and pursued him
relentlessly—her eye is part of her mind—
and though there would be patter she never would lose him
until he was gone. I don't know how she feels
about them as scavengers, I don't know if she
calls them rats with wings or if she finds them
endearing, as I do, with their gorged bodies
and drooping wings—gobbling doves—if she
forgives them, as I do, for their gluttony,
if she watches them fighting the currents, if she compares them
to hawks, if she compares them to pigeons. After

her walk on the beach she lay down with her clothes on
in one of those shingled houses, on starched sheets
with eyelets at the border, maybe flowers—
faded peas or roses. There was a roomful
of crisp white linen, there was a pear-shaped bottle
with three carnations, there was a wedding bouquet
with ivory streamers—curled up on the bureau—

and there was a drawing of Thomas Hardy's birthplace
in Dorset, and a painting above the bed
of an apple orchard in bloom, it was cloudy
and humming. She woke up at six and watched
the light get stronger in the windows, the one
a lemon pink, the other a pearl gray,
both of them filled with branches, and she thought
a little about her happiness. Day and night

the gulls eat, although they rest; they fall
asleep in a second. Even if there is some shifting,
even gurgling, they are asleep. It is
sleep that alters their rage, sleep slows down
their appetites, it is their only substitute
for pity—even as it renews
their life of greed. I think she must get up,
I think she smiles; she rummages through her suitcase
looking for something, she kneels at the foot of the bed
with one hand under her chin; her right eye catches
the lavender. I have her letter, I am
more voracious than I was seven years ago
but I am more lenient. I watch them catch the wind,
then race downstream. Why did it take so long
for me to get lenient? What does it mean one life
only? Could I not stand in the mud
beside my black willow, thinking of her and loving her?

Those Things

With one foot on the standpipe
I bend down to tie my soaking shoe
    a block from everything,
the Back Stage Deli, the Roosevelt Hotel,
    the French consulate.
I walk up Vanderbilt, across Forty-seventh
    under the canopy
of Maggie's Place, into the Paris Croissant.
    I am on the East Side
for the first time in years, in an East Side drizzle,
    pushing against umbrellas,
walking through taxicabs, touching wet dogs.
    Someone else
is going to smoke a cigarette, someone
    is going to stumble through
the olives and fettucini and spinach with some kind
    of hope—or terror—I
will put my arm on the table, I will talk
    to Tintoretto, I will smear
catawba blossoms on my cheeks, I will
    argue with Amos, I
will walk away with my head in my hands, Dio-
    nysus again, the veins still struggling,
the heart still pumping away. I have to retreat
    to West Virginia, to North Carolina,
my city in southern Mexico, my mountain
    in northern Greece. A man
has two dark stages in his life; the first
    he puts *those things* to the side;

he comes upon them lifting a stone, or turning
  a corner, something touches him,
he moans, he moans in his sleep, he turns the other
  corner, he is besieged a little,
his hair, his hair turns white, he combs it out
  of his brush, the terror of dying,
the body turned around—that is his sign;
  the second stage is later, he is
freed a little, bored a little, but still
  he is filled with passion—what
would you call it otherwise?—He leaves New York,
  he leaves the Paris Croissant, the Louvre
is pasted on the wall, the glass pyramid
  is on the other side, the solstice
is not for him, endless light, ridiculous
  chanting, he needs another table,
a cave this time, maybe that bench at last
  outside his library, every word
scorched this time, this time he listens, this time
  he has forever. What will he wear?
he thinks. What will he read? What will he drink?
  And what will he do for love this time?
For love will he bend down like a crow? Will he listen?
  Will he write three dozen letters? He
is sitting again, his hand is holding a pencil,
  and he is drinking. He has picked
a flower from a battlement, the lily
  of Spain it's called—in France it is
a weed and grows between the stones, it is

                his flower, he puts it in a glass,
he puts it in his pocket, it is better
                than a death's-head, some poor creature on
his table, a thumb in her mouth, the Bible lying
                open, a candle making shadows—
love, not death, for him to think about,
                a flower, such a pretty thing,
another year of life it means, it means
                that he will have to wait a little,
that he will live on his stomach dreaming, that he
                will turn the petals to the light,
that he will have yearning again, and greed, and sorrow.

His Song of the Green Willow

I guide my darling under the willow tree
to increase the flow of her blood.

A branch weeps, so does she, a twig breaks off
like one of her thoughts.

We are helpless together, we spend the night
listening to shameless sounds

and study the moon together, watching it spread
knowledge over the white mulberry.

Whoever lies down first, that one will hear
the cardinal first, and that one will see the streaks

above the lilacs. Whoever does not leave,
whoever is loyal, whoever stays, that one will see

the rabbits thinking, that one will see a nest
and small ones warm from living. Whoever sits up

and looks at the sky—whoever is alone—
that one will be the griever, that one will make

his song out of nothing, that one will lean on his side
and stir the ground with his stick—and break his stick—

if that is his way, and moan, if that is his way,
and go on forever—his thirty-two feet at a time—

thirty-two feet until the branches start
and the scattered twigs,

her thoughts again—for him her thoughts—his song
of the green willow, her song of pain and severance.

If the Lark Had Thorns

A ghost I know too well stands bitterly by
his own birch tree hunting for borers; his cat
comes walking by with a bird in her mouth. To say
he was offended, what does that mean? He was
astonished! All of his tolerance left him. He wanted
to kill the cat, not kick it, not just gingerly
open its mouth and free the bird. He wanted
to kill it. All of his knowledge left; he stood there
holding a leaf; he tore at the paper bark
and studied the deadly patterns like a surgeon
who knew something. He could tell by the legs
and the yellow chest it was a meadowlark
the cat had killed. The way it lay there the throat
was tilted back as if it were warbling. He could have
screamed, he could have crossed his arms with rage,
he who was once a *student*, he who watched
everything—with fascination. He studied
the row of holes; it was a machine gun
across the face of the trunk; it was a sapsucker,
not a borer; the holes were too big. That made him
happy, thinking of how the sapsucker went
for the soft inner bark or how he gobbled up
the beetles or sucked the sugar. For a minute
he almost forgot the meadowlark; he leaned
his cheek against the birch, he kissed it, he all but
forgot the meeting of two orange cats in the street
and how they *consulted*, how they accommodated
one another, how the one with the meadowlark
walked into the bushes, how the other watched

with envy—even with fear—yet *protected*
the first one, out of some ancient ritual—maybe
he was the male—I know the first one, the killer,
was purring. If you could talk about smiling, if you could
talk about pride, or property, I'd say
that she was full of pride and that she guarded
her property with all her cunning; the chest
of the meadowlark meant nothing to her nor
its speckles nor its flutelike song. Although
for him that wasn't the point exactly, it was
her growling that he hated most, he could
accept anything but her growling. That was
unjust! That was the final oppression, bending
over and growling, or looking up for a minute
with sullen eyes. It was unjust, compared
to anything, worse than the prowling, worse than
stealing the body, worse than cutting off
the music. That was vileness. It forced him
into his trap, languishing over his birch tree,
eating his liver. When he was young he could have
put up with anything. He pressed his tongue
against his bottom teeth and slightly opened
his mouth in what he thought was thought—that was
one of his gestures—but it was more coldness than thought,
it was more hesitation. It is better
hating this life if you have to; it is better
not to explain your wailing. If you have to
it is better to cut a hole yourself
and let the gum well up. The cry of justice

is greater than any other cry; all things
begin and end with that cry. What do you think the
scales are? What do you think is balanced? Ah, he
kicks at the cat; he runs into a garbage can,
he certainly slides in the mud; he certainly loses
his glasses, *that* is justice. What he does
he does in twenty square feet, between a birch
and an arbor vitae, what he does he does
with so much knowledge that he can forgive himself
for anything. One of his hands, he thinks,
stands for one thing and one of them stands for another.
He needs them both to hold up the birch. He favors
one and so he pushes the other, even
here there has to be justice, there has to be
consideration. He turns to the barberry, he picks
two berries, he has learned to watch out for thorns—
and if the lark had thorns, if it had a stench,
if it could screech—he's seen his orange cat cower
a dozen times, she runs from shadows. Sometimes
he leans against the trunk, sometimes he stretches
his shortened hamstrings; he loves a certain twilight—
that first darkness doesn't depress him—sometimes
he holds the lowest branch, for him it is
a restful position, sometimes he pulls at the bark
and reads the yellow page, sometimes he chews
on one flamboyant leaf, sometimes on another.

The Smell of Death

Green fishes swimming in the street
and white clematis climbing a wooden fence
for our last walk together.

A rose with such an odor
that to bend down and smell it
is to live again like two Babylonians,
one with her hair so heavy that when she bends over
she holds it with two hands,
one with his beard so thick and curly
that when he bends over
his chest, where the linen falls, is cool
as the ground was where the dead leaves lay.

A mulberry tree—two mulberry trees—two babies
so thin that they are thinner than weeds the doves
planted there overnight, the doves who ate
a mile away from here and flew here with food
filling their stomachs, rich and sticky food.

And two hibiscus blossoms faced two ways
on the same stem,
like trumpets, or like ears to gather in
the sounds of our grieving—

Two paper heads, I should say, two round heads
with plaited cheeks and seedy noses that have
an inch of wisdom between them,
heads that they fold at night and keep half-folded

for days on end
like wilted cabbage leaves, like thick handkerchiefs,
folded to keep the cold out—is that it?—like two
white heads on the same pillow, like two flat heads
faced eye to eye, if there were eyes, and even
mind to mind, if there were minds; for me

there are only hearts—like two red hearts then
somewhere inside those roots, unless the flowers
themselves are what they call hearts, two flowers, then, talking
for the last time, they could be from a single
bud for all I know, two brutal flowers
turning away from each other, spending their last night
plotting and thinking, barely closing, concentrating
on their own bitterness, hating, for all I know,
the concrete borders and the broomfuls of dirt,
hating the sun, for all I know, one of them—
I want to say—more bitter, I want to say
more brutal, but what do I know, one of the two
round heads myself; I want to say she is hateful
of light itself. I think, to my embarrassment,

of a flattened squirrel, a kind of glove, her mouth
more simpering every day, I think of cone flowers
lying in my garbage, a layer of plaster,
then a layer of flowers; I think of the heads
buried in glass, the pointed heads, the stalks
foolish in that position. The fishes are seedpods

that cover the street for a day or two—some tree
or other—why should I think *that* strange? My seed
would have filled three buckets—isn't that lovely?
It goes with the putrid squirrel. I stop to smell
the smell of death, I kick it a little, fumes
rise, there is a god that loves it, he smacks
his lips, like a dog; the smell of death, we say,
a catch in our voice: I smelled it once in the Bronx

walking back to the subway; there was a corpse
lying behind some bushes, I was there
for the People's Convention, Reagan came, and Carter,
they promised to rebuild the Bronx—I think the corpse
was holding his nose—he had to be either Black
or Puerto Rican; some girls, as if to test me,
as if to see if I could be shocked, guided me
back to the body; I think he had been there for three
whole days, in the heat of July; all of the buildings
were empty; that was 1980; we had

two summers, didn't we, my darling. I think of that,
my round head on the pillows. I use four now,
like a duchess, darling, flowers, stripes and always
a heavy white; I lie on my stomach sometimes
to rest my neck, I make room for my nose
by turning a fraction to the right, I free
one of my ears so I can hear the fan
mix with the music. There is one pillowcase

I love more than the others; I hunt for that one
most of the time; I think it was pale blue once
but it is almost white from so much washing,
the way the sky was after it rained; I saw that
in my part of the garden with my huge
red eye an inch or two away from you
with your red eye, and your paper head, my sweet,
trying to follow my words as I had to strain
with yours—I always had to—a foot away
from the sullen lupines and the ruthless lilies, my darling.

Red with Pink

It is a great weariness, isn't it,
almost a kind of sorrow,
getting up before you're ready
because of a babbling in the maples.
It is a great bitterness, pressing
one ear at a time to the ground
beside the green delphiniums,
calling up the worms, cocking
your own bird head, walking through
the chives, picking one or two clouds,
putting them in a crushed vase,
certainly a sadness, touching
the trunk of a dead dogwood
where a thick vine choked it
yet left an elegant imprint
as if a snake had lain there
waiting for the babbling to stop.
    My hand is in that tree,
or maybe only three fingers,
it is so narrow; I can't
be buried inside, there is
no room for my legs, I need
a cherry or a sycamore.
I break a branch off, a twig
instead of a branch, a stem—
if that is smaller—I water
the lupines, they are almost shameful,
I water the white bleeding hearts,
I turn the earth into mud,

I lift a blossom to my face,
I let one drop or two
fall on my table; I save them
for later. If I look
at the two sides of the flower
a green wedge is driven
through the middle; that is—
though I don't want to say it—a heart
broken in two; the drop
is a kind of platform, it springs
the blossom open; white drops
are everywhere, and pollen,
a kind of semen, though in this case
love had to be reversed.
      I wrap my thumb and finger
around the dogwood; that is
a way of remembering, probably
a way of thinking; even
a cane wouldn't be this thin;
there never was substance, it never
was truly a tree. Ten feet
away, as the red ant crawls—
if that—the orange roses
are snarled in honeysuckle;
that is a way of crying
in two languages at once,
Polish and Yiddish, medieval
Greek and Irish; one voice
holds up the other. We say

they cry, but they rage, they choke
on their beauty, they die in their bloom.
I say they "die" but one of them
lives, even if it is crippled.
I tried to disengage
the one from the other; I ripped
out leaves from my wire fence—
long live honeysuckle, it sticks
to wire—long live orange roses,
they came there first. Ten feet
away another rose bush
is growing; this one is free
of honeysuckle, though it is
more like a shrub, it falls
apart when you touch it, that is
a kind of freedom, isn't it,
living unsnarled, no sweetest
of sweets to hold you, falling
apart at the touch; I lived
in New York like that, falling
apart at the touch; I walked
up Avenue C or First Avenue,
I gave up ever seeing again
the bluejay under my birch,
the wind driving him crazy;
I gave up chives and poppies,
and lived in a white shirt, walking
and running by turns—oh sweetest
of sweets, I disentangled

myself from the honeysuckle,
I loosened the morning glory,
I gave up the choking feeling
east on Fourth Street, north
on Second, past the Bangladesh
laundry, past the white gunny sacks
of rice. I had to be a rose
one more time. I had to be
open and airy. I stopped
in a Polish restaurant. I first went
down three steps to the entrance—
a rose going down three steps
is quite a sight, and a rose
eating his soup, even on
First Avenue next to McDonald's
on one side and something Spanish
on the other is rare, and a rose
learning Greek so he could
talk to his neighbor from Samos
is also rare. I could have
studied Polish, or Ukrainian,
but that is not decent for this kind
of rose, whether red or yellow,
whether ivory tinged with salmon
or orange with a crimson base
or blue with pink.
                        I learned
her name while basking on a wall—
Vassilia—it is the Greek

for "royal"; if she were a rose
she would be lilac with a white edge
and when the wind blew her down
she would be more white than blue,
a modern color combining
old thoughts. I know we first met
outside the Temple to Hera
a half a century ago
when she was eighteen and I was
a few years younger. I tell her
this in English, we are sitting
with the wire fence between us
in our own courtyards an hour
from New York City. I tell her
how much I loved Samos; she smiles
when I name her village; our roses
are almost alike, they come
from the same green sticks; she sits
with shears in her hand; I sit
with a pencil in mine; her stockings
are rolled; she almost knows
my name. Her husband is blind,
he is in Samos; my wife
lives in New York. She was
pink with brown edges; she was
very dark red. I live
by myself now. I am scattered.

Someone Will Do It for Me

If that dove leaves before I do
I will have the wall to myself
and the onion sets and the wooden tulips.
I alone will swing my legs
and flap madly over the telephone wire
and through the dead maple.
I have no trouble with this
or with shrieking, when it comes,
or even with gobbling from a sunken pan
or a glass or dirty water.
I understand how, for one day,
I have the body of another,
be he a fat and nimble handyman
or she a spindle-legged half-blind hydroptic.
I carry it from one wet roof to another
and I return constantly to a certain canyon
and a certain cement sidewalk.
Poor things whose fate
is with a small-headed bird
with ruined eyes
and a way of dragging himself as if he were made of mud.
No responsibility on this end,
avoiding red bricks, paying attention to diet;
they will have to stay with me
and trust I'll live and live,
sleeping in the gutters, burying my head
under my bloodless wing.
And what about me—what bird of mine?
Where could he be? Will I slide

down the roof as gently as a man
going in for supper? Will I choke
on tongue again and this time swallow the rind
or this time when a bullet
hits my chin first, then my soft neck,
will I bleed to death just off route 24
with no one there to scream,
or will I be in my T-shirt
brushing one tooth at a time
smiling again in the cracked mirror;
or sweeping the piece of concrete
between the brick wall and the wire fence
with special gestures for the cherry stones
and the red leaves? Poor white one,
you will have to learn it all, the rashness,
the wandering, the secrecy, as I am learning the name
of the Greek next door, sitting in his tomatoes,
reading his paper; as I am planting an iris
only for him, among the hollyhocks,
as I am smiling at him, as I am writing
his name—Augoustis Bozakis—in my tablet
and the name of his wife—Vassilia—and the island
she comes from. Someone will do it for me, someone
will see me with my legs crossed and my pencil
going back and forth, he'll watch me with my orange
against the wall, looking into the sunshine,
and write my name down just as it would have been
if we had stayed in Kiev, if there had not been
one separation after another; he'll know

my American name and my embarrassment.
I wish I could see the tablet. What is it called
seeing yourself that way? Is it a final
understanding, or is it just shabby pity
and shabby revenge? There are doves colliding
in both skies; there is such interchange
it is almost frenzy, such hijinks—
heavy landing and puffing and bitter warbling—
it is almost relief.

I Would Call It Derangement

I cut a stick for my love. It is too early
to clear the yard. I pick some lilac. I hate them
dying on the vine. I plan my assault
on the dead maple. I will tie some rope
to the rotting side and pull it down so I can
cut it limb from limb without destroying
the phone connections from one state to another
or smashing the new tomato plants and ruining
the asters. She is walking from place to place
and wrapping herself in sheets. If the wind
were free up there it would lift the curtains
just as it bends the poppies and the yearning
iris. I am setting a table. I
am smiling at the Greeks next door. I put
an old gardenia in the center, something
that has some odor. We are in the flowery
state now. I spill half the petals over
her watermelon; only here are flowers
good for eating, here and India
where they are sprinkled over colored ice
and onto the half-cooked fish. I have a system
for counting bricks but this one day I study
the clouds that move from left to right and the swallows
hunting for food. They seem to fly in threes
and alternately flap their wings, then skim
the roofs; they even make a sound, some brief
chipping; I hear it when they come in range,
maybe when they fight for space. One cloud
is black, it goes from a simple skeleton

to a bloated continent. Given my inclination,
I will turn it into a blowfish before
breakfast is over—or an uprooted tree.
Upstairs she sings—she chips—I know she's dancing
with something or other. When she comes down she'll have
the static of the radio on her tongue,
she understands the *words*, she actually sings
those songs—her voice is a high soprano—I
love it going up and down. My voice is ruined
but I can do a kind of quaver. I have
unearthed the wisdom from my second decade,
and though it did the world little good and even
served as a backdrop to our horrors I don't
blame the music, I can't blame the music
if the horrors grow stronger every year.
She listens to me with one hand, eating sugary
pineapple with the other. I listen too,
under the washrag and the dead maple,
hearing the words for the first time, making her scream
with laughter at my words, almost lucid
compared to hers, as hers are labyrinthian
compared to mine. There is this much music
in eastern Pennsylvania and this much love
and this much decadence. I would call it
derangement—the swallows twice a day
have it, and the white delphiniums
turning to blue again and the orange snapdragons.
If we could lie down for a minute we would let
the bastardy of our two decades take over

just as we let the songs do; there is nothing
that doesn't belong with love; we can't help it
if anguish enters; even leaving the world
as we do there is no disgrace, that is
another kind of anguish—just as it was
following a band of swallows, just as it was
bending down to taste the flowers or turning
the clouds into overturned trees or smiling in Greek.

The Thought of Heaven

There is one blossom on my redwood table
I smell for hours, even holding it
like a handkerchief in the palm of my hand
and bringing it to my face. I recognize it
as a kind of thought, as in the black locust
the poor of the world for one or two weeks a year
have their paradise, nor is it disgraceful
nor is it weak and seedy even if the thorns
make their wrists bleed, even if the leaves
they love to strip are dry; as in the phlox,
the weightless phlox, the bees drag down, the six
colors of lavender, a field of wild ninnies
growing like grass where there is a little room
beside the road; as in the bridal wreath
that smells like honey, that covers a city with cream,
there is one day for pomp; as in the dogwood
there is one day for sadness, four curled petals
with drops of blood, growing white or pink
in the cold dirt, all the more to be
the contrast, under some maple or huge cherry,
for me a blossom of thought supreme, nothing
in the world like it; as in the colored weeds
on my dashboard; as in the flowers in all five pockets;
as in my blue jacket once I found twenty years
of thought—more than that—the election
of Lyndon Johnson, the death of Eleanor Roosevelt—
look how they are political—Americans
in Lebanon, in Hispaniola; I sit there
like a tailor, cleaning out lint, whatever

lint is, holding a stem in the air, rubbing
a golden flower through my fingers, catching
the spots of light. The sun is on my left,
the poppies are in my driveway, a wild exchange
is taking place in my yard, something between
my dwarf apples; yellow dust is falling
into the sweet-smelling glue—this is thought,
even if it's copulation, it is a tried
and true intrigue, an old flirtation; there are
swollen stamens and green lipstick; Plato
would be the first to forgive me, but I don't think
of forgiveness now these last few decades. I
struggle past my willow; someone has cursed me
with a weeping willow, it is Chinese and grows
in swamps best, that I remember, swamps and bogs,
that and the sycamore; if anything,
I'll turn away; if anything I'll sit
among the broken sticks facing the fenced-in
weeds, revenge on ground hogs; I will stare
for a minute or two at a private flower, that is
enough for one day—who is it wants to sit
forever anyhow? There are two months
left—I should say three—the wind and the sun
will help me, so will water, so will bees,
for all I know, and moths, and birds; ah what
dark thoughts once rested in our coats, all of us,
dogs and cats and humans, not only burrs,
not only prickles; how it scatters first
and then floats back; that is what they called

a germh; it was Hegelian; I have
to find the pre-Socratic, that is for me
what thought should be, I am a sucker still
for all of it to hang together, I want
one bundle still. When the sweet scent comes from the east,
though I call it a thought, it is, as it should be,
something that precedes thought—that is a way
of putting it—something that accompanies thought,
but it is *thought* as it drifts down over the Chinese
willow, as it floats above the table
and penetrates my doors and windows; I bow
down to it, I let it change me, that
is the purpose of thought—I call it all thought, whatever
changes you. Dear apple, I am ready.
What is it for you, is it dreaming, does that set you
free? I call a bursting "dreaming," I call
a rage and sundering by its sweet-smelling name,
as if I were a child domesticating
everything within a mile for purposes
of my own rage. There is a thought. It is
if not in this blossom then in another, in
the lilies of our highways, in the great
round thistles beside them, in the black-eyed susan,
the flower I always bend down for, most of all—
for two or three weeks at least—in the chicory,
blue with the dust of the universe, a blue
more like lavender—I would call it purple
if I were extreme—I would say the edges
are white from gripping the sky, or they are drained

from so much thought. I call it the thought of heaven,
not too disgraceful for the chicory,
solemn and blue as it is, such is my thinking.

4

Bread Without Sugar

In memory of Harry Stern, 1897–1969

This is what makes justice in the world—
to bring these lives into the light.

—*Grace Paley*

The first time I saw the stone
I was overjoyed that I would be
keeping him like that. I cried
at the back of my mouth—a kind of gasp,
a kind of sucking in of air,
more in the way of surprise, maybe
terror even—though I was at peace,
even though I covered my mouth
as if I were still coming out of the garden
the way it was when we were boys
together. I never put a shawl
over my lower face; it was
the delicate fingers over my lips
in front of the Rosenberg rat-strewn bakery:
my mouth was open—I stood for a while
somewhere between two continents, somewhere
on an overnight flight. I should have been freezing
in New York City or Chicago; there was
saltwater down there, there was sand
and shallow roots. I should have been standing
or kneeling a little, one knee wet—
or dirty; it was December. I long for
that staggered wall again, for the street light
that makes the garbage glow. I long for
the Plumbing and Heating sign, my own
plastic basket reflected in the glass,
a Gauguin sky, an airplane floating
through the window of a skyscraper.
And I should have sat on my haunches holding

a bowl of rice to my lips, half lost
in thought the way a Chinese teacher,
a poet, would also be lost—say one
from Hunan Province—looking over
the empty lot, the windswept garbage,
a hundred wires holding him together,
pulley and phone and electric.

                          I stood
facing a row of mean-hearted elders
who made money in the 1960s
from a sudden flutter in the stock market,
tough little boys who learned to read
the newspapers and move the columns
of wooden and metal beads. They read
the *Miami Herald*—it was two inches
thick—cars and furniture and cruises
dripped all over their rugs. I slipped
on the television buy of the century once;
I fell down on a velour sofa—
it was either a kitchen banquette
or the backseat of a Chrysler New Yorker.
The *Herald* is thicker than the *Dispatch*,
thicker than the *Star-Ledger*,
thicker than the *Post-Gazette*.
Their wives are beside them. Did I think
they'd meet on the sly and pull out names
and numbers forever? Did I think
they'd whistle a little and talk about streets

in Flatbush and Newark, and talk about houses,
how solidly they were built, some restaurant
they always stood in front of? It
was the same restaurant in Newark and Flatbush,
there was a blonde at the cash register,
she was beautiful in the style
of 1941. They ate
fruit salad sundaes—the fruit was tasteless
but pretty, the syrup was heavy—the war
was on their lips there was one battle
south of Naples and there was another
on a tiny Asian atoll; the bodies
were cut to ribbons on the coral;
there would be Japanese hidden there
for thirty years to come. Their lives
in Newark and Flatbush would always be hooked,
they would always be crisscrossed with someone
showing up at a wedding, or leaning
inside a window while a family
was eating supper, a look of meekness—
futility—on his face, his hair
unbecomingly long, exhaustion,
grief, and curiosity taking over,
the war neither won nor lost.

> My mother
walks like a sparrow; I love her at last
without vexation. I am reckless
the way I was when I was twelve,

maybe fourteen, before I broke loose,
before I started to build a cave
inside my throat, before I claimed
only stricken things to the dismay and anger—
even the admiration sometimes—
of my young parents, starched sparrows
worrying over the pockmarked bread
that looked so much like limestone, that tasted
so bland without sugar—bread without sugar,
we ate it daily. Would you believe
my food if I told you? Would you not gasp
and roll your eyes? Milk was the poison
I ate before my meat—that was
the way we did it, that was how
we pleased the Levites; how would they know
the meat wasn't already boiling in milk
once it was in my stomach? She is
more like a pigeon, my mother: she hobbles,
although I thought of her, almost in her nineties,
as some small bird; the wind must take her,
she is like wild grass, she lunges
from place to place, she runs; I lift her
into the buses, I hold her down
as if she were paper. This is the pain
I stayed away from, I could bear
the endless separation better,
the cruelty of one short phone call
a week; but I am reckless, I sing
some Edith Piaf for her, she loves

the culture between the wars, she knows
the French—we school each other; I make her
breakfast before we leave, we take
a cab, there is such sighing, I pay him
to drive us into the cemetery;
I want to see how it looks with trees
growing beside the walks; I want
to see some shadows. Oh God, in Pittsburgh
the Russian graveyard was on three hills;
the paths were narrow and twisted; it took
an hour to find someone; and there was
such a shortage of space you found
the souls on top of each other, the head
of one stone facing the foot of another
the way it was in our bedrooms in
the first brick house, the ferns half-soaring
above our faces. But in this swamp
there is such space that they can build
a city for the dead that stretches
for thirty miles if they have to: the Jews
of Bucharest, the Jews of Berlin,
the Jews of Paris with white napkins tugging
at their throats, the Jews of Lima
already looking like Indians, the Jews
of Leningrad with music in their hands,
and the Jews of Detroit and the Jews of Toronto
speaking Spanish again, going back
to the fifteenth century, bowing and lisping,
learning it, bitterly now, from the Cubans,

taking their places with the Nicaraguans
and Venezuelans, remembering words
they hadn't thought of for five hundred years—
the names for dessert, the names for love,
the names for bitter wind, and the names
for silence: there are so many good names
for that—nor was it ever lost,
in one warm place and another, the streets
going down to the water, sailors and thinkers
always with trunks on their backs, a secret
message sewn somewhere, something explained
to their joy, something overlooked to their sorrow.

There are two plots, the third is in France,
the third is in Egypt; I go from country
to country in search of a plot; I see me
buried in Poland—what a nightmare *that* is!—
I go to see my mother's city
and on the second day while waiting
for Gregor Musial, my Polish translator,
I am hit by a cab; I'll never
die of a heart attack in Warsaw,
I'll never catch pneumonia, not there;
the cab will lose its steering and jump
the curb; of course I'll be the one sitting
closest to the street, I'll be reading
the newspaper with a dictionary,
I'll be reading the principal poets
in Polish and English; the cabbie can't give

a day up to find the part, maybe have
his cousin make one in his garage—
there are no spare parts in Poland. What a
fate for a Jew from Pittsburgh, guilt
and sadness driving him for fifty years,
to join his brothers and sisters that way,
blood spreading over his cotton shirt,
a circle of Polacks around him, a cop
going through his wallet, scratching his neck
with his metal nightstick. What does it matter?
Where should my site be? In Texas? Arizona?
I am more scattered than my father was,
born in Kiev, died in Miami.
There is the crow—I thought I'd wait
for hours for him. There is the gull.
There is a robin—from Pennsylvania—
I know him by his hop, I know him by his stance,
he and a worm are struggling together,
the robin's legs are spread. The stone
is gray—and streaked—the letters are deep;
Vermont granite. I am left
with stone, my father is made of stone,
he is one of the stones half-walking
in crooked formation, in Opa-Locka;
his place is by the fence, Meyer Schwartz
is behind him, Abe Wagner is his friend—
his neighbor. There is garbage not far
from the grave; it is the people living
on the other side: their cars are there,

their saucers are there, they throw their cardboard
and plastic over the vine-strewn fence.
The cantor is dead who sang at his grave;
the rabbi is dead, the boring rabbi
with the slanting hand; I gave him the money
to split between them; they hated each other,
law and music estranged them. I learned
pity from my father, I learned silence.
I tried to master his grief.

                        I was
forty-four when he died. It was
the worst snowstorm in northern New Jersey
in fifty years—the lines were down;
it took a day to reach me; Newark
and La Guardia were closed; I had to
take a train to Philadelphia
and fly from there. The schools were shut,
the snow was over the windows. I didn't
own a suit. I walked two miles
to Robert Hall—it was the only
store open. A salesman was trapped
inside—he thought I was crazy—he had
the cuffs done for me somehow—maybe
he was a tailor too—it was
a heavy wool suit. I stood for hours
on a wooden platform, the wind was brutal,
the tracks were covered with ice. The train
was a local; it ran from New York City

to Philadelphia; we used to call it
the Pennsylvania railroad; it was
my train—I knew every stop; I worked
at the Union Station in Pittsburgh pulling
wagons, unloading boxcars; we breathed
the filthiest air in history; there was
a yellow cloud hanging over the steam
and there were cinders—clinkers—free-floating
in the grand hall; I loved it; I even
loved the disgusting smell. My father
had thirty-eight suits, the silk and the wool
were woven together—somewhere. He was
a buyer, a merchandise manager,
and he had fifty wide ties; it was
a pleasure to see him get dressed. My suit
was hot—it was in February, I think
it was eighty degrees or more—that was
the suit I wore to the funeral; he would
have felt the cloth and known where the wool
was made, and known the cheap cut; his feeling
for others he showed in how he touched
their clothes. I wanted to sit and talk
with him—all my life—I wanted to have
one day together, but he couldn't be
at peace with me, something drove him
wild. I think he was only happy
with the Godforsaken—and children. He died
in an ambulance—an error—but he
couldn't say a word to the squad; I am

rude because of him, I am violent;
I shocked him, but he was so mild
he never complained, that Aaron.

                                    The sky
is streaked tonight; I love the tropics,
the orange underneath the blue; green parrots
are flying out of the sun, voices
are rising out of the ground, it must be
Yaglom and Sosna, these are his neighbors,
and Felder and Katz; some are New Yorkers,
one is from Cincinnati, one
was born in Africa, one is from Turkey—
he would know grapefruit. When they sing
they do it as in the movies or they
do it as if they were sitting down there
in Lummus Park, on Wednesday afternoon.
Schmaltz was our downfall, schmaltz was our horror,
we wept on the streets or walked to the swimming pool
weeping, we drove to the bakery weeping.
What was it for? What did we long for
so much, what had we lost? Was it
so shocking to live here? Did we not live
like angels? Why did we need such pity?
Why was there always such odd vexation?
One voice is heavy, it loves itself
and lingers in *basso profundo*; one voice
is dark, it is the alto I dreamed of,
the sound is like a cello. They sing

about dust, they sing about mouths, they sing
about mercy; they have delicate memories,
although there is no desire for blood—
that is absurd to them; their words
are drumlike, it is the sound of boxes,
the sound of barrels—I know the music.
Do you know Abe Corn? He drove us there
the second day—we couldn't find the footstone
our first visit. He was a cop
in his other life; he came from Vienna;
he was brutal, but he waited like a chauffeur
the whole morning while we probed in the dirt
for the name. My father was the only one there
without a name.

        This petulant city
is in despair a little: there was
some burning, two blacks were shot for riding
a red motorcycle—the mayor is working
hard to legalize red motorcycles,
though red excites the police. You go
from the graveyard east to 95,
the ocean is on your left—so are
the Azores, so is Carthage, so is
India. What have we done? We don't know
who to ask for forgiveness. Far from
that, we delight in our own slaughter,
but Miami is honest at least: either rust
corrodes the metal or sunlight bleaches

the cloth or water distends the wood.
And where should I go, to the Art Deco
to see how it merges with the Spanish?
Or should I go back to Córdoba and live
with the Moslems again, or this time the Greeks
and speak Ladino? Should I not
find my own sky to stare at, white lights
burning in the water, the salt
making my red nose quiver? Fat chance
for that—fat chance for a village—I have to
go down to Baja somewhere and watch
the pigs rolling in shit and munch on
some hideous sugar wafers; or sit
in a square in the mountains of Samos sighing
over stone and smiling at Germans half
a century and more after the sorrow.
I was in a forest studying Greek
and trying to learn the symbols when the
angel Sammael squeezed onto
my rock—he stank from the sun—and whispered
six secret words—or seven—I forget;
I even forget if it was Yiddish
or Hebrew, and though I flew to Israel
by Olympia and though I ate two suppers
with the Jewish poets and though we cursed
the government and though I felt
at home with Amos and sweet Josea
and hated the same dwarf kings as they did,
I had to go back to my country, so hate me

for that—and I had to start my next wandering,
so hate me for that. I am going to live
in Chinatown now and I'm going to visit
southern France. I may even go to
Crete, that I loved so much, though I want
to live with the Spanish forever. I love
their food and I love their music; I am
not even dead and I am speaking
their language already; I hope their poets
remember me.

           Tomorrow my plane
is leaving, I'll have a thimbleful of coffee
at the jazzy airport before I walk down
the ramps. I have to make a visit
to the Charles Hotel, I have to walk through
the giant lobby and see who is sitting
on the old sofas and play with the birds
and look at the stairway going down like lightning
directly onto the floor and talk to
the woman who runs the desk and see who
is living there now; it looks like a welfare
hotel, it looks like the checks are coming
from some department or other—the porch
is full of children. I have to see
my father and mother at the same hotel
in 1940 or 1941:
we were the first to sleep in our rooms;
the doors were *louvered*; my God, we ate

at a cafeteria—Hoffman's! There was
a girl named Sonny Uncles—that was
her name—we walked underneath the coconuts;
she was the guide. My father had a plan
to move here—there was a job; there are
three steps to the porch; announcements are everywhere;
and there is a piano still, and a fish tank,
and there are ferns and stucco beams
and glass-brick walls and barbaric paintings.
What would it cost for a room—on the ocean?
Where would I eat—on a hot plate? Where
would the honor come from? Who would give
me love, and delight? What would my son
and daughter think of it? Why does shame
always overtake me? Why does destruction?
—And what would I do with my glasses on the sand?
And how would I find my towel? The wind
is blowing two boats, there must be shrimp
and turtle out there. May the turtles escape
the nets! May I find my ocean! May
the salt preserve me! May the black clouds instruct me!

for Ted Solotaroff

Acknowledgments

The following is a partial list of the periodicals or collections in which some of these poems appeared. I wish to thank the editors.

The American Poetry Review, Antaeus, Anthology of Magazine Verse and Yearbook of American Poetry 1980 & 1981, The Best American Poetry, The Black Warrior Review, Boulevard, Breadloaf Anthology of Contemporary American Poetry, Columbia, Cook College Catalogue of Rutgers University, Crazy Horse, The Enigma, Fiction International, Field, The Georgia Review, Gettysburg Review, Graham House Review, Iowa Review, Ironwood, Missouri Review, MSS, The Nation, New England Review and Breadloaf Quarterly, The New Yorker, Northwest Review, Ohio Review, On Equal Terms, Parchment Conch, Paris Review, Pequod, Poesis, Poetry, Poetry East, Poetry NOW, The Pushcart Prize, The Scotsman, The Smith, Sonora Review, South Florida Poetry Review, Terra Poetica, Three Rivers Poetry Journal, and *Tikkun.*

I also want to thank my fellow poets, friends, students, and editors for their inspiration, assistance, and support, particularly Philip Levine, Edward Hirsch, Arthur Vogelsang, William Merwin, William Matthews, Muriel Rukeyser, Patricia Stern, Carol Smith, Ted Solotaroff, and Jonathan Galassi. Particular thanks to Jill Bialosky, the inspiring editor of this book, and to Alison Liss for her help.

And thanks for the aid I received from a John Simon Guggenheim Memorial Foundation grant, a Pennsylvania Council on the Arts Fellowship, and National Endowment of the Arts Writing Fellowships.

And deep thanks to Stephanie Smith for her assistance and to Anne Marie Macari for her endless help and love.

Index

A bunch of old snakeheads down by the pond, 147

Acacia, 204

A chicken with three hearts, that is a vanished, 437

Adler, 325

After cheating each other for eighteen years, 75

After it rains you should sigh a little for the spongy world, 90

After the heavy rain we were able to tell about the mushrooms, 136

After thirty years, 297

Age of Strolling, The, 455

A ghost I know too well stands bitterly by, 508

Ah tunnel cows, 208

A hundred years from now nobody will know who Zane Grey was, 199

All I Have Are the Tracks, 341

All I have are the tracks. There were a dog's, 341

All I need is one foot in the mud, 60

All that I know about the rose, 217

Angel Poem, The, 187

Anger of Age, The, 34

Another Insane Devotion, 386

Arm over arm I swam out into the rain, 175

Arranging a Thorn, 370

Arthur's Lily, 221

Aspiring to Music, 483

At an unexpected turn in the Kiskiminetas, 22

At Bickford's, 67

At Eleventh and Euclid I stood in front of an air, 195

A thousand times I have sat in restaurant windows, 213

At Jane's, 281

Baja, 304

Bee Balm, 273

Before he opened his eyes, as he lay there under the window, 114

Before I go outside I daub my face, 491

Before I leave I'll put two sticks on the porch, 253

Before the winter is over I'll have some sticks, 294

Behaving Like a Jew, 113

Béla, 351

Berkeley, 269

Between the eighth and the seventh avenue, 37

Bird Cursing, 13

Bite, The, 48

Blessed, The, 8

Blink of an Eye, The, 388

Blue Skies, White Breasts, Green Trees, 88

Blue Tie, The, 92

Bob Summers' Body, 377

Bob Summers: The Final Poem, 124

Brain of My Heart, 446

Bread Without Sugar, 533

Bull-Roarer, The, 438

Burst of Wind Between Broadway and the River, 37

Burying an Animal on the Way to New York, 82

By Coming to New Jersey, 16

By coming to New Jersey I have discovered the third world, 16

Cemetery of Orange Trees in Crete, The, 119
Christmas Sticks, 253
Clay Dog, 239
Climbing This Hill Again, 100
Coleman Valley Road, 492
Columbia the Gem, 39
County Line Road, 77
Cow Worship, 177

Dancing, The, 270
Dangerous Cooks, 151
Days of Nietzsche, The, 81
Days of 1978, 184
Dear Mole, 218
Dear mole, I have forgotten you!, 218
Delaware West, 40
Dog in the House, 51
Dogs, The, 336
Dog, The, 372
Don't flinch when you come across a dead animal lying on the road, 82
Down in the sweet pepper bushes, 242

Each spring the long-nosed god of rain, 125
82/83, 294
Elaine Comparone, 160
Eroica, 55
Every city in America is approached, 308
Every day the dark blue sky of brother Van Gogh, 83
Every night I have to go to bed twice, 168
Everyone who dances understands what I am doing, 383
Expulsion, The, 329
Eyes Are Always Brown, The, 475

Faces I Love, The, 145
Feeding Prisoners, 107

First Day of Spring, 463
First Lewd Offering, The, 450
Forgive me for being alone, 55
For hours I sit here facing the white wall, 267
For Night to Come, 226
For Once, 419
For Song, 266
For three days now I have been watching the blue jay take over—, 18
Founder, The, 448
Four Sad Poems on the Delaware, 86
Fritz, 317
From the Pennsylvania Side, 57

Garden, A, 400
Gert's Gifts, 111
Gloves, gloves, and a tubular hat, 44
God of Rain, God of Water, 125
Going North on 202, 17
Going north on 202 I have to wait for hours, 17
Gold Flower, 108
Goodbye, Morbid Bear, 30
Goodbye, morbid bear; you will be waving your morbid arm forever, 30
Good Friday, 1977, 152
Goons Are Leaving, The, 12
Grapefruit, 397
Great little berries in the dogwood, 451
Green fishes swimming in the street, 511
Grinnell, Iowa, 488
Groundhog Lock, 333
Guy Daniels would have loved May, 488

Hanging Scroll, 197
Have you ever lived through seven fat years and grown soft, 178
Heat Rises in Gusts, The, 36
Here are about seventy snakes waiting to come to life, 109

Here I am again with one more flower, 235

Here I Am Walking, 228

Here I am walking between Ocean and Neptune, 228

Here in this huge dining room, 306

Here is a green Jew, 288

Here's a blue flower to keep me company, 131

Her Right Eye Catches the Lavender, 501

He who destroys, he who reigns, he who meditates, 8

Hidden Justice, 252

His Animal Is Finally a Kind of Ape, 10

His animal is finally a kind of ape—after all—and not an elephant, 10

His Song of the Green Willow, 506

Hobbes, 393

Home from Greece, 127

Honey Locust, 109

How strange it is to walk alone, 9

How was I to know—in 1938—that anyone but, 28

How Would It Be?, 471

How would it be at my age to burn some land, 471

Hundred Years from Now, A, 199

Hungarian, The, 123

I always remember the crone. I always think of her, 319

I always went for natural shapes, I slid, 444

I am giving instructions to my monkey, 226

I am going over my early rages again, 240

I am going to carry my bed into New York City tonight, 120

I am here again, 393

I Am in a Window, 349

I Am in Love, 383

I am letting two old roses stand for everything I believe in, 233

I am one of the squirrels--I have a dogwood, 450

I am picking the roses for next time, 236

I am serving my own head on a platter, as Ensor did, 151

I am sitting again on the steps of the burned out barrack, 15

I am sitting thirty feet above the water, 266

I Am So Exhausted, 74

I am so exhausted I can barely lift my arms over my head to pull the, 74

I am taking off my glasses, 292

I am wandering through Newark, New Jersey, 370

I began this fall by watching a thin red squirrel, 153

I Called the Wolf Josephus, 35

I called the wolf Josephus, 35

I carry the white head with me, 453

Ice, Ice, 162

I could live like that, 275

I could never feel sorry for Arthur Vogelsang, 221

I cut a stick for my love. It is too early, 523

I didn't start taking myself seriously as a poet, 48

I Do a Piece from Greece, 342

I do a piece from Greece. I haven't done that, 342

I don't know if it's the one great sadness of my life, 298

If I get up one more time in the dark, 93

If I have one gift it is rising in the dark, 461

If I waited till September, 123

If I were to pick one bird to love forever, 313

If that dove leaves before I do, 520

If the Lark Had Thorns, 508

If this is a thing of the past, 41

If You Forget the Germans, 121

If you forget the Germans climbing up and down the Acropolis, 121

If you have seen a single yellow iris, 98

If you know about the Babylonian Jews, 69

If You Saw Me Walking, 129

If you saw me walking one more time on the island, 129

If you want to live in the country you have to understand the power of maples, 65

I guide my darling under the willow tree, 506

I Hate My Moaning, 344

I hate my staring. I hate my moaning. Sometimes, 344

I have been such a follower, 463

I have been waiting for a month, 279

I have come back to Princeton three days in a row, 197

I have in mind some dust; a sprite, 479

I have moved so far into my own thought, 81

I have put my hand in a baby shepherd's mouth, 219

I have settled down to watch the branches, 442

I have to be somewhere inside those flats, 97

I heard a fluttering—just inside the door, 469

I know that body standing in the Low Library, 39

I lay forever, didn't I, behind those old windows, 274

I like the way my little harp makes trees, 251

I'll never forget the small red dog in Mexico, 239

I loved a certain period; I wore, 455

I love the cows best when they are a few feet away, 177

I love the weeds—I dream about them—, 20

I love to bend down over my love, 271

I love to sit down, 160

I'm dreaming of the dahlias up there on the radiator, 193

I'm eating breakfast even if it means standing, 397

I'm finally listening to my own radio, 276

I'm looking at the moon, I'm half resting, 411

Immanuel Kant and the Hopi, 31

Immensity, 148

I move from chair to chair. Thinking of Liszt, 349

I'm singing a song for the romeos, 355

I'm working like a dog here, testing my memory, 329

In all these rotten shops, in all this broken furniture, 270

In a month all these frozen waterfalls, 156

In Carpenter's Woods, 53

In Crete the old orange trees are cut back until they are stumps, 119

I Need Help from the Philosophers, 72

I need help from the philosophers, I am still attacked by memory, 72

I never told this—I saw Bob Summers' body, 377

In Kovalchick's Garden, 7

In locust trees the roots run along the ground, 204

In Memory of W. H. Auden, 240

In the next booth over the hairless white, 26

In These Shadows, 217

In the sunset glow and early twilight and first star-sprinkling, 402

I only saw my father's face in butchery, 438

I Pity the Wind, 292

I put the sun behind the Marlborough Blenheim, 3

I Remember Galileo, 165
I remember Galileo describing the mind, 165
I saw my first kinglet in Iowa City, 360
I see my wife struggling in the dirt, 166
I Slept Like That, 362
I Sometimes Think of the Lamb, 347
I sometimes think of the lamb when I crawl down, 347
I spend an hour watching the yellow parrots, 475
I stand like some country crow across the street, 244
I think this year I'll wait for the white lilacs, 260
It is a great weariness, isn't it, 515
It is dusk, the drive-ins are opening, the balloon is coming to rest, 7
It is my emotions that carry me through Lambertville, New Jersey, 116
It Is Not Berenson's Blood, 50
It is not Berenson's blood, it is not Cramer's, 50
It is ten years since I have seen these shirts, 170
It is this Mexican lying on his back with his, 128
It is when there is not one leather jacket left with, 110
I touch the rose to see what happens there, 281
It's Nice to Think of Tears, 246
It's nice to think of tears as polliwogs, 246
It was always a soothing position, 362
It Was a Rising, 391
It was a rising that brought the worms. They came, 391
It Was in Houston, 378
It was in Houston I saw the heavy sideboard, 378
It was in Philadelphia that I first lived a life of deferment, 146

It was in southern Florida I reached, 419
It was March third I came outside and saw, 300
It was when I went out to get an angry soul, 380
It was when the bridal wreaths were all out, 222
It will always be invisible, it will, 164
It would be worth it to go ninety miles out of your way, 155
I've been seeing these tombstone beef sticks, 284
I walk now along the mule path between the first and second locks, 40
I wanted to know what it was like before we, 216
I want to watch my sweet body go out again into the beach plums, 13
I wasn't sure—when I reached 45—, 33
I Will Be a Romantic, 14
I will have to tell you what it is like, 493
I wonder who has pissed here, 414
I Would Call It Derangement, 523

John's Mysteries, 284
Joseph Pockets, 178
July 2, 1983, 335
June First, 174
June Fourth, 186

Kissing Stieglitz Goodbye, 308
Knowledge Forwards and Backwards, 407

Last Self-Portrait, The, 66
Later Today, 234
Later today, when most of the ice is melted, 234
Leaving Another Kingdom, 260
Let Me Please Look into My Window, 71

Let me please look into my window on 103rd Street one more time—, 71

Lillian Harvey, 363

Little Did the Junco Know, 158

Little did the junco know who he was keeping company with this Christmas, 158

Little White Sister, 146

Living on the river I am able to dip my feet in darkness, 68

Lobelia, 97

Long Nose, 128

Look at our poor rhododendron, 272

Look at those poor cattails, 278

Look at Us Play with Our Meat, 42

Look at us play with our meat, 42

Lord, Forgive a Spirit, 159

Lost with Lieutenant Pike, 28

Love for the Dog, 114

Love Is the Opposite, 453

Lovesick, 340

Lucky Life, 102

Lucky life isn't one long string of horrors, 102

Lyric, 414

Magritte Dancing, 168

Making the Light Come, 390

Malagueña, 105

Margie Moser's Garden, 78

May 15, 272

Mentioning of the Souls, 93

Mine was the nettle tree, the nettle tree, 299

Modern Love, 156

Morning Harvest, 133

Moscow, 271

My broken wing is on the left near the large joint, 187

My Death for Now, 442

My Favorite Demon, 385

My favorite demon holds me by the hair, 385

My Favorite Farewell, 415

My favorite piece of dreck, 483

My First Kinglet, 360

My Flow: His Stoppage, 26

My friends, still of this world, follow me to the bottom of the river, 149

My Hand, 219

My pen was always brown or blue, with stripes, 390

My Swallows, 267

Naming of Beasts, The, 5

Near Périgord, 263

Neither English nor Spanish, 380

Nettle Tree, The, 299

New Moses, The, 278

Nice Mountain, 451

Night Again, 276

96 Vandam, 120

Nobody Else Alive, 406

Nobody else alive knows the four heart sounds, 406

Nobody Else Living, 339

Nobody else living knows that song as well as I do, 339

No Longer Terror, 402

No matter what anyone says it is I who, 137

No Mercy, No Irony, 27

Nothing is too small for my sarcasm. I know, 148

Now after all these years I am just that one pigeon, 369

Now I am reading a psalm, 473

Now I feel safe, 323

Now I know why I have kept this orange flower wrapped up in tissue, 66

No Wind, 185

Of Blessed Name, 306

Once and for all I will lie down here like a dead man, 145

One Animal's Life, 366

One Bird to Love Forever, 313

One Day an Arbor Vitae, 444

One Foot in the River, 68

One Gift, 461

One more time the hard green daf-
  fodils are growing, 163
One More Time the Lambs, 163
One Thing in Life, The, 85
One time I rose from my bed, I had
  to walk, 458
On Long Island in 1951 I fought
  against bats for hours, 51
On My Poor Road, 87
On my poor road there is nothing
  but opossum and groundhog, 87
On the Far Edge of Kilmer, 15
On the first day of viburnum, 263
On the Island, 75
Orange Roses, 233

Pair of Hands, A, 376
Peddler's Village, 135
Pennsylvania spiders, 133
Phipps Conservatory, 183
Picasso Poem, The, 222
Pick and Poke, 153
Picking the Roses, 236
Pile of Feathers, 106
Planting Strawberries, 41
Pleistocene, 33
Poem of Liberation, The, 200
Poem of Life, The, 18
Potpourri, 166
Power of Maples, The, 65
Proverbs, 110
Psalms, 115

Red Bird, 323
Red Coal, The, 210
Red with Pink, 515
Rejoicings, 3
R for Rosemary, 469
Rhododendron, 235
Richard Strauss, my hero, here you
  are, 357
Roar, The, 225
Romance, 297
Romania, Romania, 244
Rose Warehouse, The, 208
Rotten Angel, 149
Royal Manor Road, 155

Sacred Spine, The, 164
St. Patrick's Day, 1979, 193
Same Moon Above Us, The, 255
Saving My Skin from Burning, 472
Saying the First Words, 275
Seine at Night, The, 280
Self-Portrait, 94
Sending Back the Gloom, 458
Sensitive Knife, The, 83
Shaking Myself and Sighing, 374
Shirt Poem, The, 170
Shouting, 473
Silver Hand, 368
Singing, 279
Slow and Painful Recovery, A, 357
Smell of Death, The, 511
Soap, 288
Some blossoms are so white and
  luscious, when they, 174
Someone Will Do It for Me, 520
Something New, 141
Sometimes I sit in my blue chair
  trying to remember, 210
Sometimes the dogs don't hear me.
  Sometimes I walk, 336
Sometimes When I Close My Eyes, 91
Sometimes when I close my eyes in
  the late afternoon, 91
Song, 249
Song for Kenneth Burke, A, 479
Song for the Romeos, A, 355
Souls from Emerson, 248
Sounds, The, 90
So what shall we do about this
  angel, 159
Stepping Out of Poetry, 112
Steps, 427
Steve Dunn's Spider, 242
Stick of Wrath, The, 45
Stolen Face, 421
Stopping Schubert, 348
Stopping Schubert, ejecting him,
  changing the power, 348
Straus Park, 69
Suddenly there are hundreds of
  fishermen on the road, 152
Supreme Subject, The, 22

Swan Song, 147
Sweetness of Life, The, 136
Sycamore, 300
Sylvia, 435

Thank God for the walnut in 1986, 446
That is a pair of white hands I see, 376
That was the last time I would walk up those five, 225
Thaw, The, 131
The anger of age—I'll love it!, 34
The dead straw in those trees, the, 340
The false dawn in Wheeling, West Virginia, 495
The final end of all but purified souls, 206
The first time I saw the stone, 533
The goons are leaving, and the Hawaiians, and the taffy-pullers, 12
The heat rises in unpredictable gusts, 36
The Jewish King Lear is getting ready, 325
The loose poems falling like blossoms, 44
The love of concrete objects, 45
There are two hundred steps between my house, 427
There are two men I know who wander around all winter as I do, 124
There is a face stolen from the twelfth century, 421
There is a kind of mop hanging down from the tree, 415
There is one blossom on my redwood table, 526
There is that little silver hand. I wrap, 368
There Is Wind, There Are Matches, 213
There I Was One Day, 364
There I was one day, 364

There's a bird pecking at the fat, 140
There's nothing in this gardenous world more delightful, 249
There was a hole in the ground once; there was a manhole, 472
There was a kind of drooping bronze head, 448
There was a time, 31
There were two jokes played on me on my first long walk in Florida this winter, 111
These Birds, 220
These birds burst in and out of their shadows, 220
These tiny Mexican mosquitoes are like lost souls, 304
The small gray bird that fit inside the hand, 135
The smell of piss is what we have in the city, 200
The-Way-We-Were Lounge, 215
The weeds are out, 57
The weeds give up suddenly after a small struggle, 107
Thinking About Shelley, 175
This is a common plantain, the simple weed, 333
This is a corner of heaven here, 53
This is a feast, climbing this hill again, 100
This is a kind of sunflower, 248
This is an old tuxedo shirt, 86
This is how I saved one animal's life, 366
This Is It, 116
This is just what I expected, the roots above the ground, 38
This Is Lord Herbert Moaning, 6
This is Lord Herbert moaning and sighing over his lost manuscripts, 6
This is lovesick for you—Charles Koechlin, 363
This is my forest now, this Christmas cactus, 252
This is the hawk I love, 27

This is the kind of place I loved when I walked, 215

This is the only thing that clarifies my life, 184

This is the season for chrysanthemums, 108

This is too good for words. I lie here naked, 317

This is what it's come to on my primrose path, 335

This is where I had my sheep vision, 492

This is where I reach for the scarlet bud, 311

This time there was no beak, 106

This version of the starving artist, 351

This Was a Wonderful Night, 345

This was a wonderful night. I heard the Brahms, 345

This was city living in the 1930s, 407

This was gruesome—fighting over a ham sandwich, 386

This was my garden in 1985, 400

This year I sat with women, gathering up, 141

Those Things, 503

Thought of Heaven, The, 526

Thousands of ajugas marching down the hillside, 78

Three Hearts, 437

Three Skies, 319

Three Tears, 98

Today a Leaf, 277

Today as I ride down Twenty-fifth Street I smell honeysuckle, 186

Today I am sitting outside the Dutch Castle, 185

Today I'm sticking a shovel in the ground, 273

Today I saw the weird leg of Apollo, 269

Today it was just a dry leaf that told me, 277

Too Much, Too Much, 137

Top Rock, 38

To the wild grape vine, the wild hop vine, the honeysuckle and the Virginia Creeper, 14

Turning into a Pond, 60

Twilight is like the blink of an eye, 388

Two American Haikus, 44

Two Birds, 49

Two Daws, 495

Two Moons, 411

Two Trees, 311

Ukrainian, 491

Underground Dancing, 140

Unity, The, 9

Villa-Lobos, 298

Visiting Florida Again, 195

Vivaldi Years, 274

Washington Square, 369

Waving Good-by, 216

Weeds, The, 20

Weeping and Wailing, 251

What a sweet urinal it was in Narbonne, 374

What is Eros doing, 435

What is the eastern gull called? Is it the same one, 501

What It Is Like, 493

What I took to be a man in a white beard, 88

What I was doing with my white teeth exposed, 372

What would you give for one of the old yellow streetcars, 112

When I drove through the little bald hills of Tennessee, 115

When I first saw this twittering thing, 49

When I got there the dead opossum looked like, 113

When I Have Reached the Point of Suffocation, 24

When I have reached the point of suffocation, 24

When I see a man sleeping over the
  grilles, 255
When It Gets Cold, 80
When it gets cold I put my body in
  the sun, 80
When I turn the ceiling light on, 94
When I woke up this morning I
  knew there was horror, I, 162
Wherever I go now I lie down on
  my own bed of straw, 85
Whoever wants to can live a life-
  time in this herb garden, 183
With a dead turtle floating down
  my canal, 105
With one foot on the standpipe, 503

With the cry of the duck in my ears,
  92

You can have the Old Causeway Inn
  on a Saturday night, 127
Your Animal, 206
You should hear the German farm-
  ers swearing in the under-
  brush, 77
You should understand that I use
  my body now for everything,
  67
You were wrong about the blood, 5
You would have to see Virgil Thom-
  son creeping down here, 280